PC File Formats & Conversions

Kussmann

Abacus

A Data Becker Book

First Printing, March 1990
Printed in U.S.A.

Library of Congress Cataloging-in-Publication Data

Kussmann, Ralf, 1959-
      PC file formats and conversions for developers / Ralf Kussmann.
          p.   cm.
      "Data Becker book."
      ISBN 1-55755-059-X : $34.95
      1. File organization (Computer science)   2. Microcomputers-
      -Programming.   I. Title.
      QA76.9.F5K87   1990
      005.74--dc20   90-231
                                                        CIP

Foreword

When PCs were first introduced they solved many problems, and also created some new ones. The number of PC users has greatly increased over the last few years. However, these new users must broaden their knowledge of these computers to get the most constructive use out of their PCs.

Compared to the rather rigid development of mainframe computers, the PC's development includes numerous standard software packages that are constantly being updated or changed. Most users may have noticed that these standard software packages often don't permit an open exchange of data with other popular software packages.

Many users try to find a single package that will do everything. More often than not, the user has requirements that the package simply cannot meet, or can only be achieved by very intricate programming (e.g., programming graphics or statistical calculations with a database program). Therefore, the ability to transfer data from one standard package to another package is crucial. This data transfer can more easily meet the user's needs. The strengths of several individual standard programs can be fully utilized by transferring data with this method. This results in more efficiency and lower program development costs.

Although most standard software packages offer open access to other programs, these features are often poorly documented. This is partly because software manufacturers aren't interested in teaching you how to move data to a product sold by another manufacturer. This book provides this information so that you can avoid re-entry of data, as well as the creation and use of conversion programs. The book is designed for the experienced user who wants to move data between software packages, as well as for the newcomer who would like to learn more about the capabilities of these standard packages before buying. PC programmers will also find this book useful when they must automate data transfer between software packages.

Since it is intended as a practical reference and because there are many problems associated with the various ways programs store data, the book's emphasis is on the transfer of data between programs. Even though all the standard software packages cannot be covered, the book does discuss many of the most popular programs, except the integrated packages, which handle these problems internally.

While researching this book, several conversion programs for word processing software were tested. The results of these tests were unsatisfactory, so these programs were not included.

Special thanks go to W. Treyer and H. M. Mueller for their important contributions to this book.

Ralf Kussmann   July 1989

Standard Software
-different file formats-

How can we transfer data from one
application to another?

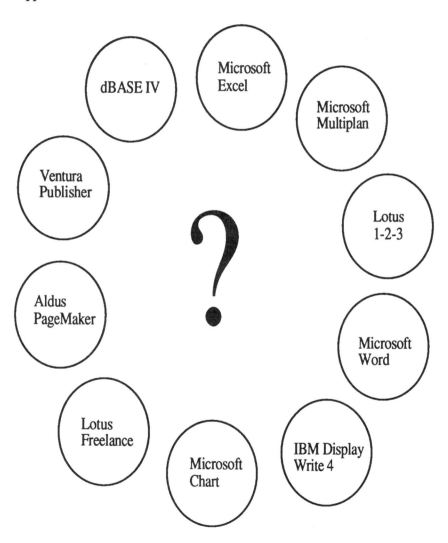

How to Use this Book

Chapter 1 categorizes the different software packages and describes their features. This chapter, which is intended for beginners, helps them decide which software best suits their needs. Readers who feel comfortable with the basics of these software packages can skip this chapter.

Chapter 2 describes and analyzes the file formats used by each standard software package, in as much detail as has been provided by the manufacturers. This chapter is especially useful for PC professionals who are faced with the task of automating data transfer between software packages.

Chapter 3 describes the standard capabilities for porting data in and out of each of the software packages discussed in this book.

Chapter 4 provides detailed instructions and examples of how to use existing commands found within each software package for data transfer.

The Appendix contains a Turbo Pascal source code listing for a program called CONVERT, which helps simplify data transfer and file conversion. In the book, this program is often used when converting data from ASCII files.

Table of Contents

Chapter 1

An Overview of the Software

In this chapter we will describe a number of software packages and their potential applications.

1.1 dBASE IV

This is a powerful and flexible database system suitable for data management applications in companies and organizations of all sizes. dBASE IV can be used by the beginner, the experienced user and the application programmer.

dBASE is a *relational database system*, which means that the individual data records in a database file are organized in a user-friendly tabular format. Think of the different data fields in each data record as columns in the table.

Since this method of organizing data enables you to change the relationships between various data elements and to change selection and search criteria, it is easier to use than hierarchical and network data models. Both its flexibility and ability to create complete application programs in its own programming language has contributed to dBASE's success.

With dBASE you can easily create databases, enter and change data records and then retrieve specific portions of the data using queries. All this can be done interactively by typing in the proper commands. When needed, help is also available at a keypress.

Sometimes you may want to use the same queries more than once. The dBASE programming language can help in these situations. dBASE applications can use all of the available commands in the interactive mode, combined with typical program control elements (such as looping, conditional statements and logical tests) in order to create structured application programs. These applications can be stored and run as needed.

Users can develop their own custom business applications to handle tasks such as inventory and bookkeeping.

Also, you don't have to program database management routines with dBASE, since that facility already exists. However, the actual database management activities are not dictated by dBASE. The environment is flexible so that it can handle most activities specified by the user.

The following is a list of some of the tasks dBASE can perform:

Data management for business needs

> Storage, retrieval and evaluation of operational data
> Accounting support
> Personnel management support

Data management for personal needs

> Phone numbers
> Addresses
> Appointments
> Personal finance

Here are several examples of database files:

> Phone number/address file
> Appointments file
> Index of magazine articles
> Customer list
> List of suppliers of goods and services

This book demonstrates how to transfer data from database files such as those listed above, and use this data in other programs. It will also show you how to load data into your database files that was created in other programs. So, you can benefit from the strengths of other programs (e.g., spreadsheets or presentation graphics) while keeping your data well organized.

1.2 Microsoft Multiplan

Multiplan is a *spreadsheet* or *worksheet* application. A spreadsheet consists of many individual fields or cells, which can contain text, numbers or formulas. The spreadsheet can be formatted in various ways by entering numbers, titles and cell labels. Multiplan replaces not only pencil and paper for many applications, but also the calculator, since the software can perform most calculations.

Multiplan is a spreadsheet program that helps with financial planning, investment decisions and calculations. The user can also create lists and tables.

The relationships between the entries in the table are stored. When one or more of the entries change, this affects the rest of the spreadsheet. One of the main strengths of a spreadsheet program is the ability to play "what if?" with your calculations.

Examples:

> What happens if we increase production?
> What happens if material costs rise?
> What if we ship by express freight? Is this cost effective?

To answer these and other questions, you must change the "critical" numbers and watch what happens to the other numbers in the spreadsheet. Since this helps you quickly analyze complex budget or capacity calculations you can make educated decisions.

Also, several tables which rely on one another for certain data can be appended.

Spreadsheet programs can save a lot of work usually done by hand because data entry is done once and the information is always available.

1.3 Lotus 1-2-3 Version 2.2

Lotus 1-2-3 is distinguished by several extra features which, until now, weren't found in any spreadsheet program. These features are the result of the integration of spreadsheet, graphics and database functions.

Lotus has all the advantages of a spreadsheet program, as discussed in Section 1.2. In addition, Lotus includes data management functions and the ability to display graphics. However, we must note that these additional functions are limited and that Lotus' real strength is as a spreadsheet program.

A Lotus worksheet can also be a data management file. One line corresponds to one record and a field corresponds to a column. There are two important functions that are available: a sort function and various query functions that allow you to search for and select data.

Lotus has five types of charts for graphics:

> Line charts
> Normal bar charts
> Stacked bar charts
> Pie charts
> X-Y charts

With the proper hardware (e.g., two monitors and correct video hardware), Lotus can simultaneously display graphics and text or numbers. Changing numbers in the worksheet immediately changes the totals on the worksheet and the appearance of the graph.

It is also possible to perform word processing tasks within Lotus, but these capabilities are very limited and cannot compete with word processing software.

1.4 Microsoft Excel Version 2.0

Microsoft Excel contains the same three integrated functions as Lotus 1-2-3: spreadsheet, database and graphics. The spreadsheet portion of the program is more powerful than both Lotus and Multiplan, and the graphics capabilities rival those of some stand alone graphics programs. Almost all the functions required for professional presentation graphics are included in Excel. You can also simultaneously display both numbers and graphics on the same screen in user definable windows. As with Lotus, changing the numbers results in an immediate change in the graphic display. The integrated database function is not as powerful as dBASE, but it is much easier to use. The extensive macro capabilities, which allow programs to be created within Excel, are also worthwhile.

Microsoft decided to use the Windows package as the user interface for Excel (PageMaker also runs under Windows). Because of its power, ease of use and graphically oriented user interface, Excel represents the future of software development.

1.5 Microsoft Chart Version 3.0

Microsoft Chart is a graphics package designed to meet a full range of business needs. Many business charts are available with eight variations per chart type. Different types of charts can be combined on a single screen. Three-dimensional presentations help produce professional looking charts.

Multiple fonts are available. These fonts can either be applied to all text in a chart or just to certain words in order to add emphasis. This feature can increase the effectiveness of the finished chart.

In addition to the graphic presentation modes, this program also offers some calculation functions that can be displayed as part of a chart. This is especially useful in applications such as trend analysis.

1.6 Lotus Freelance Plus Version 2.01

Lotus Freelance can be used to make many types of graphics quickly and easily. With Freelance Plus, you can create text charts, business graphics and drawings. You can also edit Lotus graphics and create custom characters, such as a logo for your firm.

With the functions available in Freelance, you can create entire presentations, from the simplest to the most complex. All graphics, except for the business graphics, can consist of the following nine elements:

> Text
> Lines
> Arrows
> Boxes
> Circles
> Arcs
> Curves
> Marks
> Polygons

Each graphic element has a variety of parameters, such as color, line style or font. With this flexibility, almost any type of graphic can be created.

Business graphics, such as line, bar and pie charts, can be created by entering or importing numerical data. By using other functions, you can alter these graphics.

1.7　Microsoft Word

Microsoft Word has become one of the easiest and most widely used word processing programs. It is a word processor that truly can reduce the time required to produce a perfectly formatted hardcopy.

Many functions are available to help the user enter the text and to format it as desired. For example, 4.0 offers:

A file manager that makes it easier to find files once they're saved.

An integrated outline function which makes it easier to organize concepts and manage large documents.

The ability to create macros, which can save typing time and work.

Margin lines and boxes for paragraphs, which help the user improve the look of the finished document.

Automatic creation of index and table of contents. Spell checking and hyphenation.

In addition, Word offers many other features and functions which make word processing easier.

1.8 IBM DisplayWrite 4 Version 2.0

DisplayWrite 4 is another word processing program that enables you to create, edit and print documents. This program is suitable for anything from simple letters to long books with complex formats.

Since DisplayWrite 4 stores files in EBCDIC code, documents created with DisplayWrite 4 can easily be transferred to IBM mainframe systems. The following word processing functions are available in DisplayWrite 4:

> Create, edit and print documents
> Center, underline, bold
> Change line and page formats
> Spell checking and hyphenation
> User expandable dictionary
> Merge data from files to create form letters
> Create and edit outlines
> Store and retrieve a series of keystrokes
> IBM Voice Communications Adapter Card and IBM Voice
> Communications Operating Subsystem Program support for text entry by voice

1.9   Desktop Publishing Applications

Aldus PageMaker 3.0 and XEROX Ventura Publisher 2.0 bring the capabilities of modern typesetting to the PC screen. Both of them are appropriate for either the beginner or the experienced graphic designer. They are relatively easy to use but offer powerful features for the design, layout and final creation of professional typeset publications. These packages are flexible enough to allow the user to make last minute changes without having to start a layout from scratch.

Text files and graphics from most of the popular word processing and graphics packages can be merged into either of these programs. It is also possible to import pure ASCII files from a text editor or from a mainframe computer.

Text and graphics are the raw materials which are processed together, with the help of desktop publishing software. Page layouts are done by interaction between the user and the desktop publishing application.

Once the page is properly arranged, it can be sent to a dot matrix printer, a laser printer or any device that understands the PostScript page description language.

Aldus PageMaker runs under the Microsoft Windows user interface. Ventura Publisher runs under the GEM user interface from Digital Research.

Chapter 2

An Overview of File Formats

In this chapter, the file format of each software package is described in as much detail as possible.

The basic factors of creating a file format involve finding the most economical way to access the largest amount of data quickly. For this reason, each standard software package has its own file format and special ways of storing data, which aren't easily revealed by software manufacturers.

2.1 dBASE IV

A dBASE file is like a two dimensional table with the following characteristics:

- All entries in a column are the same data type and a column is referred to as a *field*.

- The columns (fields) must have unique names.

- Each row represents a single data record and is identified with a *record number*. The record number gives the position of the record in the file.

A dBASE file would appear like this:

	Field 1	Field 2	Field 3
Field name	Name	Address	City
Record 01	Becker	125 Main	Boston
Record 02	Jones	345 Oak	Chicago
Record n	...	...	...

max. 128 fields

max. 1 million records

The internal structure of a dBASE file consists of a header and the data records. It is constructed like this:

Byte	Contents	Description
0	1 Byte	Bit 0-2:
		dBASE IV Version Number
		Bit 3-5:
		Reserved for SQL
		Bit 6-7:
		Availability of a memo file
1 - 3	3 Bytes	Last update (YY MM DD)
4 - 7	32 Bits	Number of records per file
8 - 9	16 Bits	Length of the identifying record structure
10 - 11	16 Bit Amt.	Record length
12 - 13	2 Bytes	Reserved bytes
14	1 Byte	Aborted transaction
15	1 Byte	Contents encoded
16 - 27	12 Bytes	Reserved for LAN use
28 - 31	4 Bytes	Reserved
32 - n	32 Bytes each	Field description matrix (see below)
n+1	1 Byte	0HD as field terminator

Description of a field:

Byte	Contents	Description
1 - 10	11 Bytes	Field name in ASCII, filled with zeros
11	1 Byte	Field type in ASCII (C,D,F,L,M or N)
12 - 15	4 Bytes	Reserved bytes
16	1 Byte	Field length
17	1 Byte	Decimal field counter
18 - 19	2 Bytes	Reserved bytes
20	1 Byte	Work area ID
21 - 31	11 Bytes	Reserved bytes

The data records are structured as follows:

The record is preceded by a blank character (20H) if it isn't deleted and by a star (2AH) if the record is deleted. Data fields in records do not have delimiting characters. Data types are stored in ASCII format as follows:

Data Type	Record Storage Format
Character	(ASCII characters)
Numeric	- . 0 1 2 3 4 5 6 7 8 9
Logical	Y y N n T t F f (?, if not initialized)
Memo	10 characters to represent a .DBT block number
Date	8 characters in YYYYMMDD format, for example 19850124 for January 24, 1985

The end-of-file marker is ASCII character 26 (1A).

2.2 Microsoft Word

The Basic Structure

A formatted Word file is divided into three parts:

1.   The Header: This contains an ID code that allows Word to recognize formatted texts along with other important information about the structure of the rest of the file.

2.   The Text: This is created without a format. Since the text always begins at offset 128 and its total length is given in the header, unformatted text can easily be formatted for storage.

3.   The Format Codes: These are added to the end of the text section and are divided into various groups (character, paragraph, text block formats, etc.).

These basic elements of a Word file are divided among one or more 128 byte blocks. Since a new piece of information always starts with a new block, many blocks won't be completely used so any characters may occupy the unused portions.

Since the structure of a Word file is very complex, it isn't easy to understand. We will describe the most important elements by using an example file that contains three parts.

1.   One paragraph containing the words "Text Text". The second word appears in bold type.

2.   Two paragraphs containing the word "Paragraph". The second paragraph is centered.

3.   An area where the page length has been defined as 11 inches.

The example document we have described contains text, paragraph and region format information.

Note: If two bytes are stored as a word in a file, the low byte appears first followed by the high byte. When stored as a word, the two successive bytes $10 $00 would have the value $0010, or decimal 10. A double word (dword) consists of two words, again with the low word preceding the high word.

The Structure of the Header

The header of a Word file is exactly one block (128 bytes) long and is counted as block 0.

Block 0: Header

```
0000(0000)  31BE000000AB0000-000000000000002101  1.............!.
0016(0010)  0000040005000500-0500050005004E4F    ...............NO
0032(0020)  524D414C2E535459-0000000000000000    RMAL.STY........
0048(0030)  0000000000000000-0000000000000000    ................
0064(0040)  0000000000000000-0000000000000000    ................
0080(0050)  0000000000000000-0000000000000000    ................
0096(0060)  00004550534F4E4C-5131060040003E4B    ..EPSONLQ1..@.>K
0112(0070)  D002000004010500-0500000005000000    ................
```

Note: In the following table, the numbers in the "Value" column are the proper values for our example file. The value "Strg" points to a character string.

HEX	DEC	Value	Name	Description
0000	0000	BE31	V_IdWord1	ID word $BE31 = 48689
0002	0002	0000	V_Reserv1	Reserved, must be 0
0004	0004	AB00	V_IdWord2	ID word $AB00 = 43776
0006	0006	0000	V_Reserv2	Reserved, must be 0
000E	0014	009D	V_TxtLnght	Number of characters in text + 128
0012	0018	0003	V_BnpFmt	Block number of paragraph format (block number 3)
0014	0020	0004	V_BnfTbl	Block number of footnote table (4)
0016	0022	0004	V_BnrFmt	Block number of region format (4)
0018	0024	0005	V_BnrTbl	Block number of region table (5)
001A	0026	0006	V_BnPBTbl	Block number page bread table (6)
001C	0028	0006	V_BnFMngr	Block number of file manger
001E	0030	Strg	V_Sty	Path+name of stylesheet+0 (= "C:\WORD\STANDARD.STY"+0)
0060	0096	0000	V_WinWrite	Reserved for Windows Write
0062	0098	Strg	V_PntrDrvr	Printer driver name without path name or file extension
006A	0106	0007	V_BlkCnt	Number of blocks in the file
006C	0108	0000	V_MarkRev	Revised text is marked by this bit field. In bit fields, individual bits are interpreted one at a time rather than as a complete field.
006E	0110	0000	V_Reserv3	Reserved, must be 0. Offset address 110 through 127 (28 byte).

The field V_TxtLnght contains the number of characters in the text plus 128. Since the text always begins at position 128 (directly following the header), V_TxtLnght always points to the first unused byte after the text. In our example, the file contains 29 characters, which gives us the value of 29 + 128 = 157, or $009D in hex.

In order for Word to easily find the formats used by the text, the block numbers of the format codes are given in the header (V_BnpFmt through V_BnPBTbl). The order of the formats in the header corresponds to the order in which they are stored in the file.

The paragraph format doesn't come directly after the text, as one might assume from studying the table. Instead, the character formats usually come first. Since the length of the text and its start address are known, the block number of the character formats can be calculated. So the block number doesn't need to be stored in the header. If the file doesn't contain text, there won't be a text block.

The field V_MarkRev contains all the information for text that has been processed with the Format revision-Marks option set on.

V_MarkRev

Bit	Name	Meaning
0	Vmr_Just	Justification 1 = Yes
1-3	Vmr_Attrib	Text attributes 0 = Underline 1 = Upper case 2 = Normal 3 = Bold 4 = not used 5 = not used 6 = Double underline 7 = not used
4-5	Vmr_Jtype	Type of justification 0 = no justification 1 = left justified 2 = right justified 3 = alternating justification
6,7	Vmr_Rsrv1	reserved 0
8-15	Vmr_Rsrv2	reserved 0

The Structure of the Text

The second block of a Word file contains the actual text. This is constantly stored and always begins with block 1 (if the file contains text). The last block of text usually isn't completely filled and may contain any characters. However, this doesn't matter since the variable V_TxtLnght in the header points to the first byte that doesn't belong to the text.

Block 1: Text

```
0128 (0080)    5465737420546578-7420546573742054    Test Text Test T
0144 (0090)    6578742054657374-2054657874205465    ext Test Text Te
0160 (00A0)    7374205465787420-5465737420546578    st Text TestTex
0176 (00B0)    7420546573742054-6578742054657374    t Test Text Test
0192 (00C0)    2054657874205465-7374205465787420     Text Test Text
0208 (00D0)    5465737420546578-7420546573742054    Test Text Test T
0224 (00E0)    6578742054657374-2054657874205465    ext Test Text Te
0240 (00F0)    7374205465787420-5465737420546578    st Text Test Tex
0256 (0100)    7420546573742054-6578742054657374    t Test Text Test
0272 (0110)    2054657874205465-737420546578740D     Text Test Text.
0288 (0120)    0ADCDCDCDCDCDCDC-DCDCDCDCDCDCDCDC    ................
```

HEX	DEC	Value	Name	Explanation
0080	0128	Strg	T_Txtbeg	The text begins here. The text may take up several blocks.

There are 29 characters in our example file. The last character ($0C for end of region /page break) is in bold type.

The text is stored in expanded ASCII code and contains no format codes. The following characters have special meanings:

ASCII Code	Meaning
9	Tab
11	End of line
12	Page break
13,10	End of paragraph (CR/LF)
31	Conditional hyphen (hyphenation function)
32	Unprotected space
45	Dash
196	Protected hyphen (not separable)
255	Protected space

The CR/LF character (10,13) should always be available, otherwise it may have an unusual effect on Word (double characters, disappearing cursor).

The basic functions supplied by Word also have special codes.

ASCII Code	Meaning
1	(Page)
2	(Print date)
3	(Print time)
5	(Footnote)

Note: A footnote is created with ASCII value 5 only if you do not specify a footnote number. If you do enter a footnote number and thereby override the automatic footnote numbering feature, your footnote number will appear as normal text in the text block.

The Structure of the Format Information

The format information is stored in several different blocks, as we have already seen by examining the header.

The "Character Format" Block

The block following the final text block contains the character formats. The block number can be found by adding the header to the number of text blocks:

```
TxtBlkNr = (V_TxtLnght + 127) / 128
```

This gives the following relationship:

Number of Characters	V_TxtLnght	Block Number of Character Format
0	$0080	1
1 - 128	$0081 - $0100	2
129 -	$0101 -	3 -

Therefore, if no text is in the file, the character formats are found in block 1.

Block 2: Character Formats

```
00000100  80 00 00 00 85 00 00 00 FF FF 89 00 00 00 78 00   .........x.
00000110  9D 00 00 00 FF FF 06 00 3F 05 16 01 4A 12 00 00   ....?...J...
00000120  41 3A 5C 00 00 2C 1D 2E 1D 32 1D 37 1D 3C 1D 40   A:\..,...2.7.<.@
00000130  1D 22 00 20 63 6D 00 20 70 31 30 00 20 70 31 32   .". cm. p10. p12
00000140  00 20 70 74 00 20 7A 67 00 A0 05 37 02 90 00 78   . pt. zg..7..x
00000150  00 14 00 F0 00 5E 1D 60 1D 63 1D 66 1D 6A 1D 6E   ...=.^.`.c.f.j.n
00000160  1D 71 1D 22 00 69 6E 00 63 6D 00 70 31 30 00 00   .q.".in.cm.p10..
00000170  31 BE 00 00 00 AB 00 00 00 00 00 02 00 01 03   1.............
```

The following character formats are given in this block:

HEX	DEC	Value	Name	Explanation
0100	0256	0080	Z_FmtBegin	This contains the offset address of the first character whose format is described by this block. The first character for this file will be found at address 128 ($80).
0104	0260	0085	Z_FmtTbl	A table, which contains format information for groups of identically formatted characters, begins here.
017E-	382-	0006	Z_FmtLst	The list of format descriptions is not added to the end of Z_FmtTbl- it is built from the end to the beginning.
017F	383	0003	Z_FmtLstNr	The number of elements in Z_FmtTbl.

The character formats describe a group of characters that have the same format. A group can also consist of a single character. If all characters except one have the same format in a given text, then three format descriptors (Z_FmtLst) are needed. One descriptor is for all characters up to the one with a different format, one is for the different character and another is for the remaining characters in the text. This applies to our example file.

The entries in the table Z_FmtTbl always have the same length (6 bytes); new entries are simply added on to the end. However, the length of the list of format types (Z_FmtLst) is variable and begins before Z_FmtLstNr. Additional entries are inserted before the first entry.

Structure of the Z_FmtTbl Table

HEX	DEC	Value	Name	Explanation
0000	0000	0085	ZFT_Next	First character to which this format does not apply.
0004	0004	0078	ZFT_DstNxt	Distance to corresponding Z_FmtLst,or FFFF if standard format.

The entries in the table always contain two pieces of information: a pointer to the first character which does not belong to the group (and is therefore described by the next entry in the table) and a pointer to the corresponding format type (Z_FmtLst). Therefore, several groups of identically formatted text require only one format type (Z_FmtLst) entry. The distance to the format type (ZFT_DstNxt) is calculated as the distance from the first entry in Z_FmtTbl to the first byte of the corresponding format type. In our example, the Z_FmtTbl table has three entries:

ZFT(1)	$85 $00 $00 $00 $FF $FF	Applies to characters $80-$84, standard format, no ZFA <character format type>.
ZFT(1)	$89 $00 $00 $00 $78 $00	Applies to characters $85-$88, ZFA begins with $0104+$78=$017C.
ZFT(2)	$9D $00 $00 $00 $FF $FF	Applies to characters $89-$9C, standard format, no ZFA.

Structure of Z_FmtLst Table

HEX	DEC	Value	Name	Explanation
0000	0000	02	ZFA_NrChar	Number of characters without this byte
0001	0001	00	ZFA_STY	Code (variant) in stylesheet (0=standard character)
0002	0002	01	ZFA_Font	Bold/Italics/Font number (see table)
0003	0003	NA	ZFA_FontPt	Size of font in half points (e.g. 8 point = $10 = 16)
0004	0004	NA	ZFA_Attrib	Other character attributes
0005	0005	NA	ZFA_Reserv1	
0006	0006	NA	ZFA_Pos	Character position 1-127=high, 128-255=low, 0=normal
0007-000A	0007-0010	NV	ZFA_Reserv2	

Note: NA = not applicable to our example.

In order to save as much space as possible, only the values that are absolutely necessary are given. A group of characters formatted with the same print format needs only a 2 byte ZFA <character format type> (1 byte for length, 1 byte for variant). This is also the smallest possible length for a ZFA, since the ZFA_STY must follow the length.

If the character position is changed (for example, increased by one character), all values from 0 - 6 must be given (including zeros and standard values).

The Structure of ZFA_STY

Bit	Meaning
0	1 = character formatted with stylesheet
1-7	Variant number (0=standard)

Character Format Variants (ZFA_STY bit 1-7)

Bit 1-7	Use	Variant
0	Character	Reserved Standard character
1-12	Character	1-12
13	Character	Footnote reference
14-18	Character	13-17
19	Character	Number of pages
20-27	Character	18-25
28	Character	Brief information
29	Character	Line numbers

Structure of ZFA_Font

Bit	Meaning
0	1 = bold
1	1 = italics
2-7	Font number

Bits 2 - 7 give the index in the font table (in the Word manual, under printer drivers: font table). Here are some examples for the EPSONFX printer driver:

ZDA_Font	Bit 2 - 7	Font Name
$04-$07	$01	Elite = ModernB
$08-$0B	$02	NLQ = ModernC
$40-$43	$10	PS = RomanA

Structure of the ZFA_Attrib

Bit	Meaning
0	1 = underline
1	1 =strikeout
2	1 = double underline
3	1 = character in edit mode
4-5	Character size
	00 - Normal
	01 - Upper case
	03 - Small upper case
6	1 - Special character: (page), (print date), (print time) etc.
7	1 - hidden character

Paragraph Format

The way to describe paragraph formats is similar to that of character formats. One block handles the description of one or many paragraphs. In the first paragraph block, the paragraphs are described beginning with the first character in the text and continuing through to the paragraph containing the last character. Word obtains the block number of the first block with paragraph formats from the V_BnpFmt field in the header. This field has a value of 3 in our example file.

Block 3: Paragraph Formats

```
00000180   80 00 00 00 8C 00 00 00 FF FF 94 00 00 00 FF FF    .........
00000190   9C 00 00 00 78 00 9D 00 00 00 FF FF 9E 00 00 00    ...x.......
000001A0   FF FF 5C 00 00 2C 1D 2E 1D 32 1D 37 1D 3C 1D 40    ..,...2.7.<.@
000001B0   1D 22 00 20 63 6D 00 20 70 31 30 00 20 70 31 32    .". cm. p10. p12
000001C0   00 20 70 74 00 20 7A 67 00 A0 05 37 02 90 00 78    . pt. zg..7..x
000001D0   00 14 00 F0 00 5E 1D 60 1D 63 1D 66 1D 6A 1D 6E    ...=.^.`.c.f.j.n
000001E0   1D 71 1D 22 00 69 6E 00 63 6D 00 70 31 30 00 00    .q.".in.cm.p10..
000001F0   31 BE 00 00 00 AB 00 00 00 00 00 00 02 3C 01 05    1...-.......<..
```

The format table A_FormTab has the same structure as the Z_FmtTbl table from the character formats. The structural differences begin with the A_FmtTbl table.

Structure of A_FmtTbl Table

HEX	DEC	Value	Name	Explanation
0000	0000	02	AFA_NrChar	Number of characters without this byte
0001	0001	3C	AFA_STY	Code (variant) in STY
0002	0002	01	AFA_Attrib	Paragraph attribute (alignment, etc.)
0003	0003	NA	AFA_Var	Character format variant for this paragraph (standard format)
0004	0004	NA	AFA_OutLvl	Outline: level and description
0005		NA	AFA_RghtInd	Right indentation in 1/20 point (pt)
0007	0007	NA	AFA_Leftind	Left indentation in 1/20 point (pt)
0009	0009	NA	AFA_LeftInd1	Left indentation of first line in 1/20 point (pt)
0011	000B	NA	AFA_LineSpc	Spacing between lines in 1/20 point (pt)
0013	000D	NA	AFA_TopMar	Top margin in 1/20 point (pt)
0015	000F	NA	AFA_BotMar	Bottom margin in 1/20 point (pt)
0017	0011	NA	AFA_Special	Header, footer and border
0018	0012	NA	AFA_LinePos	Line positions
0019	0013	NA	AFA_Reserv1	Reserved, must be 0
0023	0017	NA	AFA_TabTbl	Table with tab values
-102	-66			

AFA_STY

This field also keeps its value if the paragraph is formatted directly after it is entered. But bit 0 is also set to 0, which shows that this paragraph is not formatted with a print format. Example: A paragraph is formatted with print format variant 1 -> AFA_STY = $3F (:2=31=variant1), and directly formatted afterwards -> AFA_STY = $3E (:2=31=variant1).

AFA_Var

This field is similar to AFA_STY, except that bit 0 doesn't need to be set. Therefore, this field contains half the value of AFA_STY.

Character formatting is retrieved from the paragraph format, even if the formatting is done directly. So, if the character formatting in the print format changes, the character formatting for a directly formatted paragraph also changes. The character formatting is determined by the print format unless the characters themselves are directly formatted.

As with character formatting, the fields from AFA_STY through the last field are stored only if their values differ from the default values. In our example file, only the field AFA_Attrib has a non-default value. It contains a value of 1, since the paragraph is centered. So only the values up through this field are recorded: $02, $3C, $01.

Word uses the following defaults:

Name	Hex	Dec	Meaning
AFA_STY	$3C	60	For paragraphs not formatted with stylesheet; bit 0 = 0
	$3D	61	For paragraphs formatted with the variant standard format (Bit 0 = 1, Bit 1-7 = $1E = 30 = paragraph standard)
AFA_Var	$1E	30	Character formatting as paragraph standard
AFA_LineSpc	$F0	240	240 * 1/20 point = 12 point

The Structure of AFA_STY

Bit	Meaning
0	1 = Paragraph was formatted with stylesheet
1-7	Number of the variant (0 = standard)

Bit 0 indicates whether the paragraph has been formatted with a print format. If the bit contains the value 1, then bits 1-7 contain the variants of the paragraph. The number thirty stands for standard paragraph format.

Paragraph Variants and the Values for Bits 1-7:

Bit 1-7	Use	Variant
30	Paragraph	Standard
31-38	Paragraph	1-8
39	Paragraph	Footnote text
40-87	Paragraph	9-56
88-94	Paragraph	Titles level 1-7
95-98	Paragraph	Index level 1-7
99-102	Paragraph	Tables level 1-7
103	Paragraph	Header/footer lines

Structure of AFA_Attrib

Bit	Meaning
0-1	Justification of paragraph
	0 = left justified
	1 = centered
	2 = right justified
	3 = block
2	1 = same page
3	1 = next paragraph same page
4	1 = next to one another
5-7	Reserved, must be 0

AFA_Var

Word assigns a standard character format to each paragraph. If a paragraph is directly formatted later, AFA_Var points to the paragraph-print format from which the character format is retrieved.

AFA_OutLvl

This entry determines the position of the paragraph in outline mode:

Bit	Meaning
0-6	Number of outline level (0=text body)
7	1 = paragraph is left out (outline level or text body)

AFA_Special

AFA_Special contains information about the margins and indicates whether or not there are headers or footers.

Bit	Meaning
0	0 = header
	1 = footer
1	1 = header/footer on odd pages
2	1 = header/footer on even pages
3	1 = header/footer on the first page
4-5	Border type
	0 = no border
	1 = compete border
	2 = border pages defined with AFA_LinePos
	3 = not used
6-7	Style of border
	0 = simple border
	1 = double border
	2 = bolded simple border
	3 = not used

AFA_LinePos

If bits 4-5 in AFA_Special have the value 2, then the AFA_LinePos bit field contains the position of the lines:

Bit	Meaning
0	1 = line on the left margin
1	1 = line on the right margin
2	1 = line on the top margin
3	1 = line on the bottom margin
4-7	not used

Tabs

The field AFA_NrChar, which gives the number of bytes in the format description, also specifies whether the paragraph contains tabs which are not noted in the print format (directly formatted tabs). If so, then the field AFA_NrChar will contain a value larger than 22. This means that there will be tab information in AFA_TabTbl. Each entry in the table AFA_TabTbl is four bytes long. Therefore, the value of AFA_NrChar will also give the number of tabs:

```
Number of tabs = (AFA_NrChar - 22) / 4
```

Note: Since the last tab may be described with less than 4 bytes, the number calculated with this formula must be rounded. Later, this, along with the structure of the table, will be described in more detail.

From the provided length of the tab table, we can see that a total of 19 directly formatted tabs is possible. The total number of possible tabs (sum of the tabs in the print format and the directly formatted tabs) is also only 19. We can see the large amounts of storage space required for direct tab formatting by looking at the tab table at the end of A_FmtTbl, since A_FmtTbl is at least $18 = 24 bytes long for each paragraph.

Structure of an Element in the Tab Table

HEX	DEC	Value	Name	Explanation
0000	0000	NA	AFAT_Dist	Distance from left edge of page in 1/20 point
0002	0002	NA	AFAT_Attrib	Tab attribute
0003	0003	NA	AFAT_Reserv	Reserved, should be 0

If there are several tabs in a paragraph, all AFATs have a length of 4 bytes, except for the last tab. For the last tab, the description can be 2 (only for AFAT_Dist) to 4 bytes long, since Word can determine the length of the last tab description from the length given in AFA_NrChar.

AFAT_Attrib

Bit	Meaning
0-2	Position
	0 = left
	1 = centered
	2 = right
	3 = decimal
	4 = vertical
3-5	Fill character
	0 = space <blank>
	1 = period
	2 = dash
	3 = underscore
6-7	Reserved, must be 0

Footnotes

Footnote numbers and the corresponding text are stored as normal text. The information about the footnotes must also be stored. Footnote tables (FNTB) are created for this purpose. The V_BnfTbl field in the header contains the block number where the footnote table (if present) begins. If this field contains the same value as V_BnrFmt, then there is no footnote table.

The Structure of the Footnote Table FNTB

HEX	DEC	Value	Name	Explanation
0000	0002	NA	FNTB_Nr	Number of footnotes + 1
0002	0002	NA	FNTB_Max	Number of available footnotes in text + 1
0004	0004	NA	FNTB_DescTbl	Footnote descriptor table

The reason why Word adds 1 to the values of FNTB_Nr and FNTB_Max relates to the management of footnotes. This will be described with the structure of the table.

The FNTB_Max field has a special meaning because it contains the largest value that FNTB_Nr ever contained during processing of the text. If the text currently has one footnote, but had 10 that were deleted, the contents of the first 4 bytes in FNTB would be $02 $00 $0B $00.

The size of the footnote table and the number of blocks it occupies can be calculated from the number of footnotes:

Number of blocks = (4 + 8 * (FNTB_Nr - 1)) / 128

If one block isn't enough to hold a FNTB, the storage is continued in the next block. The remaining portion of the last page is filled with zeros.

The Structure of FNTB_DescTbl

HEX	DEC	Value	Name	Explanation
0000	0000	NA	FNTBFT_Ofc	Offset of the footnote characters starting from the beginning of the text
0004	0004	NA	FNTBFT_Oft	Offset of the footnote text starting from the beginning of the text.

Note: The offsets given in this table are not taken from the start of the file. They are counted, starting with 0, from the first character in the text.

Word always enters a value increased by 1 in FNTB_Nr and makes two entries in the FNTB_FnTb for this "dummy footnote": the offset of the first character after the footnote text of the last footnote and the offset of the last character of the footnote text. Word needs this information in order to determine the length of the last footnote so that it knows where to insert the next footnote text.

Except for the last valid footnote, this information can be obtained from the following footnote for all footnotes. The dummy footnote contains this information only for the last footnote.

Regions

If a Word document is divided into several regions or if some regional format is used, then Word will store certain information in the region table. The V_BnrTbl field in the file header contains the block number in which the region table (RT) begins (if one is present). If this field contains the same value as V_BnPBTbl, then there is no region table in the file.

Structure of a Range Table

```
00000280   02 00 02 00 1D 00 00 00 06 00 00 02 00 00 1E 00   ...............
00000290   00 00 02 00 FF FF FF FF 00 03 10 00 00 00 10 00   ...........  ....
000002A0   00 00 10 00 00 00 10 00 00 00 10 00 00 00 10 00   ...............
000002B0   00 00 00 00 50 69 63 61 00 00 9C 00 04 00 0C 00   ....Pica..E.....
000002C0   06 FF 06 FF 06 FF 06 FF 10 00 00 03 13 00 00 03   ...............
000002D0   16 00 00 00 16 00 00 00 16 00 00 00 16 00 00 00   ...............
000002E0   16 00 00 00 16 00 00 00 00 00 14 00 0A FF 0A FF   ...............
000002F0   0A FF 0A FF 16 00 00 02 18 00 00 02 1A 00 00 00   ...............
```

HEX	DEC	Value	Name	Explanation
0000	0000	0200	RT_Nr	Number of regions (2)
0002	0002	0200	RT_Max	Maximum available regions; contains the highest value that RT_Nr ever had during processing of the document.
0004	0004	Tab	RT_DescTbl	Region descriptors table

Note: The entry "Tab" in the "Value" column means that the region descriptors table (listed below) follows.

Structure of the RT_DescTbl Table (RTT)

HEX	DEC	Value	Name	Explanation
0000	0000	ID	RTT_Next	First character which no longer belongs to this region (counted from start of text, not start of file)
0004	0004	06	RTT_Reserv	Not used
0006	0006	0200	RTT_FdPos	Position of the corresponding format descriptor (RF) in the file (for our example $02000 = 512)

The first entry in the RTT describes the first region. This consists of the characters from the start of the text to the start of the region and the characters after the region to the end of the text.

Unlike with the character and paragraph formatting, the first character of the text is at address 0, not at 128.

As with character and paragraph formatting, the region is not described directly in the RTT. Instead, it points to the correct format descriptor RF. In this way, many regions can be described with one format descriptor.

Structure of a Region Format (RF)

In our example, the block contains only one region format. Its last valid byte is $40.

HEX	DEC	Value	Name	Explanation
0000	0000	6	RF_Nr	Number of byte in the format descriptor not including this byte
0001	0001	D2	RF_STY	Stylesheet
0002	0002	02	RF_Attrib1	Region format
0003	0003	8E43	RF_PgLen	Page length 1/20 point (pt)
0005	0005	832E	RF_PgWidth	Page width 1/20 point (pt)
0007	0007	FFFF	RF_FstPgNr	First page number (or $FFFF for continual)
0009	0009	8A05	RF_TopMarg	Top margin in 1/20 point (pt)
000B	0011	9639	RF_LnTxtReg	Length of text region in 1/20 point (pt)
000D	0013	6E04	RF_LeftMarg	Left margin in 1/20 point (pt)
000F	0015	A725	RF_WidthTxt	Width of text region in 1/20 point (pt)
0011	0017	00	RF_Attrib2	Region format
0012	0018	01	RF_NrCol	Number of columns in regions
0013	0019	C502	RF_DistHdr	Distance of header from top margin in 1/20 point (pt)
0015	0021	C940	RF_DistFtr	Distance of footer from bottom of page in 1/20 point (pt)
0017	0023	NA	RF_DistCol	Distance between columns in 1/20 point (pt)
0019	0025	NA	RF_WdthBin	Width of gutter margin in 1/20 point (pt)
001B	0027	NA	RF_DstPgNr	Distance of page number from top of page in 1/20 point (pt)
001D	0029	NA	RF_DstPgNrL	Distance of page number from left edge of page in 1/20 point (pt)
001F	0031	NA	RF_DstLnNrL	Distance of line numbers from left edge of page in 1/20 point (pt)
0021	0033	NA	RF_IntvLnNr	Interval of line numbers

Block 4: Region Format (RF)

As with character and paragraph formatting, fields from RF_STY to the last fields are stored only if their values differ from the defaults.

RF_STY

Bit	Meaning
0	1 = Region was formatted with a region format from the print format codes
1-7	Variant number

RF_DFV	Use	Variant
105	Region	Standard
106-126	Region	1-21

RF_Attrib1

Bit	Meaning
0-2	Change region 0 = continuous 1 = column 2 = page 3 = even 4 = odd
3-5	Page number format 0 = Arabic numbers 1 = Roman numerals, upper case 2 = Roman numerals, lower case 3 = upper case letters 4 = lower case letters
6-7	Begin pagination with: 0 = page 1 = region 2 = continuous

RF_Attrib2

Bit	Meaning
0-4	Reserved, should be 0
5	1 = line numbering on
6	Reserved
7	1 = print footnotes at end of text

2.3 Microsoft Symbolic Link (SYLK) Format

The idea behind the SYLK format is to allow the transfer of data between Microsoft products. The format is easy to analyze and can be reproduced by other programs.

A Multiplan spreadsheet can be completely represented as lines stored in SYLK format. The command TRANSFER OPTIONS with the format (Symbolic) selected will tell the program to store the file in SYLK format.

SYLK files are stored in ASCII format. The records in the file are separated by line feed (LF) or carriage return (CR) characters.

Each record begins with a character that identifies the record type. There are three basic types of records: Records used for general file description (for example record types ID, E), records that store the position, value and contents of the data elements (record type C), and records that store special attributes of the Multiplan spreadsheet (records types W, F, NN, etc.).

Each record contains one or more fields, each of which begins with a semicolon (;). After the semicolon comes a field identification character. Except for two exceptions, there are no restrictions on the contents of the fields: LF and CR may not be used and if a semicolon is desired, it must be doubled.

Programs that read SYLK files must be able to skip over unrecognized record and field types.

An example file is printed on the following pages:

Multiplan File

```
#1         1          2       3    4      5        6        7        8
    1 NAME       STREET    CTY  SALES  DATE
    2 Burns      64 24th St. NY  370.00   1/1/90
    3 Bear       12 Elm St.  LA  378.00   2/1/89
    4 Fischer    34 D St.    GR  260.00 12/23/89
    5 Hoffman    2 Apple Rd. DM  250.00   3/1/89
    6 Huber      1 Plum Dr.  KZ  190.00   4/1/89
    7 Miller     23 23rd St. GR  100.00   5/1/89
    8 Mylor      81 Tuo Dr.  LA  299.00   7/1/89
    9 Micheal    9 Umm Ave.  NY  150.00   8/1/89
   10 Smith      99 Gem Rd.  LA  500.00  7/20/89
   11 Stevens    10 Apso Ln. LA  300.00  7/30/89
   12
   13
   14
   15
   16
   17
   18
   19
   20
COMMAND: Alpha Blank Copy Delete Edit Format Goto Help Insert Lock Move
         Name Options Print Quit Run Sort Transfer Value Window Xternal
Select option or type command letter
R1C1      "NAME"                    100% Free     Multiplan: DATA.MP
```

SYLK File

```
ID;PMP
P;PNONE
P;Pm/d/yy
P;Pm/d
P;Pd-mmm-yy
P;Pd-mmm
P;Pmmm-yy
P;Ph:mm\ AM/PM
P;Ph:mm:ss\ AM/PM
P;Ph:mm
P;Ph:mm:ss
P;Pm/d/yy\ h:mm
F;DG0G10
F;W1 1 10
F;W2 2 12
F;W3 3 4
F;W4 4 7
F;W5 5 9
B;Y11;X5
NN;Nname;ER2:11C1;K
NN;NStreet;ER2:11C2;K
NN;NCty;ER2:11C3;K
NN;NSales;ER2:11C4;K
NN;NDate;ER2:11C5;K
C;Y1;X1;K"NAME"
C;X2;K"STREET"
C;X3;K"CTY"
C;X4;K"SALES"
C;X5;K"DATE"
C;Y2;X1;K"Burns"
C;X2;K"64 24th St."
C;X3;K"NY"
C;X4;K370
F;FF2D
C;X5;K32874
F;P1;FD0D
C;Y3;X1;K"Bear"
C;X2;K"12 Elm St."
C;X3;K"LA"
C;X4;K378
F;FF2D
C;X5;K32540
F;P1;FD0D
C;Y4;X1;K"Fischer"
C;X2;K"34 D St."
C;X3;K"GR"
C;X4;K260
F;FF2D
C;X5;K32865
F;P1;FD0D
C;Y5;X1;K"Hoffman"
C;X2;K"2 Apple Rd."
C;X3;K"DM"
```

```
C;X4;K250
F;FF2D
C;X5;K32568
F;P1;FD0D
C;Y6;X1;K"Huber"
C;X2;K"1 Plum Dr."
C;X3;K"KZ"
C;X4;K190
F;FF2D
C;X5;K32599
F;P1;FD0D
C;Y7;X1;K"Miller"
C;X2;K"23 23rd St."
C;X3;K"GR"
C;X4;K100
F;FF2D
C;X5;K32629
F;P1;FD0D
C;Y8;X1;K"Mylor"
C;X2;K"81 Tuo Dr."
C;X3;K"LA"
C;X4;K299
F;FF2D
C;X5;K32690
F;P1;FD0D
C;Y9;X1;K"Micheal"
C;X2;K"9 Umm Ave."
C;X3;K"NY"
C;X4;K150
F;FF2D
C;X5;K32721
F;P1;FD0D
C;Y10;X1;K"Smith"
C;X2;K"99 Gem Rd."
C;X3;K"LA"
C;X4;K500
F;FF2D
C;X5;K32709
F;P1;FD0D
C;Y11;X1;K"Stevens"
C;X2;K"10 Apso Ln."
C;X3;K"LA"
C;X4;K300
F;FF2D
C;X5;K32719
F;P1;FD0D
W;N1;A1 1;C7 0 7
E
```

Record Type: ID (e.g. ID;PMP)

The record type ID is the identifying record in a SYLK file. It contains the name of the program that created the file.

Record Type: P (e.g. P;Pd/m/yy)

Record type P provides information on the possible date formats.

Record Type: B (e.g. B;Y11;X5)

Record type B contains the dimensions of the spreadsheet. It is given in the lower right corner of the spreadsheet as x-y coordinates.

;Xn;Ym
          n = number of columns m = number of rows

Record Type: F

Record type F describes the format of one or more Multiplan fields or the format of the entire spreadsheet.

The possible fields within record type F are:

;X;Y*   Same as record type B

;Pn   Gives information on the stored date format (e.g. F;P1;FD0D).

  n   Numerical position of the date format within the P record (P;PNONE corresponds to a value of 0).

;F<anb>*
          Format field: (Format/Cells) e.g. F;FF2D.

a	Format code: (a character)	
	D	Default
	C	Continuous
	E	Exponentiation
	F	Fixed decimal point
	G	General
	I	Integer <?>
	$	Currency
n	Number of digits after the decimal	
b	Position format:	
	D	Default
	C	Center
	G	General
	L	Left
	R	Right

;D(anbm>*
> Default format: (Format/Default, F;DG0G10)
>
> Default field: The same rules apply here as for format fields except that code D may not be used with a and b. The parameter m gives the column width.

;K   Commas separating thousands turned on (Format/Options).

;E   Formula display is turned on (Format/Options).

;W<nmo>*
> Column width of a region in the spreadsheet (Format/Width). Columns that have no W format field are stored with the default width.

n	Number of the first column
m	Number of the last column
o	Column width in characters

Record Type: C

Record type C contains the position and contents of the individual cells of the spreadsheet. Each cell that is not empty must be described using a C record (e.g. C;Y1;X1;K"NAME").

The possible fields within a C record are:

;X;Y*   Same as record type B.

;K   This field contains the value of a cell. If this value is calculated with a formula, then the record will have an E field which contains the formula. Text is placed in quotes.

;E   If the cell value is calculated with a formula, this field contains the formula.

;P   If a C record has a P field, the cell is "protected".

;S   If a C record contains an S field, then the cell value is determined by the contents of the cell with coordinates ;Rn;Cm. The C record for the cell with ;Rn;Cm must then contain a D or a G field.

;Rn;Cm
> Coordinate fields: n is the row number, m is the column number. These coordinates give the location of the cell that contains the value of the current cell (used only in connection with the S field).

;D   The formula in field ;E is also used to calculate the value of other cells.

;G   The value in field ;K is also used by other cells.

Record Type: NN

Record type NN contains the logical names of spreadsheet ranges assigned by the Multiplan command Name. For example:

NN;Nname;ER2:11C1)

The possible fields within record type NN are:

;Nname Name is the logical name for the spreadsheet range.

;Ex   x describes the range to which the name is assigned.

Record Type: NE

This record type describes relationships with other spreadsheets. (Xternal command.)

The possible fields for record type NE are:

;Ftab   Tab is the name of the external table.

;Sa   a describes the logical name of the position of the source range within the external table.

;Ex   x describes the location of the target range.

Record Type: NU

Record type NU is used to rename external tables. (Mulitplan Xternal/Use command.)

The possible field types are:

;La   a is the name of the external table.

;Fb   b describes the new name for the external table, which will be used in place of the name given under ;L.

Record Type: W

Record type W describes the contents of each window in a divided Multiplan screen.

The possible field types are:

;Nn   n is the number of windows.

;Ayx   yx are the coordinates of the cells in the upper left corner of the window.

;B   If the record has a B field, then the window has a border.

The S fields describe the division:

;STcycx
> The screen was split by specifying the size of the new window (Multiplan command: Window/Split/Titles). cy is the number of rows in the new window, cx is the number of characters.

;SHLcy The screen was split horizontally (Multiplan command: Window/Split/Horizontal). cy is the number of rows in the new window. If the letter L is present, then there is a relationship between the two windows. If no L is present there is no relationship.

;SVLcx The screen was split vertically (Multiplan command: Window/Split/Vertical). cx is the number of characters in the new window. If the letter L is present, then there is a relationship between the two windows. If no L is present there is no relationship.

Record Type: E

Record type E marks the end of a SYLK file.

Note: The field types marked with * do not have to appear if their values are unchanged from the last record in which they were given.

A SYLK file must be organized as follows:

1.   The record type ID must be stored as the first record in a SYLK file.

2.   Record type B should be present in order for the file to be read by Multiplan, but this is not absolutely necessary.

3.   The following applies to record type C in Multiplan: A C record with a D or a G field must come before a C record with an S, R or C field.

4.   The records containing name definitions should come before the records that use names, but this is not absolutely necessary.

5.   Records that describe the contents of windows must contain the order of the window numbers.

6.   Record type NU must never come before record type NE.

7.   The E record must always be the last in the file.

2.4 ASCII Files

There are two different formats of ASCII files used for data transfer between standard software applications.

These formats are not used by the applications to store files. They are only used for data exchange. Each software package described in this book has the ability to port data in at least one of these formats.

2.4.1 ASCII(DELIMITED) Files

The ASCII(DELIMITED) format is an ASCII file with field and text delimiting characters. For example, dBASE uses an ASCII(DELIMITED) format with commas (,) as field delimiters and quotes (") as alphanumeric text delimiters. Numerical and data fields are not delimited with the text delimiter.

As an example, we have included a file containing the fields NAME, ADDRESS and CITY (alphanumeric), and SALES and PROFIT (numeric):

ASCII(DELIMITED) File

NAME   ADDRESS   CITY   SALES   PROFIT

"Burns","64 24th St.","NY",370.00,290.00
"Bear","12 Elm St.","LA",378.00,584.00
"Fischer","34 D St.","GR",260.00,470.00
"Hoffman","2 Apple Rd.","DM",250.00,350.00
"Huber","1 Plum Dr.","KZ",190.00,280.00
"Miller","23 23rd St.","GR",100.00,300.00
"Mylor","81 Tuo Dr.","LA",299.00,560.00
"Michael","9 Umm Ave.","NY",150.00,200.00
"Smith","99 Gem Rd.","LA",500.00,789.00
"Stevens","10 Apso Ln.","LA",300.00,100.00

2.4.2 ASCII(SDF) Files

ASCII(SDF) stands for ASCII file with standard data format. This means that each column has a definite length. Data records are organized in rows. The logical structure of an ASCII(SDF) file looks like this:

	Field 1(8)	Field 2(12)	Field 3(9)	Field 4(9)
Record 1				
Record 2				
Record 3				
Record 4				

As an example, we'll use a file with the following structure:

NAME (10), ADDRESS (12), CITY (10), SALES (6,2), PROFIT (6,2)

The numbers in parentheses are the column widths. The number before the comma is the entire width and the number after the comma gives the number of decimal places (e.g. 6,2 means a 6 character column with 2 decimal places).

ASCII(SDF) File

```
NAME       ADDRESS      CITY SALES   PROFIT
Burns      64 24th St.  NY   370.00  290.00
Bear       12 Elm St.   LA   378.00  584.00
Fischer    34 D St.     GR   260.00  470.00
Hoffman    2 Apple Rd.  DM   250.00  350.00
Huber      1 Plum Dr.   KZ   190.00  280.00
Miller     23 23rd St.  GR   100.00  300.00
Mylor      81 Tuo Dr.   LA   299.00  560.00
Michael    9 Umm Ave.   NY   150.00  200.00
Smith      99 Gem Rd.   LA   500.00  789.00
Stevens    10 Apso Ln.  LA   300.00  100.00
```

2.5 DCA/RFT Formats

Document Content Architecture (DCA) is an IBM standard that defines word processing file format rules.

There are two distinct formats within DCA:

1. **RFT (Revisable Form Text)**

   If a document is in RFT format, further changes can be made.

2. **FFT (Final Form Text)**

   Documents in FFT format can no longer be revised. It can only be displayed, printed or mailed electronically. In this book, we will only be concerned with RFT format.

Chapter 3

Exporting Data

In this section, the capabilities each software package has for exporting data are analyzed and described in detail.

3.1 dBASE IV

dBASE has the ability to convert database files or parts of files to various formats. This allows data from dBASE to be processed in other programs such as spreadsheets or word processors.

dBASE can import and export data in the following file formats:

- ASCII files (with fixed field lengths or with field delimiters)

- SYLK files

- Lotus 1-2-3 files

- VisiCalc files

- Framework 2 files

- dBASE III Plus files

The general syntax for the command is:

```
COPY TO <Destination> FIELDS <Field1,Field2,> FOR <Conditions> <Filetype>
```

Destination

The file where the data is to be stored.

FIELDS   <Field1,Field2,>

This allows you to restrict the fields copied to the destination file. Only the fields specified will be copied.

dBASE IV
Interfaces

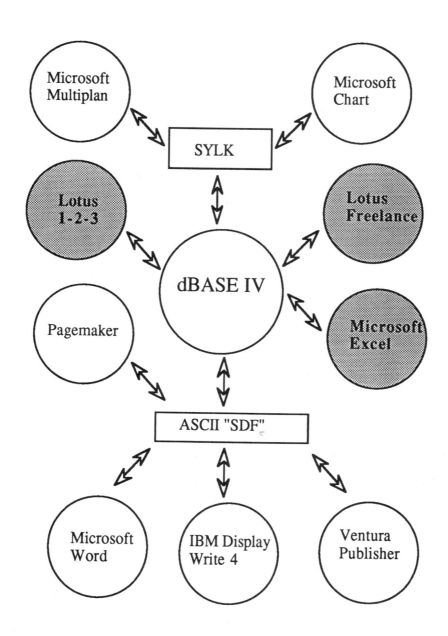

FOR <Conditions>

This clause allows you to restrict the records copied to those which meet the specified condition(s).

<Filetype>

This option determines the format of the destination file.

The following file types are available in dBASE:

SDF

This type creates an ASCII file with fixed field and record lengths.

DELIMITED

This type creates an ASCII file which uses a comma (,) as the field delimiter and quotes (") to surround alphanumeric text.

DELIMITED WITH <Special_Character>

This type allows you to select the separator character used to separate alphanumeric text.

SYLK

This type creates a file which can be read by Microsoft Multiplan or Microsoft Chart.

WKS

This type creates a file which can be read by Lotus 1-2-3.

DIF

This type creates a file which can be read by VisiCalc.

DBASEII

This type creates a file which can be read by dBASE II.

To further clarify how dBASE can transfer data to other file formats, the following dBASE file will be used as an example:

```
01 Burns           64 24th St.       NY          370.00
02 Bear            12 Elm St.        LA          378.00
03 Fischer         34 D St.          GR          260.00
04 Hoffman         2 Apple Rd.       DM          250.00
05 Huber           1 Plum Dr.        KZ          190.00
06 Miller          23 23rd St.       GR          100.00
07 Mylor           81 Tuo Dr.        LA          299.00
09 Michael         9 Umm Ave.        NY          150.00
10 Smith           99 Gem Rd.        LA          500.00
11 Stevens         10 Apso Ln.       LA          300.00
```

Structure of the dBASE file			
Field name	Type	Width	Dec
1 CUST_NR	Character	2	0
2 NAME	Character	20	0
3 ADDRESS	Character	20	0
4 CITY	Character	15	0
5 SALES	Numeric	7	2

The following command:

```
COPY TO word SDF
```

creates the following ASCII SDF file:

WORD.TXT

```
01Burns            64 24th St.       NY          370.00
02Bear             12 Elm St.        LA          378.00
03Fischer          34 D St.          GR          260.00
04Hoffman          2 Apple Rd.       DM          250.00
05Huber            1 Plum Dr.        KZ          190.00
06Miller           23 23rd St.       GR          100.00
07Mylor            81 Tuo Dr.        LA          299.00
09Michael          9 Umm Ave.        NY          150.00
10Smith            99 Gem Rd.        LA          500.00
11Stevens          10 Apso Ln.       LA          300.00
```

The following command:

```
COPY TO dell DELIMITED
```

creates the following ASCII(DELIMITED) file:

DEL1.TXT

```
"01","Burns","64 24th St.","NY",370.00
"02","Bear","12 Elm St.","LA",378.00
"03","Fischer","34 D St.","GR",260.00
"04","Hoffman","2 Apple Rd.","DM",250.00
"05","Huber","1 Plum Dr.","KZ",190.00
"06","Miller","23 23rd St.","GR",100.00
"07","Mylor","81 Tuo Dr.","LA",299.00
"09","Michael","9 Umm Ave.","NY",150.00
"10","Smith","99 Gem Rd.","LA",500.00
"11","Stevens","10 Apso Ln.","LA",300.00
```

The following command:

```
COPY TO del2 DELIMITED WITH *
```

creates the following ASCII file with * delimiters:

DEL2.TXT

```
*01*,*Burns*,*64 24th St.*,*NY*,370.00
*02*,*Bear*,*12 Elm St.*,*LA*,378.00
*03*,*Fischer*,*34 D St.*,*GR*,260.00
*04*,*Hoffman*,*2 Apple Rd.*,*DM*,250.00
*05*,*Huber*,*1 Plum Dr.*,*KZ*,190.00
*06*,*Miller*,*23 23rd St.*,*GR*,100.00
*07*,*Mylor*,*81 Tuo Dr.*,*LA*,299.00
*09*,*Michael*,*9 Umm Ave.*,*NY*,150.00
*10*,*Smith*,*99 Gem Rd.*,*LA*,500.00
*11*,*Stevens*,*10 Apso Ln.*,*LA*,300.00
```

The following command

```
COPY TO mplan FIELDS name,sales FOR name>"H" SYLK
```

creates this SYLK format file:

MPLAN

NAME	SALES
Hoffman	250.00
Huber	190.00
Miller	100.00
Mylor	299.00
Michael	150.00
Smith	500.00
Stevens	300.00

The following command:

```
COPY TO lotus FIELDS cust_nr,sales FOR sales>2700 WKS
```

creates this .WKS file:

LOTUS.WKS

NAME	SALES
Mylor	299.00
Smith	500.00
Stevens	300.00

The following command imports ASCII files or other files into dBASE:

```
APPEND FROM <Srce_File> <File type>
```

For this to work, a dBASE file with fields that correspond in number and length with those of the source file must already exist. The field names do not matter. Field delimiters and markers for alphanumeric fields (if file type = DELIMITED) are automatically removed by dBASE. These characters are not counted in the field length.

When ASCII files are imported, the records are added to the end of the existing dBASE file, just as the normal dBASE APPEND command does.

TEST.TXT

```
01Burns          64 24th St.        NY        370.00
02Bear           12 Elm St.         LA        378.00
03Fischer        34 D St.           GR        260.00
04Hoffman        2 Apple Rd.        DM        250.00
05Huber          1 Plum Dr.         KZ        190.00
06Miller         23 23rd St.        GR        100.00
07Mylor          81 Tuo Dr.         LA        299.00
09Michael        9 Umm Ave.         NY        150.00
10Smith          99 Gem Rd.         LA        500.00
11Stevens        10 Apso Ln.        LA        300.00
```

To import this file into dBASE, a dBASE file which corresponds to the structure of the ASCII file must be created. This file would have the following structure:

Field name	Type	Width	Dec
1 CUST_NR	Character	2	0
2 NAME	Character	20	0
3 ADDRESS	Character	20	0
4 CITY	Character	15	0
5 SALES	Numeric	7	2

If this dBASE file already exists, the dBASE command USE will open the file. The following command imports the ASCII file shown above and adds the records to any records which may already have been in the dBASE file:

```
APPEND FROM Test SDF
```

The following ASCII file has the same structure but a different data storage format:

```
"01","Burns","64 24th St.","NY",370.00
"02","Bear","12 Elm St.","LA",378.00
"03","Fischer","34 D St.","GR",260.00
"04","Hoffman","2 Apple Rd.","DM",250.00
"05","Huber","1 Plum Dr.","KZ",190.00
"06","Miller","23 23rd St.","GR",100.00
"07","Mylor","81 Tuo Dr.","LA",299.00
"09","Michael","9 Umm Ave.","NY",150.00
"10","Smith","99 Gem Rd.","LA",500.00
"11","Stevens","10 Apso Ln.","LA",300.00
```

The command

```
APPEND FROM Test2 DELIMITED
```

will copy the records into dBASE.

3.2 Microsoft Multiplan

Multiplan can process data from ASCII files, from files created on other spreadsheets or from SYLK files. SYLK files are loaded as follows: Select the Transfer command from the main menu, then the Options command. Select the Symbolic command and press the <Enter> key to confirm. Now Multiplan will read SYLK format files into the work area the next time you select Transfer/Load. This can also be done using a macro.

Lotus 1-2-3 files are loaded as follows: Select the Transfer command from the main menu, then the Options command. Select the Other command and press the <Enter> key to confirm. The 1-2-3 file loads into the work area the next time you select Transfer/Load. This can also be done using a macro.

ASCII files are loaded as follows: The ASCII file must be divided into lines (i.e., records), where every line contains one or more data fields. Select the Transfer command from the main menu, then the Import command. Enter the name of the ASCII file in the File name: command field. Press the <Tab> key to move on to the at: command field. If you don't enter a number, Multiplan defaults to the upper left corner of the area. The numbers: command field specifies whether to treat all entries as numbers. If you select (Yes), Multiplan interprets all numeric data as values. If you select (No), Multiplan interprets all data as text.

The query: command field specifies how to handle data already in the program. Selecting (Yes) instructs Multiplan to ask the user whether it should overwrite existing cells with the new data. Selecting (No) overwrites existing cells without asking the user. The delimiters: command field specifies the characters used in the ASCII file to delimit (divide) data. The defaults are the tab (^t) and space (^s) characters. You may include almost any characters as delimiters, with the exception of the following characters:

?   @   ;   !

Multiplan can also save data as SYLK files, Lotus 1-2-3 files or ASCII files. SYLK files are saved as follows: Select the Transfer command from the main menu, then the Options command. Select the Symbolic command and press the <Enter> key to confirm. Multiplan saves the file to disk as a SYLK file the next time you select Transfer/Save. This can also be done using a macro.

Lotus 1-2-3 files are saved as follows: Select the Transfer command from the main menu, then the Options command. Select the Other command and press the <Enter> key to confirm. Multiplan saves the file to disk as a 1-2-3 file the next time you select Transfer/Save. This can also be done using a macro.

ASCII (SDF) files are saved as follows: Select Print/File from the main menu, enter the filename of the ASCII (SDF) file to which you want the data saved and press the <Enter> key to confirm.

Microsoft Multiplan
Interfaces

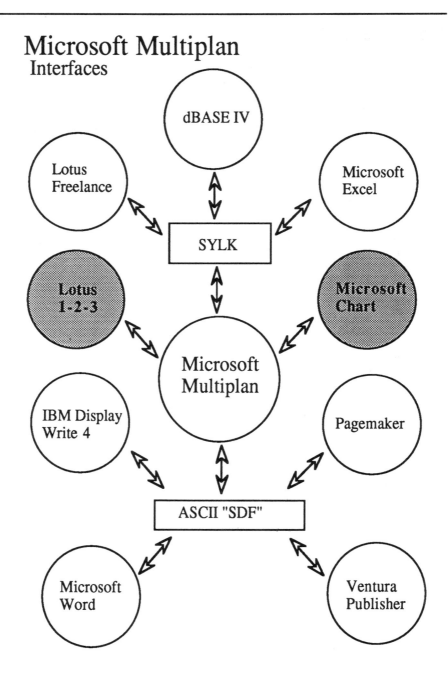

3.3 Microsoft Excel

Excel can process data from ASCII files, from files created in other spreadsheet programs, dBASE files or SYLK files.

Excel loads all these files from the same menus. Select the File menu and select the Open command. A window opens, displaying files with extensions of .XL*.

Enter *.* in the File_Name: text box. Excel displays all the filenames in the directory specified. Select the filename you want to load and select the OK button. Excel will automatically determine what the file type is and load it if it is one that it recognizes.

Excel can also save files to these formats. Select the File menu and select the Save As command. Select the Options button. A dialog box appears, listing the following file formats:

Normal	SYLK	DIF
Text	WKS	DBF 2
CSV	WK1	DBF 3

Select a file format and select the OK button. Excel adds the correct extension to the filename.

Microsoft Excel
Interfaces

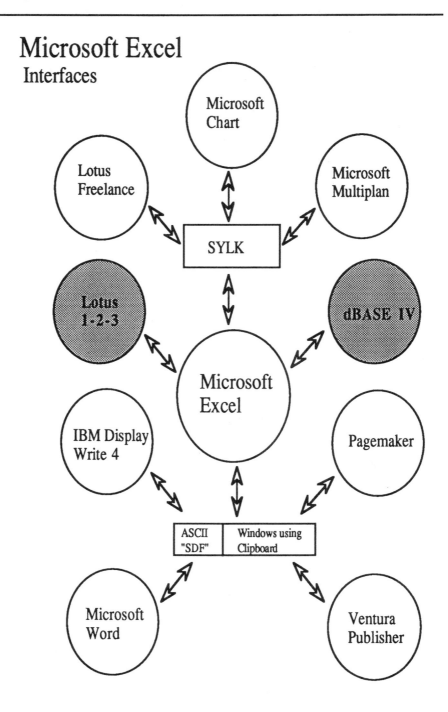

3.4 Microsoft Chart

Microsoft Chart accepts data from other files and interprets this data graphically. Chart accepts the following file types:

•   Microsoft Multiplan worksheet files

•   SYLK files

•   Lotus 1-2-3 or Lotus Symphony files

•   dBASE ASCII(DELIMITED) files

•   ASCII files with predefined field lengths

•   ASCII files with other delimiters. Chart's Xternal command allows the selection of one of these files (Multiplan, Lotus, dBASE, SYLK/DIF, text) based on the following data:

Filename

Whether the source file should be merged with an existing chart file

Data types

•   Sequence of the data. If the data of the source file are edited or revised, the source file should be merged with a new Chart file. Each change to the source file's data is accepted by the existing Chart file. If a merge has already occurred between the source file and Chart file, the data of the Chart file cannot be edited directly.

The data must form a rectangular range before the source file can be prepared in graphic form:

Microsoft Chart
Interfaces

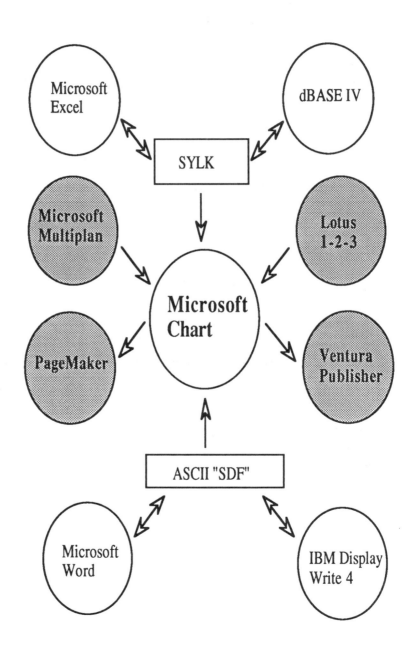

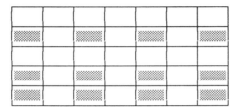

Several blocks of data can be copied into Chart, provided they result in a rectangular range:

3.4.1 The Xternal dBASE Command

The Xternal/dBASE command lets Chart accept dBASE files that were created using the following command in dBASE:

```
COP Y TO < filename > DELIMITED
```

Run Chart and select the Xternal/dBASE command.

Enter the name of the ASCII dBASE file in the filename: command field.

The linked: command field specifies whether Chart should merge the incoming data with an existing Chart file. Press <Y> or <N> for yes or no.

The selected rows: command field specifies the starting row of the source file. If two or more rows are stated the first and the last row are specified with a colon separating them. Several adjacent rows may be specified by entering these rows, separating them using commas (,).

For example, the following transfers only rows 1,3,4 to 8 and 11 to 16:

```
1,3,4:8,11:16
```

The line length is limited to 255 characters.

The selected columns: command field specifies the starting column of the source file. If two or more columns are stated the first and the last column are specified with a colon separating them. Several adjacent columns may be specified by entering these rows, separating them using commas (,).

For example, the following transfers only columns 1,3,4 to 8 and 11 to 16:

```
1,3,4:8,11:16
```

The row and column specifications help Chart establish the structure of the source file.

For example, if you transfer columns 1,3 and 5 and rows 2 and 4 from your dBASE ASCII file, the following is the result:

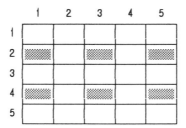

Chart treats the fields as individual rectangular blocks of data.

Empty areas between transferred fields have no effect on the structure of the diagram.

The orient series by: command field allows you to select rows or columns for data orientation. This controls the sequence of data on which the chart is based. For example, if you select rows for a data set, the chart is displayed as two data sets with three data points:

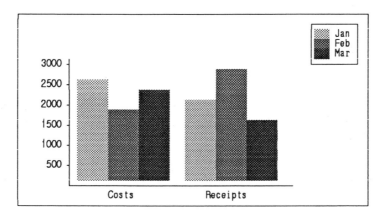

If you select a data sequence based on columns, Chart creates a series of three data items, each with two data points:

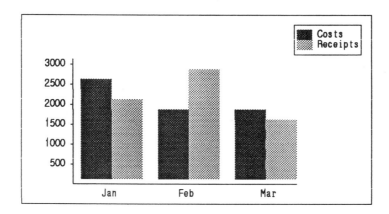

The series names from: command field specify the locations of the data series names. If the data sets were based on rows, you must enter the column at which these set names must appear. If the data sets were based on columns, you must enter the row at which these set names must appear.

The category type: command field specifies whether a text and/or value should be used from the dBASE file as descriptions in the chart.

3.4.2 The Xternal Lotus Command

This command allows the transfer of Lotus 1-2-3 or Lotus Symphony data.

Enter the filename of the Lotus data in the filename: command field.

The linked: command field specifies whether Chart should merge the incoming data with an existing Chart file. Press <Y> or <N> for yes or no.

The type: command field specifies the Lotus data type (Worksheet or Graph).

The named area or reference: command field specifies the rectangular data range to be used by Chart. This field can accept numerous unconnected ranges, provided the ranges are separated by commas.

The orient series by: command field allows you to select rows or columns for data orientation. This controls the sequence of data on which the chart is based (rows or columns).

The series names from: command field specify the locations of the data series names. If the data sets were based on rows, you must enter the column at which these set names must appear. If the data sets were based on columns, you must enter the row at which these set names must appear.

The categories from: command field specify the row or column location of the categories.

The category type: command field specifies whether a text and/or value should be used from the Lotus file as a description in the chart.

3.4.3 The Xternal Multiplan Command

This command allows the transfer of Microsoft Multiplan data into Chart.

Enter the filename of the Multiplan worksheet in the filename: command field.

The linked: command field specifies whether Chart should merge the incoming data with an existing Chart file. Press <Y> or <N> for yes or no.

The named area or reference: command field specifies the rectangular data range to be used by Chart. This field can accept numerous unconnected ranges, provided the ranges are separated by commas.

The orient series by: command field allows you to select rows or columns for data orientation. This controls the sequence of data on which the chart is based (rows or columns).

The series names from: command field specify the locations of the data series names. If the data sets were based on rows, you must enter the column at which these set names must appear. If the data sets were based on columns, you must enter the row at which these set names must appear.

The categories from: command field specify the row or column location of the categories.

The category type: command field specifies whether a text and/or value should be used from the Lotus file as a description in the chart.

3.4.4 The Xternal SYLK/DIF Command

This command allows the transfer of SYLK files into Chart.

Enter the name of the SYLK file in the filename: command field.

The linked: command field specifies whether Chart should merge the incoming data with an existing Chart file. Press <Y> or <N> for yes or no.

The selected rows: and selected columns: command fields specify the starting row and column of the source file.

The linked: command field specifies whether Chart should merge the incoming data with an existing Chart file. Press <Y> or <N> for yes or no.

The orient series by: command field allows you to select rows or columns for data orientation. This controls the sequence of data on which the chart is based (rows or columns).

The series names from: command field specify the locations of the data series names. If the data sets were based on rows, you must enter the column at which these set names must appear. If the data sets were based on columns, you must enter the row at which these set names must appear.

The categories from: command field specify the row or column location of the categories.

The category type: command field specifies whether a text and/or value should be used from the Lotus file as a description in the chart.

3.4.5 The Xternal Text Command

This command allows the transfer of text files in either SDF (Delimited) or columnar (specific columns) form.

Selecting Xternal/Text/Columnar displays a set of command fields similar to those displayed by Xternal/dBASE or Xternal/SYLK/DIF. One additional command field appears: The column width: command field, which prompts the user for the default width of each column.

Selecting Xternal/Text/Delimited displays a set of command fields similar to the set displayed by Xternal/Text/Columnar. Two additional command fields appear: The text quote character: command field, which prompts the user for the text quote used in the text file, and the delimiter character: command field, which prompts the user for the character used as a delimiter.

3.5 Lotus 1-2-3

Lotus 1-2-3 can read and write ASCII files. These ASCII files should be saved with ^t and " as delimiters. dBASE creates these delimiters when you enter the following command:

```
COPY TO <filename> DELIMITED
```

The /File Import command loads an ASCII file into Lotus 1-2-3 as follows:

Move the cell pointer to the upper left corner of the area in which you would like the data to appear. Press the </> key, the <F> key and the <I> key. Press either <N> (Numbers) or <T> (Text). Enter the filename and press the <Enter> key.

If you select Numbers, Lotus 1-2-3 interprets alphanumeric data as values and text. If you select Text, Lotus 1-2-3 interprets both values and numbers as text.

The /Print File command writes data to diskette or hard disk as an ASCII file. The user must enter a filename under which the ASCII file should be stored, including a drive specifier and path if needed.

Lotus 1-2-3 also includes a Translate program, which allows file format exchanges between Lotus 1-2-3 Version 2.2, earlier versions of 1-2-3, dBASE II, dBASE III+, Lotus Symphony and other formats. Translate can be started from the 1-2-3 Access utility. A menu appears, allowing the option of accessing 1-2-3, Translate or other Lotus utilities.

```
┌──────────────────────────────────────────────────────────────┐
│ 1-2-3 PrintGraph Translate Install Exit                        │
│ Use 1-2-3                                                       │
└──────────────────────────────────────────────────────────────┘
```

```
┌──────────────────────────────────────────────────────────────┐
│              Lotus 1-2-3 Release 2.2 Translate Utility         │
│      Copr. 1985, 1989 Lotus Development Corporation  All Rights Reserved │
│                                                                │
│ What do you want to translate FROM?                            │
│              1-2-3 1A                                           │
│              1-2-3 2, 20.1 or 2.2                               │
│              dBASE II                                           │
│              dBASE III                                          │
│              DIF                                                │
│              Multiplan (SYLK)                                   │
│              Symphony 1.0                                       │
│              Symphony 1.1, 1.2 or 2.0                           │
│              VisiCalc                                           │
│                                                                │
│                                                                │
│              Highlight your selection and press ENTER          │
│               Press ESC to end the Translate Utility           │
│                Press HELP (F1) for more information            │
└──────────────────────────────────────────────────────────────┘
```

Lotus 1-2-3
Interfaces

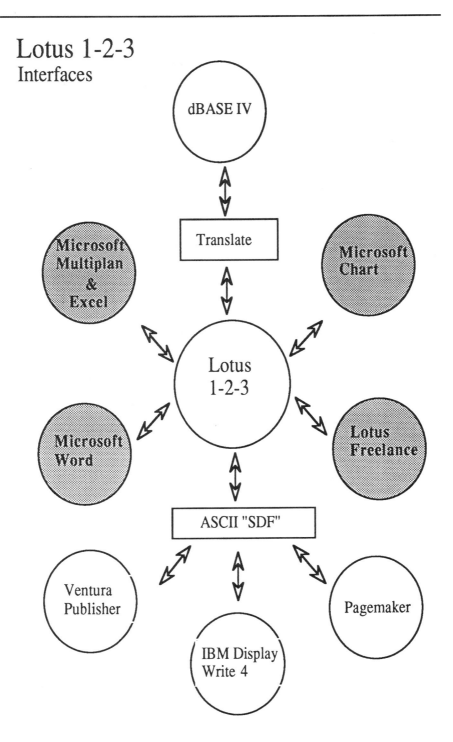

3.6　Lotus Freelance Plus Version 3.01

Freelance can read dBASE files, SYLK files, ASCII text files and Lotus 1-2-3 worksheet files and interpret this data graphically. In addition, it can also import .PIC (graphic) files from Lotus 1-2-3 and display the graphic. Freelance can import metafiles to other applications.

3.6.1　SYLK, dBASE and 1-2-3 Data

Freelance can read data directly from dBASE, SYLK or Lotus 1-2-3 for graphic display. To do so, the user must select the Chart New-data command. A chart form appears.

The Chart type: item specifies the type of chart you want displayed.

Pressing the <Tab> key moves you to the DATALINKS bar. Press <Space> to see a set of file parameters. The File type: item prompts the user for the type of file from which data must be taken. Pressing <Space> lists the following file types: Worksheet (Lotus 1-2-3), dBASE, ASCII Numbers, ASCII Text and SYLK. Highlight the desired file using the <Cursor up> and <Cursor down> keys, then press the <Enter> key.

The File path: item lists the drive specifier and path of the file. Pressing <Space> displays a list of available paths. Highlight the desired path using the <Cursor up> and <Cursor down> keys, then press the <Enter> key.

The File name: item specifies the filename. Pressing <Space> displays a list of available filenames. Highlight the desired filename using the <Cursor up> and <Cursor down> keys, then press the <Enter> key.

The Type of import: item specifies whether specific ranges or Lotus-compatible graphics should be imported. Specified ranges refers to Lotus 1-2-3, dBASE or SYLK data. The Named graph option instructs Freelance to load an existing Lotus 1-2-3 graphic.

If you select the Named graph option, press <Space>, enter the name of the graph in the Name of graph: item and press the slash key (/) or the less-than key (<) to load the graphic. Graphic captions and axis legends are NOT transferred.

Lotus Freelance
Interfaces

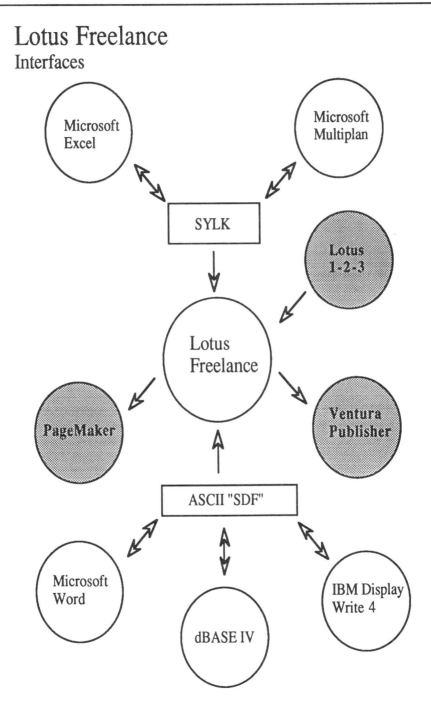

If you select the Specified Ranges option, the Destination options may be completed or skipped as necessary. Select the DONE item when finished.

Some rules must be followed when importing ranges:

- When importing SYLK files, the range must follow a specific syntax of R#C#:R#C#. For example, to transfer the Multiplan range R1C1:R10C16, you must enter A1..P10. Multiplan ranges must be converted to Lotus 1-2-3 compatible format. Columns 1-26 used in Multiplan must be converted to A-Z, 27-53 become AA-AZ, 54-80 become BA-BZ and so on. For example, the Multiplan range R1C1:R50C79 must be converted to A1..BY50.

- Lotus 1-2-3 and Multiplan also allow names for the individual ranges.

- Lotus Freelance will only allow the transfer of alphanumeric and numeric fields. Logical or memo fields are ignored.

Specification of a dBASE range allows the following:

- Records can be read as fields, including field names.

- A range of records can be given for a dBASE field by including the field name, a color and the range. For example, if you want Chart to read values from records 5 to 45 of the ENTRIES field, enter ENTRIES:5..45.

- A group of fields within a record can be read by including the range of fields, a colon and the record number. For example, if you have a dBASE file containing the fields NAME, STREET, CITY, SALES1, SALES2, SALES3, SALES4 and SALES5, and you want to read the fields from SALES1 to SALES3 in the fifth record of the file, enter SALES1..SALES3:5.

- After entering the importation format, press either the slash key (/) or the less-than key (<). Freelance then asks whether the graphic format should be activated by the import file. Press the <Y> key. If the load is successful, the information is then converted to graphic form. If you press the slash key (/) or the less-than key (<), Freelance returns you to the main menu, which allows you to then edit the imported graphic data in Freelance.

3.6.2 Transferring a Lotus 1-2-3 Chart

Freelance imports Lotus 1-2-3 graphics (.PIC files) direct from Lotus 1-2-3. This option allows the transfer of 1-2-3 charts, complete with titles, axis descriptions and labels.

Select the File Import command from the main menu of Freelance.

Select either PIC or Raw PIC from the File type item to load a 1-2-3 graphic and convert it to Freelance format. The PIC option loads the Lotus 1-2-3 graphic directly into Freelance and converts it. The Raw PIC option converts all the PIC graphic information into Freelance format, but leaves line segments and text as they appeared in the original format. Raw PIC offers an alternative method of loading graphics. This is handy when you cannot load a PIC file by normal means (e.g., the file is corrupted).

Select a drive specifier, path and filename, and press either </> or <F10> to load the chart.

3.6.3 Transferring ASCII File Data

Freelance can accept ASCII file data and display this data in graphic form.

Select the File Import command from the main menu. Select either the ASCII option (7-bit ASCII) or 8-bit ASCII.

The ASCII option loads a 7-bit ASCII file and converts it to Freelance format.

The 8-bit ASCII option loads an 8-bit ASCII file (i.e., one created using the extended ASCII character set) and converts it to Freelance format.

You can then edit the imported graphic data in Freelance.

3.6.4 Exporting Metafiles from Freelance

Freelance also allows the exportation of metafiles (a graphics format created by ANSI). Once you have prepared a graphic in Freelance, select the File Export command. Select the Metafile option from the File type item, enter a filename in the Name item and press the <Enter> key to save the graphic in metafile format.

3.7 Microsoft Word

Microsoft Word can load standard ASCII files without problems. The WORD_DCA utility converts DCA files and RFT files into Word format, and Word files into RFT format.

3.7.1 ASCII Files

Microsoft Word directly accepts ASCII files. When creating ASCII files for loading into Word, avoid using such delimiters as quotation marks, since Word treats these as normal characters. SDF ASCII files are best, such as those created from Lotus 1-2-3, Microsoft Multiplan and dBASE (generated using dBASE's COPY TO <filename> SDF), or unformatted ASCII files.

Word defaults to the .DOC file extension when handling files. If you assign an alternate file extension to an ASCII file (e.g., .TXT), you'll need to enter the filename and extension when attempting to load this file into Word.

ASCII files are loaded into Word as follows: Select the Transfer/Load command. Enter the filename (and extension if necessary) and press the <Enter> key. Word loads the ASCII file. You can then edit the file as you would a standard Word file. The Transfer/Merge command allows you to combine multiple files into one large file.

Word 5.0 can save files in ASCII format as follows: Select the Transfer/Save command. Enter a filename if this is a new file. Use the <Tab> key to move to the format: command field. Select the Text-only either by pressing <Space> or by pressing the <T> key. Press <Enter> to confirm.

Word 4.0 can save files in ASCII format as follows: Select the Transfer/Save command. Enter a filename if this is a new file. Use the <Tab> key to move to the Formatted: command field. Press the <N> key. When Word asks for confirmation, press <Y>. Press <Enter> to confirm.

A portion of a Word document can be printed to diskette as an ASCII file. Select the Print/Options command. Press the <F1> key to see the printer driver list. Highlight the word PLAIN using the cursor keys. Press the <Tab> key until the cursor reaches the range: command field. Press the <S> key to highlight the word Selection. Press the <Enter> key, then the <Esc> key to exit. Move the cursor to the starting point of the text segment you want to print to diskette. Press the <F6> key (Extend mode). Move the cursor keys until the cursor has highlighted the text you want saved. Select the Print/File command. Enter a filename and extension and press the <Enter> key to save to disk.

Microsoft Word
Interfaces

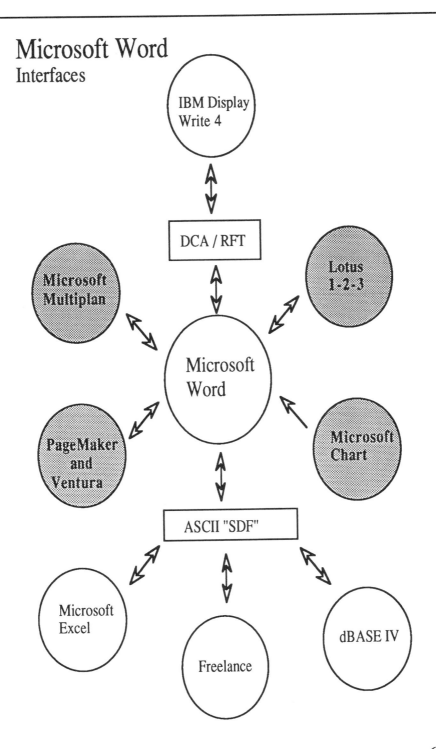

Word 5.0 can save files in ASCII format with line breaks at the end of each line as follows: Select the Transfer/Save command. Enter a filename if this is a new file. Use the <Tab> key to move to the format: command field. Select the Text-only-with-line-breaks either by pressing <Space> or by pressing the <T> key until this option is highlighted. Press <Enter> to confirm.

3.7.2 WordStar Files

Some versions of Microsoft Word included a conversion utility called WSCONV, which converted files created in earlier versions of WordStar to Word format. To convert WordStar 2000 files to Word format, save the files as DCA files and use the WORD_DCA conversion program described below.

3.7.3 RFT Files

The WORD_DCA program converts RFT (DCA) files into Word files and vice versa.

Call the WORD_DCA program from the DOS prompt. The program displays the following menu:

```
WORD_DCA 5.0 - DCA RFT File Conversion Utility for Microsoft (R) Word 5.0
Copyright (C) Systems Compatibility Corp., 1988-1989. All rights reserved.



                        - INTERACTIVE MODE -
Select Conversion Type:
A = Microsoft Word to DCA/RFT
B = DCA/RFT to Microsoft Word
Enter A or B ==>
```

Once you select a conversion, Word asks for the input file list and output file list (file/pathnames and directory).

3.7.4 Print Files and Word

Word also accepts printer files from other systems. Some of these printer files can be text (see Section 3.7.1 for information on generating a printer file in Word) or graphics (e.g., from Microsoft Chart). Other printer files can contain commands for the page description language known as PostScript, provided that the application generating the printer file supports PostScript.

Here are some ground rules for printer files:

- Printer files can contain almost any type of printer escape code.

- No page breaks should occur at the beginning or end of the file.

- A D code must precede a document printer file. For example:

    `.d.:external.asc`

- A G code must precede the citation of a graphic printer file. For example:

    `.g.a:graphic.gfc`

    If you enter a G code without a filename, Word leaves a blank range.

Word 5.0 allows the entry of external files as follows: Select the Library/Link command. The command field displays the options Document, Graphics and Spreadsheet. Select the desired file type, enter a filename and press <Enter>. Word ignores any bold and centered text from the external file.

HPGL and PostScript graphic data can be inserted in this manner.

3.7.5 Graphics

This option is available in Version 5.0 of Word. It allows the insertion of graphics in a Word document. Word currently accepts graphic data from Lotus (.PIC files), PC Paintbrush (.PCX files), HPGL plotter, PostScript, TIFF and Microsoft Windows. You can insert these graphics using the Library/Link/Graphics command.

The command fields in the Library/Link/Graphics command control the file format, width of the graphic, alignment within the frame, height and width of the graphic. Default settings create a centered graphic six inches high by six inches wide.

3.7.6 Spreadsheet Data

Word also accepts data from spreadsheet applications such as Microsoft Multiplan and Lotus 1-2-3. This data can be merged at any time as follows: Move the cursor to the location where you want the spreadsheet file to begin. Select the Library/Link/Spreadsheet command. Enter the filename and the cells of the range if you want to load a range of a file (in the area: command field) and press the <Enter> key.

If you can't remember the filename, press the <F1> key to see a list of files in the current directory. Select the filename using the cursor keys or mouse and press the <Enter> key.

```
.1.C:\LOTUS\TEST\L-CODE-1.WK1,A1
Costs:         Jan     Feb     Mar
Material:      1000    2000    3000
Labor:         200     300     400
Overhead:      300     400     500

Totals:        1500    2700    3900
.1.
```

The first and last line of the inserted data are formatted as hidden text. Select the Options command and select (Yes) for the show hidden text: command field. Pressing the <Enter> key reveals a L code at the beginning and end of the file.

3.8   IBM DisplayWrite 4

DisplayWrite 4 saves documents to disk in EBCDIC format, but can also read other file formats (i.e., 7-bit ASCII, 8-bit ASCII and RFT).

Files are loaded into DisplayWrite 4 by calling the Get function (pressing <Ctrl><F6>).

```
                           Get File

 If no pages are specified, the entire document will be included.
 When specifying multiple pages, separate page numbers with a space.

 File Name..............[                                      ]
 System Page Number (s).[                                      ]

 Insert Included Text...[N]    Y = Yes      N = No
 File Type..............[1]    1 = Document or DisplayWrite File
                               2 = ASCII
                               3 = 7-Bit ASCII
                               4 = Revisable-Form Text

 Enter   Esc=Quit   F1=Help   F3=List
```

This menu prompts the user for the filename, including the drive specifier and path if needed. Pressing the <Cursor down> key, the user then enters the number of pages that DisplayWrite 4 should load. If you omit this parameter, DisplayWrite will load the entire file.

The Insert Included Text parameter specifies whether you want to insert text from the Notepad.

The File type parameter specifies the type of file you want to load:

> 1: Normal DisplayWrite file
> 2: ASCII file
> 3: 7-bit ASCII file
> 4: Revisable-Form Text (RFT)

Press the number key corresponding to the file format you want loaded and press the <Enter> key to load the file into the current document.

After getting a file, you can then edit the file using the Document options (<Ctrl><F7>).

DisplayWrite 4 allows you to save an ASCII file to disk, allowing you to transfer this file to another application. You can do this through the Notepad. Move the cursor to the beginning of the text you want saved in ASCII format.

IBM Display Write 4
Interfaces

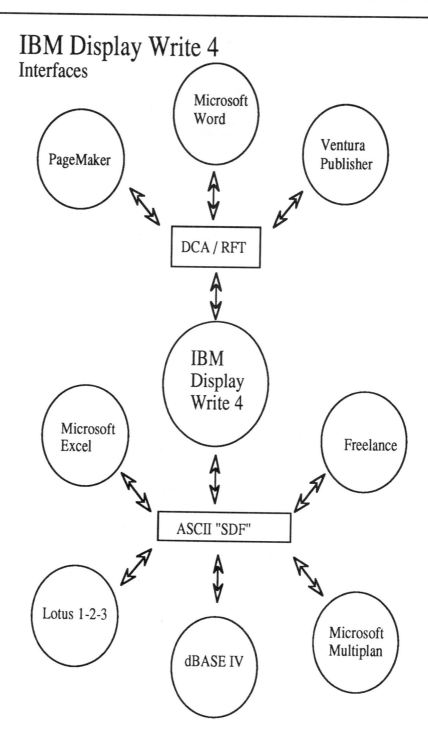

Press <Ctrl><F4> to invoke the Notepad.

```
┌─────────────────────────────────────────────┐
│                   Notepad                     │
├─────────────────────────────────────────────┤
│ * 1. Move to Notepad                          │
│ * 2. Move and Append to Notepad               │
│                                               │
│ * 3. Copy to Notepad                          │
│ * 4. Copy and Append to Notepad               │
│                                               │
│ * 5. ASCII Copy to File                       │
│ * 6. ASCII Copy and Append to File            │
│                                               │
│ * 7. Recall from Notepad                      │
├─────────────────────────────────────────────┤
│   Enter   Esc=Quit   F1=Help                  │
└─────────────────────────────────────────────┘
```

Select the ASCII Copy to File option. DisplayWrite 4 prompts you to move the cursor to the desired end of the text. Press the <Enter> key.

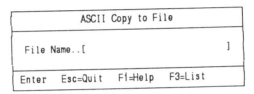

```
┌─────────────────────────────────────────────┐
│            ASCII Copy to File                 │
├─────────────────────────────────────────────┤
│                                               │
│   File Name..[                            ]   │
│                                               │
├─────────────────────────────────────────────┤
│   Enter   Esc=Quit   F1=Help   F3=List        │
└─────────────────────────────────────────────┘
```

Enter the filename you want assigned to the ASCII file, including the drive specifier and path name if necessary. DisplayWrite 4 automatically appends a file extension of .ASC if you do not enter a file extension.

Press the <Enter> key to save the file. After the command finishes execution, DisplayWrite 4 allows you to continue with the document currently in memory.

DisplayWrite 4 also offers the option of saving a file in RFT (Revisable-Form Text) or FFT (Final-Form Text) format. Select the main menu in DisplayWrite 4:

```
┌─────────────────────────────────────────────┐
│          DisplayWrite 4 Version 2             │
├─────────────────────────────────────────────┤
│   1.   Create Document                        │
│   2.   Revise Document                        │
│   3.   View Document                          │
│                                               │
│   4.   Print                                  │
│   5.   Spell                                  │
│   6.   Utilities (Copy, Erase, ...)           │
│                                               │
│   7.   Merge                                  │
│                                               │
│   8.   DOS Commands                           │
│   9.   Profiles                               │
├─────────────────────────────────────────────┤
│   Enter   Esc=Quit   F1=Help                  │
└─────────────────────────────────────────────┘
```

Select option 6 (Utilities):

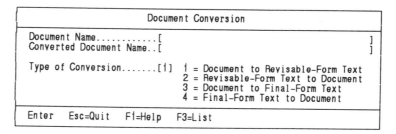

```
                    Utilities
  ┌──────────────────────────────────────────┐
  │  1. Copy                                  │
  │  2. Erase                                 │
  │  3. Rename                                │
  │                                           │
  │  4. Compress                              │
  │  5. Recover                               │
  │                                           │
  │  6. Document Conversion                   │
  ├──────────────────────────────────────────┤
  │  Enter   Esc=Quit   F1=Help               │
  └──────────────────────────────────────────┘
```

From Utilities select option 6 (Document Conversion). The following menu appears:

```
  ┌────────────────────────────────────────────────────────────────┐
  │                   Document Conversion                           │
  ├────────────────────────────────────────────────────────────────┤
  │  Document Name............[                                  ]   │
  │  Converted Document Name..[                                  ]   │
  │                                                                  │
  │  Type of Conversion.......[1]  1 = Document to Revisable-Form Text │
  │                                2 = Revisable-Form Text to Document │
  │                                3 = Document to Final-Form Text   │
  │                                4 = Final-Form Text to Document   │
  ├────────────────────────────────────────────────────────────────┤
  │  Enter   Esc=Quit   F1=Help   F3=List                           │
  └────────────────────────────────────────────────────────────────┘
```

Enter the name of the original document in the Document Name command field. Use the <Cursor down> key to move to the Converted Document name command field. Enter the name of the destination (converted) file here, including the drive specifier and path if necessary.

Use the <Cursor down> key to move to the next command field and select the desired conversion type. Press the <Enter> key to complete the task.

3.9 Aldus PageMaker

PageMaker can load files created by the following applications:

- Microsoft Word (.DOC extension)

- RFT files (.RFT or. DCA extension)

- ASCII files (.DOC or .TXT extension)

- Microsoft Windows/Write (.WRI extension)

- Lotus 1-2-3 graphics (.PIC extension)

- Lotus Freelance Plus metafiles

- Microsoft Chart print files (HPGL format)

- Microsoft Windows Paint (.MSP extension)

File loading procedures are similar for all filetypes when in PageMaker. The general procedure is as follows:

- Run PageMaker and either open an existing publication or create a new publication.

- Select the File/Place... command. Click on the filename and click OK.

- When the page reappears, the mouse pointer changes into a manual flow text pointer. Click once at the location in the publication at which you would like the text block to start.

PageMaker generates a block of text.

- If not all the text can be displayed, the bottom windowshade handle displays a plus sign (+). Add a page to the publication, move to the next page and click on this page.

PageMaker can also load files direct from Lotus 1-2-3 worksheets, dBASE database information and other application files, provided the proper import/export filters have been installed (see your PageMaker installation instructions for more information about filters).

3.10 Ventura Publisher

Xerox Ventura Publisher directly accepts the following file formats, among others:

Text

- Microsoft Word (.DOC extension)

- RFT files (.RFT or. DCA extension)

- ASCII files (.DOC extension)

- Lotus 1-2-3 graphics (.PIC extension)

- Lotus Freelance Plus metafiles

Graphics

- Microsoft Chart printer files in HPGL format

- Microsoft Windows Paint (.MSP extension)

- Microsoft Chart printer files in HPGL format

File loading procedures are the same in Ventura Publisher for all file types. Select the File menu and the Load Text/Picture... option. Depending on the type of file you wish to load, click on the Text button, the Line-Art button or the Image button. You can select the file type from one of the buttons that appear (e.g., Microsoft Word). Click on the filename when the ITEM SELECTOR box appears and click on the OK button.

When loading ASCII files, Ventura Publisher reads <u>two</u> end of paragraph markers as one paragraph break. This means that if you load an ASCII file with only one marker separating each paragraph, Ventura ignores the single markers, making the document one long paragraph delimited by protected spaces.

The simplest solution is to click on the WS 4.0/5.0 button instead of the ASCII button. This automatically adds the data needed to split paragraphs.

Another solution is to insert double end of paragraph markers in ASCII files. Ventura Publisher will then read this data as single end of paragraph markers. If you cannot do this, you'll have to enter the Text Editing function of Ventura Publisher after loading the file, and insert end of paragraph markers at the conclusion of each paragraph.

Some versions of Ventura Publisher include a file utility called CLIP2VP, which operates in a manner similar to the clipboard in Microsoft Windows.

3.11   Programming Languages

Applications can be programmed in different languages to generate ASCII(SDF) files.

The Appendix of this book includes a source code written in Turbo Pascal which converts files from ASCII(DELIMITED) to ASCII(SDF) and vice versa. This utility is a good example of file conversion using Pascal.

You can also find this CONVERT program on the companion disk for this book as a Turbo Pascal source code and as an executable program.

This utility converts SDF into DELIMITED as follows: Start the CONVERT application from the DOS prompt. The program prompts the user for the name of the source file, the format of the source file (SDF or DELIMITED) and the number and lengths of the fields involved. For DELIMITED files, the CONVERT program also requests the field separators and text delimiters for the source file. The user must enter these single characters (usually a comma and quotation mark). In some cases, no text delimiter may be needed. Press either the <Enter> key or the <Space> key.

The program then prompts for the name of the target file. If a file by that name already exists, the program asks the user whether the existing file can be overwritten. If the user responds negatively, the program stops.

If the user responds affirmatively the target file type (SDF or DELIMITED) is requested, as are the separator characters, text delimiters and file type (T for TEXT, N for NUMBERS and D for DATE). The target file is then generated.

Chapter 4

Exchanging Data

This chapter describes methods of transporting data from one application to another, including concrete examples of file transfer.

4.1 dBASE IV

The following data will be used for most of this section. It states the last name of a salesperson, the street address, the two-character abbreviation for a city (e.g., NY=New York, KZ=Kalamazoo, DM=Des Moines), the sales on a particular date and the date of those sales:

```
Record  NAME      STREET        CTY  SALES   DATE
  1     Burns     64 24th St.   NY   370.00  01/01/88
  2     Bear      12 Elm St.    LA   378.00  02/01/88
  3     Fischer   34 D St.      GR   260.00  12/31/87
  4     Hoffman   2 Apple Rd.   DM   250.00  03/01/88
  5     Huber     1 Plum Dr.    KZ   190.00  04/01/88
  6     Miller    23 23rd St.   GR   100.00  05/01/88
  7     Mylor     81 Tuo Dr.    LA   299.00  07/01/88
  8     Michael   9 Umm Ave.    NY   150.00  08/01/88
  9     Smith     99 Gem Rd.    GR   500.00  07/20/88
 10     Stevens   10 Apso Ln.   LA   300.00  07/30/88
```

This database uses the following structure:

```
Structure for database: DATA.DBF
Number of data records:      10
Date of last update: 01/19/90
Field    Field Name  Type       Width  Dec.  Index
   1     NAME        Character     10           N
   2     STREET      Character     12           N
   3     CTY         Character      4           N
   4     SALES       Numeric        6    2      N
   5     DATE        Date           8           N
** TOTAL **                        41
```

4.1.1 dBASE—Multiplan

There are two methods of transferring data to Microsoft Multiplan. The period must first be selected as the decimal point (you can do this through the Format/Units—Currency command). Select the period in the decimal separator: command field and press the <Enter> key to confirm.

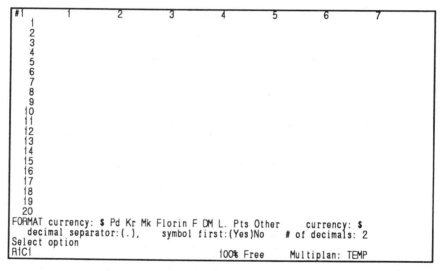

Figure 4.1.1a: Selecting decimal points in Multiplan

You must add an extra date field for a date number (more on this below).

- If you haven't already done so, activate the DATA.DBF file using the USE command, enter the MODIFY STRUCTURE command and create a new field for accepting numerical data (name this field DATNUMBER).

```
 Layout   Organize   Append   Go To   Exit              12:36:52 am
                                                Bytes remaining:   3954
 ┌─────┬────────────┬────────────┬───────┬─────┬───────┐
 │ Num │ Field Name │ Field Type │ Width │ Dec │ Index │
 ├─────┼────────────┼────────────┼───────┼─────┼───────┤
 │  1  │ NAME       │ Character  │  10   │     │   N   │
 │  2  │ STREET     │ Character  │  12   │     │   N   │
 │  3  │ CTY        │ Character  │   4   │     │   N   │
 │  4  │ SALES      │ Numeric    │   6   │  2  │   N   │
 │  5  │ DATE       │ Date       │   8   │     │   N   │
 │  6  │ DATNUMBER  │ Numeric    │   6   │  0  │   N   │
 │     │            │            │       │     │       │
 │     │            │            │       │     │       │
 └─────┴────────────┴────────────┴───────┴─────┴───────┘
 Database‖A:\DATA                   ‖Field 1/6
          Enter the field name. Insert/Delete field:Ctrl-N/Ctrl-U
 Field names begin with a letter and may contain letters, digits and underscores
```

Figure 4.1.1b: Modifying database structure in dBASE

- Enter the following command to create the numeric data:

```
REPLACE ALL  datnumber WITH date-CTOD ( "12/30/1899")
```

This command "subtracts" 12/30/1899 from the current date, since Multiplan begins its date system at 0 (0 = 1/1/1900). The field DATNUMBER is filled with the numerical date, which can be interpreted by Multiplan as a date.

After this change, the database contains the following structure:

Record	NAME	STREET	CTY	SALES	DATE	DATNUMBER
1	Burns	64 24th St.	NY	370.00	01/01/88	32143
2	Bear	12 Elm St.	LA	378.00	02/01/88	32174
3	Fischer	34 D St.	GR	260.00	12/31/87	32142
4	Hoffman	2 Apple Rd.	DM	250.00	03/01/88	32203
5	Huber	1 Plum Dr.	KZ	190.00	04/01/88	32234
6	Miller	23 23rd St.	GR	100.00	05/01/88	32264
7	Mylor	81 Tuo Dr.	LA	299.00	07/01/88	32325
8	Michael	9 Umm Ave.	NY	150.00	08/01/88	32356
9	Smith	99 Gem Rd.	GR	500.00	07/20/88	32344
10	Stevens	10 Apso Ln.	LA	300.00	07/30/88	32354

The DATNUMBER field contains the date format recognized by Multiplan.

4.1.1.1 dBASE (SYLK)—Multiplan

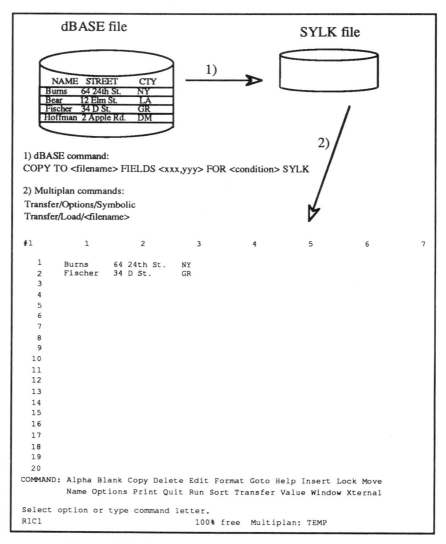

Figure 4.1.1.1: Transferring data to Multiplan (SYLK format)

•   Activate the database with the USE command.

•   Enter the following to create a dBASE (SYLK) file named
     DB-MP-1.SLK:

```
COPY TO db-mp-1.slk FIELDS name,sales,datnumber FOR CTY="GR" SYLK
```

This SYLK file has the following structure:

```
ID;PDB3
F;DG0G10
B;Y4;X3
C;Y1;X1;K"NAME"
C;X2;K"SALES"
C;X3;K"DATNUMBER"
C;Y2;X1;K"Fischer     "
C;X2;K260.00
C;X3;K 32142
C;Y3;X1;K"Miller      "
C;X2;K100.00
C;X3;K 32264
C;Y4;X1;K"Smith       "
C;X2;K500.00
C;X3;K 32344
W;N1;A1 1
E
```

The SYLK data looks something like this when laid out as records:

```
NAME      SALES  DATNUMBER
Fischer   260.00    32142
Miller    100.00    32264
Smith     500.00    32344
```

This dBASE (SYLK) file can be loaded into Multiplan as follows:

•   Select the Transfer/Options command. Select the Symbolic option and press the <Enter> key. Select the Transfer/Load command. Enter the filename DB-MP-1.SLK and press the <Enter> key.

```
#1        1         2          3        4         5
  1    NAME      SALES     DATNUMBER
  2    Fischer      260        32142
  3    Miller       100        32264
  4    Smith        500        32344
  5
***
  20
R1C1     "NAME"     ? 100% free     Multiplan: DB-MP-1.SLK
```

•   The date fields in column 3 must be formatted as true dates. Select the Format/Time-Date command. Select the cells containing the date numbers, and select a format (we used mm/dd/yy). Press the <Enter> key.

```
#1        1         2          3        4         5
  1    NAME      SALES     DATNUMBER
  2    Fischer      260     12/31/87
  3    Miller       100       5/1/88
  4    Smith        500      7/20/88
  5
***
  20
R1C1     "NAME"     ? 100% free     Multiplan: DB-MP-1.SLK
```

You can now edit the information from within Multiplan.

4.1.1.2　dBASE　(ASCII)—Multiplan

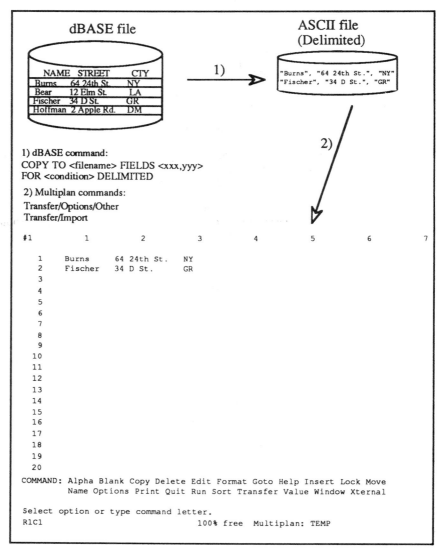

Figure 4.1.1.2: Transferring ASCII data from dBASE to Multiplan

Create a dBASE ASCII (DELIMITED) file and copy it to Multiplan as follows:

- Activate the dBASE database application using the USE command.

- Enter the following to copy the NAME, SALES of over 250.00 and DATNUMBER data to a file named DB-MP-2.DEL:

```
COPY TO DB-MP-2.DEL FIELDS name,sales,datnumber FOR sales>250 DELIMITED
```

The resulting dBASE ASCII file named DP-MP-2.DEL contains the following data:

```
"Burns",370.00,32143
"Bear",378.00,32174
"Fischer",260.00,32142
"Mylor",299.00,32325
"Smith",500.00,32344
"Stevens",300.00,32354
```

Load the above dBASE ASCII file into Multiplan as follows:

•   Select the Transfer/Import command. Enter the filename. The at: command field indicates the upper left corner of the range into which the data will be loaded. If this field doesn't display R1C1, enter that data now.

•   Make sure that the (Yes) option is selected in the numbers: command field. The query: command field specifies whether Multiplan should ask the user before overwriting an existing file (Yes) or not (No). For now make sure that the query: command field has (Yes) selected.

•   The delimiters: command field should have a comma listed. Enter a comma in this command field if this is not the case.

```
#1           1          2          3          4          5
    1
    2
   ***
   19
   20
TRANSFER IMPORT filename:                    at: R1C1
     numbers:(Yes)No      query:(Yes)No  delimiters:,
Enter filename or use direction keys to select from list
R1C1                        ? 100% free  Multiplan:
```

•   Press the <Enter> key to load the file at row 1, column 1.

```
#1           1          2          3          4          5
    1     Burns      370.00     32143
    2     Bear       378.00     32174
    3     Fischer    260.00     32142
    4     Mylor      299.00     32325
    5     Smith      500.00     32344
    6     Stevens    300.00     32354
    7
   ***
   20
   ***
R1C1      "Burns"         ? 100% free  Multiplan: TEMP
```

•   Select the Format/Time-Date command to change the date format.

- Select the cells containing the date numbers, and select a format (we used mm/dd/yy). Press the <Enter> key.

```
#1         1         2         3         4         5
   1    Burns      370.00     1/1/88
   2    Bear       378.00     2/1/88
   3    Fischer    260.00    12/31/87
   4    Mylor      299.00     7/1/88
   5    Smith      500.00     7/20/88
   6    Stevens    300.00     7/30/88
   7
  ***
|  20                                                    |
  ***
| R1C1     "Becker"        ? 100% free  Multiplan: TEMP  |
```

You can now edit the information from within Multiplan.

4.1.2 dBASE—Microsoft Excel

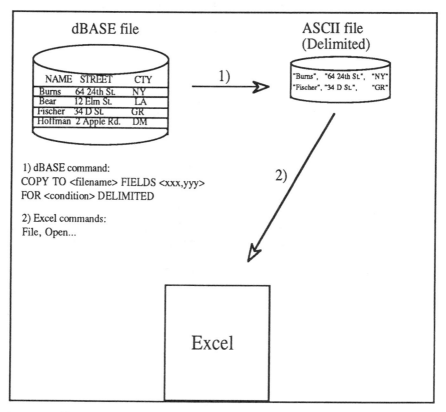

Figure 4.1.2: Transferring data from dBASE to Microsoft Excel

Microsoft Excel can read dBASE files almost directly. One small change must be made to a dBASE file before conversion to Excel—conversion of dates to date numbers.

- If you haven't already done so, activate the DATA.DBF file using the USE command, enter the MODIFY STRUCTURE command and create a new field for accepting numerical data (name this field DATNUMBER).

```
 Layout    Organize    Append    Go To    Exit                          12:36:52 am
                                                           Bytes remaining:    3954
  ┌─────┬────────────┬────────────┬───────┬──────┬───────┐
  │ Num │ Field Name │ Field Type │ Width │ Dec  │ Index │
  ├─────┼────────────┼────────────┼───────┼──────┼───────┤
  │  1  │ NAME       │ Character  │  10   │      │   N   │
  │  2  │ STREET     │ Character  │  12   │      │   N   │
  │  3  │ CTY        │ Character  │   4   │      │   N   │
  │  4  │ SALES      │ Numeric    │   6   │  2   │   N   │
  │  5  │ DATE       │ Date       │   8   │      │   N   │
  │  6  │ DATNUMBER  │ Numeric    │   6   │  0   │   N   │
  │     │            │            │       │      │       │
  └─────┴────────────┴────────────┴───────┴──────┴───────┘

 Database║A:\DATA                  ║Field 1/6      ║            ║
          Enter the field name. Insert/Delete field:Ctrl-N/Ctrl-U
 Field names begin with a letter and may contain letters, digits and underscores
```

Figure 4.1.2a: Structure change in dBASE

- Enter the following command:

```
REPLACE ALL datnumber WITH date-CTOD ( "12/30/1899")
```

This command "subtracts" 12/30/1899 from the current date, since Multiplan begins its date system at 0 (0 = 1/1/1900). The field DATNUMBER is filled with the numerical date, which can be interpreted by Excel as a date.

After this change, the database contains the following structure:

```
 Record  NAME      STREET        CTY  SALES   DATE       DATNUMBER
    1    Burns     64 24th St.   NY   370.00  01/01/88     32143
    2    Bear      12 Elm St.    LA   378.00  02/01/88     32174
    3    Fischer   34 D St.      GR   260.00  12/31/87     32142
    4    Hoffman   2 Apple Rd.   DM   250.00  03/01/88·    32203
    5    Huber     1 Plum Dr.    KZ   190.00  04/01/88     32234
    6    Miller    23 23rd St.   GR   100.00  05/01/88     32264
    7    Mylor     81 Tuo Dr.    LA   299.00  07/01/88     32325
    8    Michael   9 Umm Ave.    NY   150.00  08/01/88     32356
    9    Smith     99 Gem Rd.    GR   500.00  07/20/88     32344
   10    Stevens   10 Apso Ln.   LA   300.00  07/30/88     32354
```

The DATNUMBER field contains the date format recognized by Multiplan.

- Activate the database in dBASE using the USE command.

- Enter the following to save the data to an ASCII delimited file named DB-EX-1.DBF:

```
COPY TO DB-EX-1.DBF FIELDS name,street,cty,sales,datnumber DELIMITED
```

```
Record  NAME      STREET        CTY  SALES    DATNUMBER
  1     Burns     64 24th St.   NY   370.00   32143
  2     Bear      12 Elm St.    LA   378.00   32174
  3     Fischer   34 D St.      GR   260.00   32142
  4     Hoffman   2 Apple Rd.   DM   250.00   32203
  5     Huber     1 Plum Dr.    KZ   190.00   32234
  6     Miller    23 23rd St.   GR   100.00   32264
  7     Mylor     81 Tuo Dr.    LA   299.00   32325
  8     Michael   9 Umm Ave.    NY   150.00   32356
  9     Smith     99 Gem Rd.    GR   500.00   32344
 10     Stevens   10 Apso Ln.   LA   300.00   32354
```

- Start Microsoft Excel.

- Select the File menu and click on the Open... option. A window appears, listing a set of files. In addition, you'll see a text box listing a file wildcard of *.XL*. Change this wildcard to read *.*, press the <Enter> key and watch the change.

- Select the desired path from the Directories window.

- Select the filename DB-EX-1.DBF and either press <Enter> or click on the OK button to load the file.

Excel loads the worksheet, but the DATNUMBER fields are out of order.

- Select all the date numbers in the DATNUMBER column. Select the Format/Number... command, select the format you want for the date and click on the OK button. You may have to adjust the column width to compensate for date length using the Format/Column Width... command.

The file can now be edited from within Excel.

4.1.3 dBASE—Microsoft Chart

The following database DATA2.DBF will be used for these examples:

```
Record  NAME      STREET        CTY  SALES   CREDIT
   1    Burns     64 24th St.   NY   370.00  290.00
   2    Bear      12 Elm St.    LA   378.00  584.00
   3    Fischer   34 D St.      GR   260.00  470.00
   4    Hoffman   2 Apple Rd.   DM   250.00  350.00
   5    Huber     1 Plum Dr.    KZ   190.00  280.00
   6    Miller    23 23rd St.   GR   100.00  300.00
   7    Mylor     81 Tuo Dr.    LA   299.00  560.00
   8    Michael   9 Umm Ave.    NY   150.00  200.00
   9    Smith     99 Gem Rd.    GR   500.00  789.00
  10    Stevens   10 Apso Ln.   LA   300.00  100.00
```

The database has the following structure:

```
Structure for database: DATA2.DBF
Number of data records:      10
Date of last update: 01/22/90
Field    Field Name  Type       Width   Dec.   Index
  1      NAME        Character     10             N
  2      STREET      Character     12             N
  3      CTY         Character      4             N
  4      SALES       Numeric        6      2      N
  5      CREDIT      Numeric        6      2      N
** TOTAL **                        39
```

You can transfer data from dBASE into Chart in three ways.

One item must be remembered when transferring dBASE data to Microsoft Chart: The period must be used as the decimal character. To do this, select the Options command, move to the Decimal point: command field, select the period using <Space> and press the <Enter> key to accept.

4.1.3.1 dBASE (SYLK)—Microsoft Chart

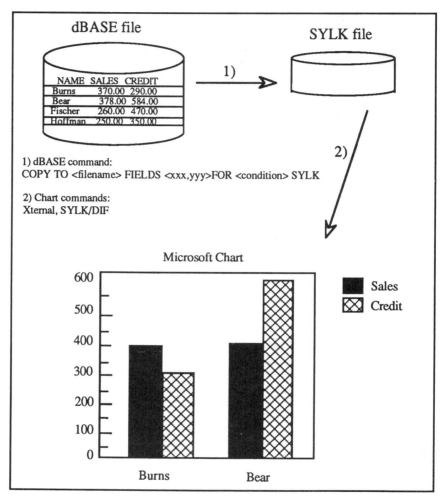

Figure 4.1.3.1: Accepting Chart Data (SYLK Format)

Create a SYLK file in dBASE and load it into Microsoft Chart as follows:

*   Activate the database in dBASE with the USE command.

*   Enter the following command to save a file named DB-CH-1.SLK to disk:

```
COPY TO db-ch-1.slk fields name,sales,credit FOR cty="GR" SYLK
```

The file DB-CH-1.SLK has the following contents:

```
ID;PDB3
F;DG0G10
B;Y4;X3
C;Y1;X1;K"NAME"
C;X2;K"SALES"
C;X3;K"CREDIT"
C;Y2;X1;K"Fischer      "
C;X2;K260.00
C;X3;K470.00
C;Y3;X1;K"Miller      "
C;X2;K100.00
C;X3;K300.00
C;Y4;X1;K"Smith      "
C;X2;K500.00
C;X3;K789.00
W;N1;A1 1
E
```

The file contains the following records:

NAME	SALES	CREDIT
Fischer	260.00	470.00
Miller	100.00	300.00
Smith	500.00	789.00

•   Run Chart.

•   Select the Xternal command. Press the <S> key (SYLK/DIF). When the filename: command field appears, enter the name DB-CH-1.SLK with the drive specifier and path if needed.

•   Press the <Tab> key to move to the next command field. Press the <Y> key to link Chart data with the file.

•   Press the <Tab> key to move to the selected rows: command field. Enter 2:4 and press the <Tab> key to move to the selected columns: command field. Enter 2:3.

•   Press the <Tab> key to move to the orient series by: command field. Press the <R> key to orient the chart by rows.

•   Press the <Tab> key to move to the series name(s) from: command field. Press the <1> key.

•   Press the <Tab> key to move to the categories from: command field. Press the <1> key.

•   Press the <Tab> key to move to the category type: command field. Press the <T> key to select Text.

•   Press the <Enter> key.

The List screen then displays the following entries:

Incl.(*)	Name	Source of data	Type	# pts.
1 *	Fischer	Linked: a:db-ch-1.slk:R2C2:3	Text	2
2 *	Miller	Linked: a:db-ch-1.slk:R3C2:3	Text	2
3 *	Smith	Linked: a:db-ch-1.slk:R4C2:3	Text	2

- Press the <C> key.

Chart generates the following graphic:

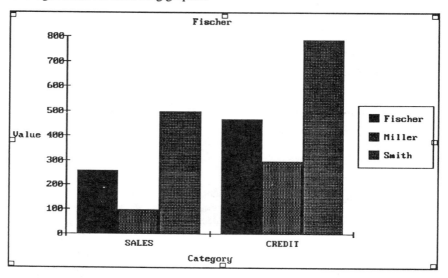

Figure 4.1.3.1a: dBASE-Chart graphic (row orientation)

Chart can also generate charts based on column orientation.

- Select Transfer/Clear/All. Press the <Y> key to confirm.

- Select the Xternal command. Press the <S> key (SYLK/DIF). When the filename: command field appears, enter the name DB-CH-1.SLK with the drive specifier and path if needed.

- Press the <Tab> key to move to the next command field. Press the <Y> key to link Chart data with the file.

- Press the <Tab> key to move to the selected rows: command field. Enter 2:4 and press the <Tab> key to move to the selected columns: command field. Enter 2:3.

- Press the <Tab> key to move to the orient series by: command field. Press the <C> key to orient the chart by columns (two series of three rows).

- Press the <Tab> key to move to the series name(s) from: command field. Press the <1> key.

- Press the <Tab> key to move to the categories from: command field. Press the <1> key.

- Press the <Tab> key to move to the category type: command field. Press the <T> key to select Text.

- Press the <Enter> key.

The List screen then displays the following entries:

Incl. (*)	Name	Source of data	Type	# pts.
1 *	SALES	Linked: a:db-ch-1.slk:R2:4C2	Text	3
2 *	CREDIT	Linked: a:db-ch-1.slk:R2:4C3	Text	3

- Press the <C> button.

Chart generates the following graphic:

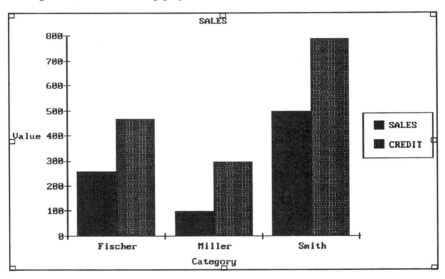

Figure 4.1.3.1b: dBASE-Chart graphic (column orientation)

4.1.3.2 dBASE ASCII(SDF)—Microsoft Chart

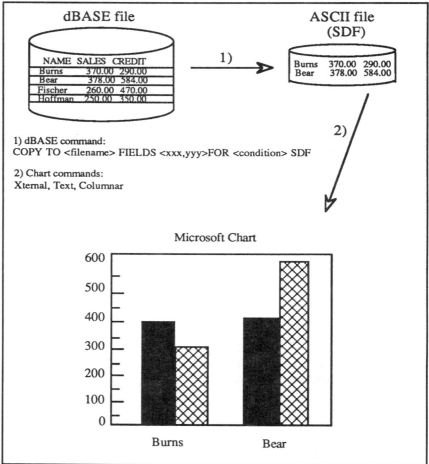

Figure 4.1.3.2: Accepting data in Chart (ASCII-SDF format)

Convert the dBASE file DATA2.DBF to an ASCII(SDF) file and load the converted file into Microsoft Chart as follows:

- Activate the DATA2.DBF database in dBASE with the USE command.

- Use the following command to create a file named DB-CH-2.SDF:

```
COPY TO DB-CH-2.SDF FIELDS name,sales,credit FOR cty="GR" .OR. cty="NY" SDF
```

The file DB-CH-2.SDF has the following contents:

```
Burns       370.00290.00
Fischer     250.00350.00
Miller      100.00300.00
Michael     150.00200.00
Smith       300.00100.00
```

•   Quit dBASE and run Microsoft Chart.

•   Select the Xternal/Text/Columnar command. Enter the filename DB-CH-2.SDF in the filename: command field. Press the <Tab> key to move to the linked: command field and press the (Y) key to link the Chart data with the ASCII file.

•   Press the <Tab> key to move to the selected rows: command field. Enter 1:5.

•   Press the <Tab> key to move to the selected columns: command field. Enter 2:3.

•   Press the <Tab> key twice to move to the column width: command field. Enter <10,6,6> and press the Tab key. The numbers and commas compensate for the lengths of the NAME, SALES and CREDIT fields.

•   Press the <Tab> key to move to the series name(s) from: command field. Press the <1> key and press the <Tab> key.

•   Since the titles were not carried over from the dBASE file, leave the categories from: command field blank.

•   Press the <Tab> key to move to the category type: command field. Make sure that the Sequence item is selected.

•   Press the <Tab> key until the cursor moves to the orient series by: command field. Press the <R> key (Row). Press the <Enter> key.

The list screen contains the following entries when based on rows:

```
Incl.(*) Name     Source of data              Type      # pts.

1    *   Burns    Linked: a:db-ch-2.sdf:R1C2:3 Sequence  2
2    *   Fischer  Linked: a:db-ch-2.sdf:R2C2:3 Sequence  2
3    *   Miller   Linked: a:db-ch-2.sdf:R3C2:3 Sequence  2
4    *   Michael  Linked: a:db-ch-2.sdf:R4C2:3 Sequence  2
5    *   Smith    Linked: a:db-ch-2.sdf:R5C2:3 Sequence  2
```

•   Use Chart to edit the titles as needed.

The graphic created by Chart has the following structure:

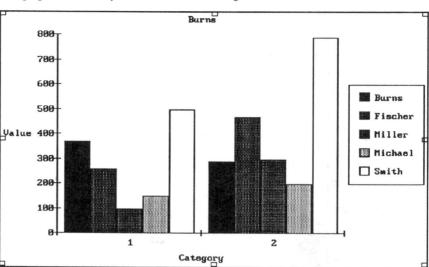

Figure 4.1.3.2a: Chart graphic created from dBASE data (row orientation)

- Select the Xternal/Text/Columnar command. Enter the filename DB-CH-2.SDF in the filename: command field. Press the <Tab> key to move to the linked: command field and press the (Y) key to link the Chart data with the ASCII file.

- Press the <Tab> key to move to the selected rows: command field. Enter 1:5.

- Press the <Tab> key to move to the selected columns: command field. Enter 2:3.

- Press the <Tab> key twice to move to the column width: command field. Enter <10,6,6> and press the Tab key. The numbers and commas compensate for the lengths of the NAME, SALES and CREDIT fields.

- Press the <Tab> key to move to the series name(s) from: command field. Leave this blank (you'll have to enter the title by hand).

- Press the <Tab> key to move to the categories from: command field. Press the <1> key.

- Press the <Tab> key to move to the category type: command field. Make sure that the Text item is selected.

- Press the <Tab> key until the cursor moves to the orient series by: command field. Press the <C> key (Columns). Press the <Enter> key.

The list screen contains the following entries when based on columns:

```
 Incl.(*) Name      Source of data               Type    # pts.
 1    *             Linked: a:db-ch-2.sdf:R1:5C2 Text      5
 2    *             Linked: a:db-ch-2.sdf:R1:5C3 Text      5
```

The graphic created by Chart has a structure similar to the following:

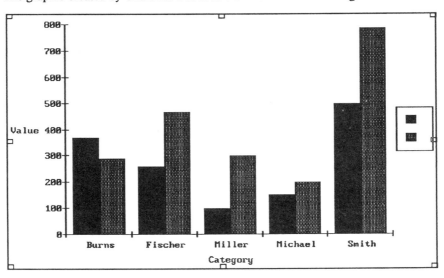

Figure 4.1.3.2b: Chart graphic from dBASE data (column orientation)

4.1.3.3 dBASE ASCII(DELIMITED)—Microsoft Chart

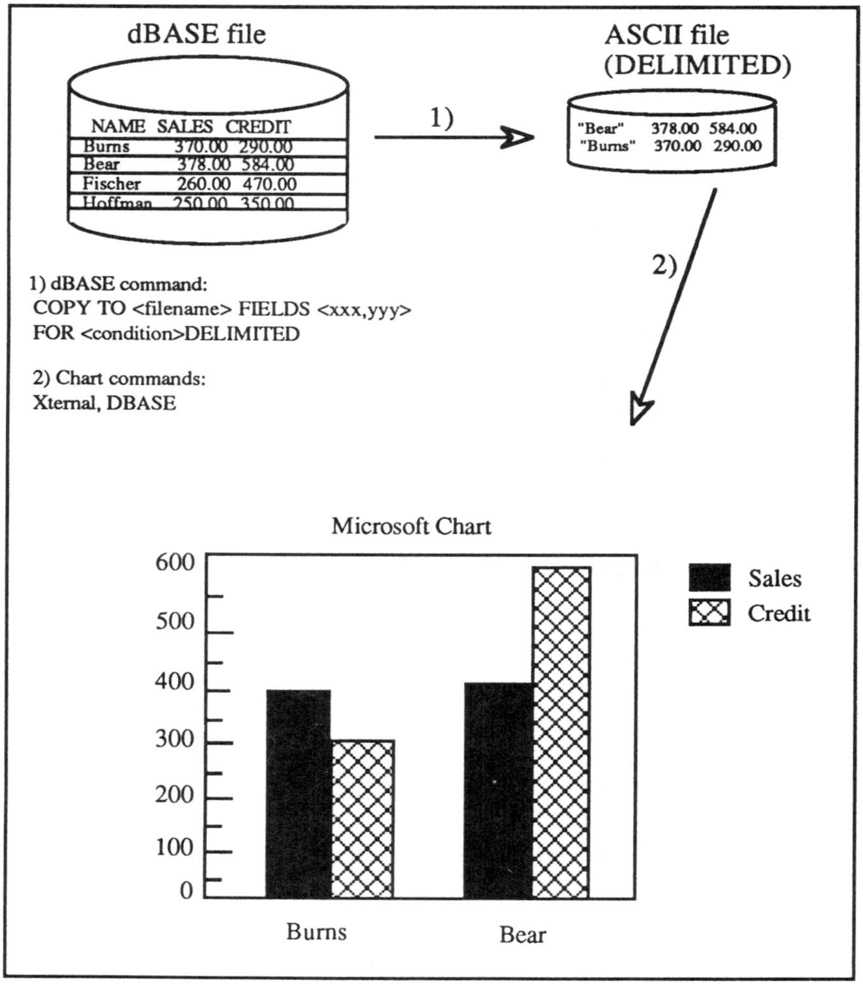

Figure 4.1.3.3: Importing dBASE data to Chart (ASCII(DELIMITED) format)

Create an ASCII file with delimiters and quotation marks from DATA2.DBF, and load this ASCII file into Chart as follows:

- Activate the DATA2.DBF database with the USE command.

- Enter the following command to create a file named DB-CH-3.DEL:

```
COPY TO db-ch-3.del FIELDS name,sales,credit FOR cty="KZ" .OR. cty="DM" DELIMITED
```

- Exit dBASE.

The file DB-CH-3.DEL has the following contents:

```
"Hoffman",250.00,350.00
"Huber",190.00,280.00
```

This file is loaded into Chart as follows:

• Run Chart.

• Select the Xternal/Text/Delimited command. Enter the filename DB-CH-3.DEL in the filename: command field. Press the <Tab> key to move to the linked: command field and press the (Y) key to link the Chart data with the ASCII file.

• Press the <Tab> key to move to the selected rows: command field. Enter 1:2.

• Press the <Tab> key to move to the selected columns: command field. Enter 2:3.

• Press the <Tab> key twice to move to the text quote character: command field. Press the <"> key.

• Press the <Tab> key to move to the delimiter character: command field. Press the <,> key.

• Set the orientation and category parameters as described in Section 4.1.3.2 above.

4.1.4 dBASE—Lotus 1-2-3

The DATA.DBF database will be used for this example:

```
Record  NAME      STREET        CTY SALES   DATE
  1     Burns     64 24th St.   NY  370.00  01/01/88
  2     Bear      12 Elm St.    LA  378.00  02/01/88
  3     Fischer   34 D St.      GR  260.00  12/31/87
  4     Hoffman   2 Apple Rd.   DM  250.00  03/01/88
  5     Huber     1 Plum Dr.    KZ  190.00  04/01/88
  6     Miller    23 23rd St.   GR  100.00  05/01/88
  7     Mylor     81 Tuo Dr.    LA  299.00  07/01/88
  8     Michael   9 Umm Ave.    NY  150.00  08/01/88
  9     Smith     99 Gem Rd.    GR  500.00  07/20/88
 10     Stevens   10 Apso Ln.   LA  300.00  07/30/88
```

This database uses the following structure:

```
Structure for database: DATA.DBF
Number of data records:      10
Date of last update: 01/19/90
Field     Field Name  Type        Width   Dec.   Index
   1      NAME        Character     10             N
   2      STREET      Character     12             N
   3      CTY         Character      4             N
   4      SALES       Numeric        6      2      N
   5      DATE        Date           8             N
** TOTAL **                         41
```

You have two options for converting dBASE data into Lotus 1-2-3 format. Bear in mind two simple rules in either case:

1)   Labels longer than 240 characters are truncated.

2)   You are limited to a maximum of 8191 converted records.

4.1.4.1 dBASE—ASCII—Lotus 1-2-3

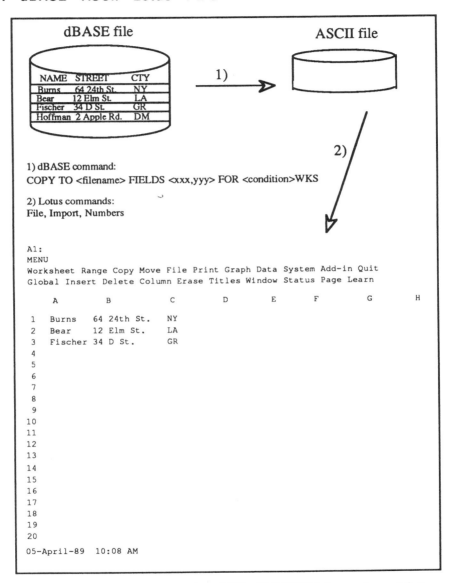

Figure 4.1.4.1: Importing dBASE ASCII(DELIMITED) data to Lotus 1-2-3

Create a dBASE ASCII(DELIMITED) file and convert the data to Lotus 1-2-3
format as follows:

- The period must be chosen as the decimal character in Lotus 1-2-3. To do this, select / Worksheet Global Default International Punctuation, select F and press the <Enter> key.

To accept the date in the corresponding format, the database must be changed in the following way:

- Add a new field for the numerical date named DATNUMBER with the MODIFY STRUCTURE command.

```
Layout   Organize   Append   Go To   Exit                        12:36:52 am

 ┌─────┬────────────┬─────────────┬───────┬─────┬────────┐  Bytes remaining:   3954
 │ Num │ Field Name │ Field Type  │ Width │ Dec │ Index  │
 ├─────┼────────────┼─────────────┼───────┼─────┼────────┤
 │  1  │ NAME       │ Character   │  10   │     │   N    │
 │  2  │ STREET     │ Character   │  12   │     │   N    │
 │  3  │ CTY        │ Character   │   4   │     │   N    │
 │  4  │ SALES      │ Numeric     │   6   │  2  │   N    │
 │  5  │ DATE       │ Date        │   8   │     │   N    │
 │  6  │ DATNUMBER  │ Numeric     │   6   │  0  │   N    │
 │     │            │             │       │     │        │
 │     │            │             │       │     │        │
 │     │            │             │       │     │        │
 │     │            │             │       │     │        │
 │     │            │             │       │     │        │
 │     │            │             │       │     │        │
 └─────┴────────────┴─────────────┴───────┴─────┴────────┘

 Database‖A:\DATA              ‖Field 1/6      ‖              ‖
          Enter the field name. Insert/Delete field:Ctrl-N/Ctrl-U
 Field names begin with a letter and may contain letters, digits and underscores
```

Figure 4.1.4.1a: Structure change in dBASE

- Enter the following command to create the numerical date:

```
REPLACE ALL datnumber WITH date-CTOD("12/30/1899")
```

This command subtracts 12/30/1899 from the existing date so that Lotus 1-2-3 begins on 01/01/1900, and places the numerical date in the DATNUMBER field.

After this change, the database contains the following structure:

```
Record  NAME      STREET        CTY SALES   DATE      DATNUMBER
  1     Burns     64 24th St.   NY  370.00  01/01/88   32143
  2     Bear      12 Elm St.    LA  378.00  02/01/88   32174
  3     Fischer   34 D St.      GR  260.00  12/31/87   32142
  4     Hoffman   2 Apple Rd.   DM  250.00  03/01/88   32203
  5     Huber     1 Plum Dr.    KZ  190.00  04/01/88   32234
  6     Miller    23 23rd St.   GR  100.00  05/01/88   32264
  7     Mylor     81 Tuo Dr.    LA  299.00  07/01/88   32325
  8     Michael   9 Umm Ave.    NY  150.00  08/01/88   32356
  9     Smith     99 Gem Rd.    GR  500.00  07/20/88   32344
 10     Stevens   10 Apso Ln.   LA  300.00  07/30/88   32354
```

The DATNUMBER field contains the date format recognized by Multiplan.

Create an ASCII file in dBASE and load it in Lotus as follows:

•   Activate the database with the USE command.

•   Enter the following command to save an ASCII file named DB-LO-1.TXT to disk:

```
COPY TO db-lo-1 FIELDS name,cty,sales,datnumber FOR sales>250 DELIMITED
```

The file DB-LO-1.TXT has the following contents:

```
"Burns",370.00,32143
"Bear",378.00,32174
"Fischer",260.00,32142
"Mylor",299.00,32325
"Smith",500.00,32344
"Stevens",300.00,32354
```

Load this dBASE (ASCII) file into Lotus 1-2-3 as follows:

•   Call the / File Import command from the main menu.

•   Select the Numbers option.

•   Press the <Esc> key until the Enter name of file to import: field is empty.

•   Enter the filename, the drive specifier and path and press the <Enter> key.

```
A1:  'Burns                                                        READY

         A        B       C        D        E      F      G      H
 1   Burns    NY          370    32143
 2   Bear     LA          378    32174
 3   Fischer  GR          260    32142
 4   Mylor    LA          299    32325
 5   Smith    GR          500    32344
 6   Stevens  LA          300    32354
 7
 8
 9
10
11
12
13
14
15
16
17
18
19
20
23-Jan-89   08:55 AM           UNDO
```

•   The date field in column D must be formatted as a date. Move the cell pointer to column D.

- Select the / Range Format Date command, and the (Long intn'l) format. When 1-2-3 prompts you for the range to format, select all the date numbers in column D and press the <Enter> key.

- Now let's change the sales figures to match currency. Move the cell pointer to column C. Select the / Range Format Fixed command, select 2 for the number of fixed decimal places and press the <Enter> key.

- Highlight column C and press the <Enter> key.

```
D1: (D4) 32143                                                    READY

          A        B        C        D        E     F      G      H
1     Burns     NY       370.00 01/01/88
2     Bear      LA       378.00 02/01/88
3     Fischer   GR       260.00 12/31/87
4     Mylor     LA       299.00 07/01/88
5     Smith     GR       500.00 07/20/88
6     Stevens   LA       300.00 07/30/88
7
8
9
10
11
12
13
14
15
16
17
18
19
20
23-Jan-89  09:21 AM           UNDO
```

Note: Instead of / Range Format Fixed, you may prefer to format column C using the / Range Format Currency command, which inserts the two decimal places and adds a currency sign to each amount.

The data can now be edited from within Lotus 1-2-3.

4.1.4.2 dBASE—Translate—Lotus 1-2-3

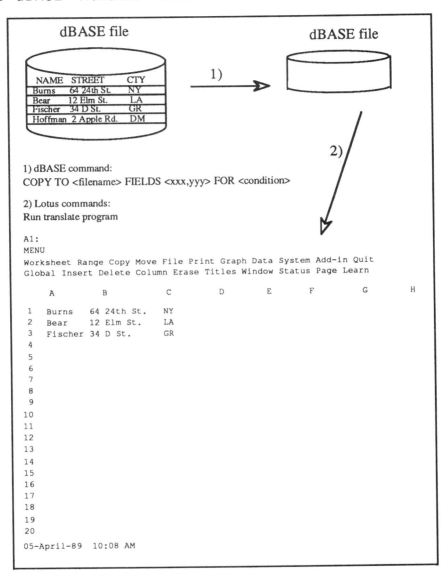

Figure 4.1.4.2: Importing dBASE data to Lotus 1-2-3 using Translate

dBASE files can be converted into Lotus 1-2-3 files using the Translate utility supplied with Lotus 1-2-3. It can only convert entire files. To convert just a section of a dBASE file, a new dBASE file must be created, then this must be converted with the Translate utility. Translate also converts the date.

For example, to get the same result as illustrated in Section 4.1.4.1, you must do the following:

- Activate the database with the USE command.

- Enter the following command to save an ASCII file named DB-LO-2.DBF to disk:

```
COPY TO db-lo-2 FIELDS name,cty,sales,date FOR sales>250
```

The file DB-LO-2.DBF has the following contents:

```
"Burns",NY,370.00,01/01/88
"Bear",LA,378.00,02/01/88
"Fischer",GR,260.00,12/31/87
"Mylor",LA299.00,07/01/88
"Smith",GR,500.00,07/20/88
"Stevens",LA,300.00,07/30/88
```

The entire Translate utility is menu driven. There are several built-in security checks, to confirm whether you actually want to continue with certain operations.

- Start the 1-2-3 Access System utility.

- Select Translate from the main menu.

- Select the type and the name of the source file and the target file. You can enter the source file as the target file provided it is given a different extension.

- The percent of the conversion is displayed. The Translate utility informs the user of whether the file conversion was successful or not.

- Press the <Esc> key to exit the Translate utility and run Lotus 1-2-3.

- The file can then be loaded using / File Retrieve:

```
A1: [W10] 'NAME                                                              READY
          A      B      C       D          E        F        G        H
1        NAME    CTY   SALES    DATE
2        Burns   NY    370.00   01-Jan-888
3        Bear    LA    378.00   01-Feb-88
4        Fischer GR    260.00   31-Dec-87
5        Mylor   LA    299.00   01-Jul-88
6        Smith   GR    500.00   20-Jul-88
7        Stevens LA    300.00   30-Jul-88
8
9
10
11
12
13
14
15
16
17
18
19
20
22-Jan-90  03:59 PM            UNDO
```

The data can now be edited from within Lotus 1-2-3.

4.1.5 dBASE—Lotus Freelance Plus

Data from other programs can be displayed in Freelance as graphics. Data from Lotus 1-2-3, Multiplan, Excel and dBASE can be shown as presentation graphics in Freelance.

This section uses the database created in Section 4.1.3.

4.1.5.1 dBASE—Freelance Graphics

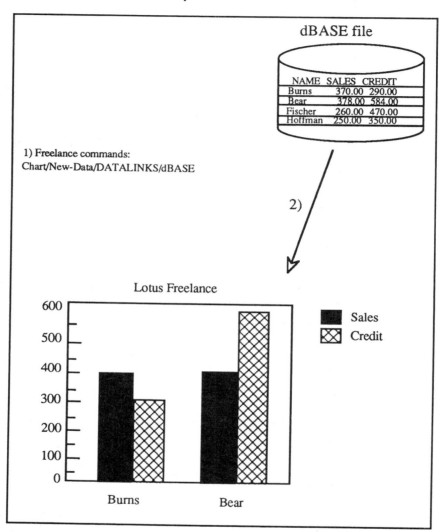

Figure 4.1.5.1: dBASE data as a Freelance graphic

Freelance can read data from a dBASE file and convert it to a Freelance graphic.

- Run dBASE and access the DATA2.DBF database with the USE command.

- Enter the following from the dot prompt:

```
COPY TO db-fl-1.dbf FIELDS name,sales,credit FOR sales>200
```

The DB-FL-1.DBF database has the following contents:

```
Burns    370.00  290.00
Bear     378.00  584.00
Fischer  260.00  470.00
Hoffman  250.00  350.00
Mylor    299.00  560.00
Smith    500.00  789.00
Stevens  300.00  100.00
```

- Exit dBASE and run Freelance. Select the Charts and Drawings command.

- Select the Chart New-Data command.

- The cursor should be in the Chart type item. Press the <Tab> key to move to the DATALINKS bar. Press <Space> to see the Datalinks menu.

- The cursor should be in the File type: item. Press <Space> to see a list of file types available. Select the dBASE option and press the <Enter> key.

- Press the <Tab> key or the <Cursor down> key to move to the File path: item. Enter the proper drive specifier and path.

- Move the cursor down to the File name: item using the <Tab> key or the <Cursor down> key. Enter the name DATA2.DBF in this line.

- The default name in the Type of import: item should read Specified Ranges.

- Leave the Headings:, Notes:, Legends: and axis Title: items blank.

- Move the cursor to the Cluster Labels: item and enter NAME.

- Move the cursor to the Bar 1 Values: item and enter SALES.

- Move the cursor to the Bar 2 Values: item and enter CREDIT.

- Press the <End> key to move to the DONE bar. Press <Enter> to accept the above data.

- Press the <F10> key for the menu. Press the <G> key (Go) to generate the chart. If a confirmation message appears, press the <Y> key to go on.

- Freelance may ask you to adjust the chart size or shape. For now, just press the keys required to draw the chart (usually <Enter>).

- Press the <Enter> key to accept the chart.

- Select the File Save command. Select the Both parameter. Enter the name DB-FL-1 in the Drawing Name item. Press <Tab> and enter the path. Press <Tab> two more times to move to the Chart File Name item.

Enter the name DB-FL-1 and press <Tab>. Enter the path of the chart file. Press the <F10> key to save the data.

Some precautions must be observed when entering ranges:

- Only numeric and character fields can be imported from dBASE files. Logical or memo fields are not allowed.

- When entering dBASE areas, data from all of the records for a field are read by entering the field names.

- A record area for a dBASE field is given by entering the field name, a colon and the record range.

- Enter the field range, a colon and the record number to import a group of fields in a record.

- After entering the import formula, press either the </> key or the <<> key. Freelance then asks whether the graphic data should be updated with the data from the import file. Press the <Y> key (Yes). If required, the information in the graphic formula can be changed. Pressing the </> or <<> key returns you to the main menu.

4.1.5.2 dBASE—Freelance Text Chart

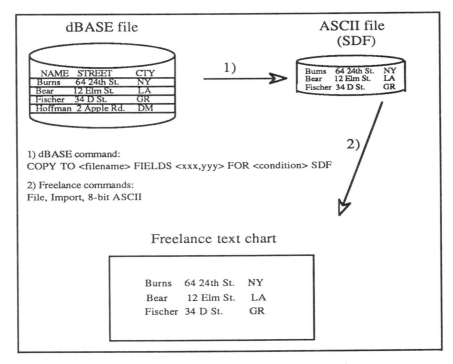

Figure 4.1.5.2: dBASE data as a Freelance text chart

Create a dBASE ASCII(SDF) file from DATA2.DBF and import this new file to Freelance.

•   Activate the DATA2.DBF database with the USE command.

•   Enter the following command to save a dBASE ASCII(SDF) file named DB-FL-2.SDF to disk:

```
COPY TO db-fl-2.sdf Fields name,street,cty,sales,credit FOR cty="GR" .or. cty="NY"
.or. cty="KZ" SDF
```

The file DB-FL-2.SDF has the following contents:

```
Burns      64 24th St. NY  370.00   290.00
Fischer    34 D St.    GR  260.00   470.00
Huber      1 Plum Dr.  KZ  190.00   280.00
Miller     23 23rd St. GR  100.00   300.00
Michael    9 Umm Ave.  NY  150.00   200.00
Smith      99 Gem Rd.  GR  500.00   789.00
```

•   Exit dBASE and run Lotus Freelance.

- Select Charts and Drawings, then select the File Import command.

- The cursor should be in the File type: item. Press <Space> to see the available options. Highlight the 8-bit ASCII option and press the <Enter> key.

- Press the <Tab> key or the <Cursor down> key to move the cursor to the Name: item. Enter the name DB-FL-2.SDF.

- Press the <Tab> key to move to the Path: item. Enter the path and press <F10> to load the file.

The data can then be processed as a Freelance text chart.

4.1.6 dBASE—Microsoft Word 5.0

Word can edit data, as well as accept data file information for creating form letters.

4.1.6.1 dBASE—Word Document

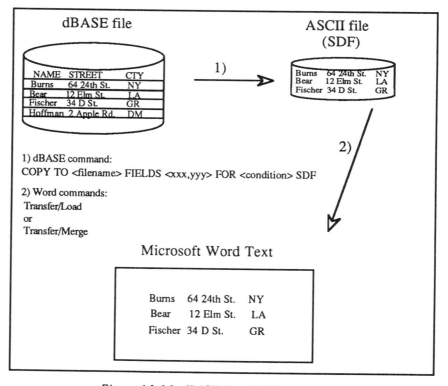

Figure 4.1.6.1: dBASE data in Microsoft Word

Create a dBASE ASCII(SDF) file and load this into Word as follows:

- Activate the database with the USE command.

- Enter the following command to save a file named DB-WO-1.SDF to disk:

```
COPY TO db-wo-1.sdf FIELDS name,sales FOR cty="GR" .or. cty="NY" SDF
```

The file DB-WO-1.SDF has the following contents:

```
Burns          370.00
Fischer        260.00
Miller         100.00
Michael        150.00
Smith          500.00
```

- Exit dBASE IV and start Word. This file can be loaded into Microsoft Word using the Transfer/Load command, or merged to an existing file using the Transfer/Merge command.

4.1.6.2 dBASE—Word Form Letters

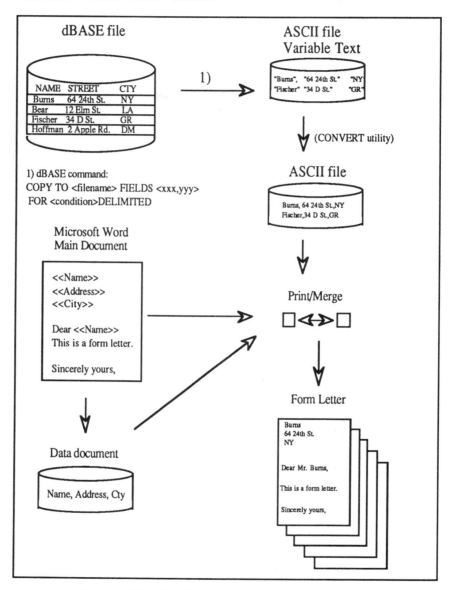

Figure 4.1.6.2: Word form letters using data from dBASE

The following dBASE file named ADDRESS.DBF is used as an example:

```
NO   NAME        FIRST_NAME STREET         CITY_STATE
357  Burns       Robert     64 24th Street New York NY 10011
421  Bear        Max        12 Elm Street  Los Angeles CA 90911
852  Fischer     Thomas     34 D Street    Grand Rapids MI 49500
147  Hassled     Phil        65 Linwood    Princeton NJ 48504
267  Cantare     Paul       12 Parrot Drive Paterson NJ 49300
741  Hoffman     Jim        2 Apple Road   DesMoines IA 60010
258  Humbug      Bart       666 Scrooge Way Strasburg PA 10500
234  Huber       Tim        1 Plum Drive   Kalamazoo MI 48001
963  Knoll       Fred       99 Appian Way  DesMoines IA 60020
159  Morgan      Maxwell    5 Jeremiah     Seattle WA 99999
345  Miller      Roderick   23 23rd Street Grand Rapids MI 49502
123  Mylor       Frank      81 Tuo Drive   Los Angeles CA 99900
369  Michael     Ed         9 Umm Avenue   New York NY 10019
 98  Smith       Kane       99 Gem Road    Los Angeles CA 99100
761  Stevens     Steven     10 Apso Lane   Los Angeles CA 92011
```

This database has the following structure:

```
Structure for database: ADDRESS.DBF
Number of data records:       15
Date of last update: 01/23/90
Field    Field Name  Type       Width   Dec.   Index
  1      NO          Numeric      3              N
  2      NAME        Character   10              N
  3      FIRST_NAME  Character   10              N
  4      STREET      Character   15              N
  5      CITY_STATE  Character   30              N
** TOTAL **                      69
```

•   Enter the following command to create an ASCII(DELIMITED) file
        named DB-FORM1.DEL:

```
COPY TO db-form1.del FIELDS no,name,first_name,street,city_state DELIMITED
```

The file DB-FORM1.DEL has the following contents:

```
357,"Burns","Robert","64 24th Street","New York NY 10011"
421,"Bear","Max","12 Elm Street","Los Angeles CA 90911"
852,"Fischer","Thomas","34 D Street","Grand Rapids MI 49500"
147,"Hassled","Phil","65 Linwood","Princeton NJ 48504"
267,"Cantare","Paul","12 Parrot Drive","Paterson NJ 49300"
741,"Hoffman","Jim","2 Apple Road","DesMoines IA 60010"
258,"Humbug","Bart","666 Scrooge Way","Strasburg PA 10500"
234,"Huber","Tim","1 Plum Drive","Kalamazoo MI 48001"
963,"Knoll","Fred","99 Appian Way","DesMoines IA 60020"
159,"Morgan","Maxwell","5 Jeremiah","Seattle WA 99999"
345,"Miller","Roderick","23 23rd Street","Grand Rapids MI 49502"
123,"Mylor","Frank","81 Tuo Drive","Los Angeles CA 99900"
369,"Michael","Ed","9 Umm Avenue","New York NY 10019"
98,"Smith","Kane","99 Gem Road","Los Angeles CA 99100"
761,"Stevens","Steven","10 Apso Lane","Los Angeles CA 92011"
```

Note: A conditional branch added to the end of the above command (e.g., FOR
        CITY_STATE="Grand Rapids MI 49502" DELIMITED) would ensure
        that letters are only addressed to the residents of one particular city, state
        and zipcode.

This ASCII file must be converted so that it is recognized by Word as the data file.
This is done using the CONVERT program, found on the companion disk for this
book, and printed in the Appendix as a Turbo Pascal source code.

- Exit dBASE and start the CONVERT utility from the DOS prompt. The program prompts the user for the name of the source file. Enter the source filename and press the <Enter> key.

- The CONVERT utility then prompts the user for the ASCII format of the source file: Press the <D> key (DELIMITED).

- Next the program prompts the user for the number of fields in each record (press the <5> key, then the <Enter> key), field separator (press the <,> key) and text delimiter (press the <"> key).

- The program then prompts the user for the type of each field. Press the <T> key for a text field, the <N> key for a number field, or the <D> key for a date field. Follow each letter key with <Enter>. In this case, press the <N> key for the first field and <T> for the remaining fields.

- CONVERT displays a test record. Press <Y> to accept this layout or <N> to repeat the preceding steps.

- The program prompts the user for the name of the target file. Enter the target filename (in this case, FORMDATA.DOC) and press the <Enter> key. If CONVERT finds an existing file of the same name, it will ask if you want to overwrite the existing file with the new data. Press the <Y> key to overwrite the existing file or the <N> key to end the program.

- The CONVERT utility then prompts the user for the ASCII format of the target file: Press the <D> key (DELIMITED). Next the program prompts the user for the field separator character (press the <,> key) and the text delimiter (press the <Enter> key).

- CONVERT prompts the user for each field type: press the <N> key for the first field and the <T> key for the remaining fields.

CONVERT then converts the file to the proper format.

A sample conversion could look like this:

```
A:\> CONVERT
Please enter the name of the source file
(e.g., C:\DBASE\MYDATA.DBF)
Source: a:\db-form1.del

Please enter source file format (<S>DF or <D>ELIMITED): D
How many fields does each record have? 5

Source file defined as DELIMITED:
Enter the field separator character (usually ,) ,
Enter the text delimiter character (usually ") "

Please enter the field type: <T>ext, <N>umber or <D>ate:
Field 1 type? N
Field 2 type? T
Field 3 type? T
Field 4 type? T
Field 5 type? T
```

```
Test read:
Field 1 :357:
Field 2 :Burns      :
Field 3 :Robert     :
Field 4 :64 24th Street :
Field 5 :New York NY 10011                :

Definition correct (y/n)? y

Please enter the name of the target file
(e.g., C:\DBASE\CONVDATA.DBF)
Target: a:\formdata.doc

ERROR: File already exists.
Do you want to overwrite it (y/n)? y

Please enter target file format (<S>DF or <D>ELIMITED): D
Source file defined as DELIMITED:
Enter the field separator character (usually ,) ,
Enter the text delimiter character (usually ")

Please enter the field type: <T>ext, <N>umber or <D>ate:
Field 1 type? N
Field 2 type? T
Field 3 type? T
Field 4 type? T
Field 5 type? T

File converted.
Press any key to continue.
A:\>
```

The result of the conversion is the following file:

```
357,Burns,Robert,64 24th Street,New York NY 10011
421,Bear,Max,12 Elm Street,Los Angeles CA 90911
852,Fischer,Thomas,34 D Street,Grand Rapids MI 49500
147,Hassled,Phil,65 Linwood,Princeton NJ 48504
267,Cantare,Paul,12 Parrot Drive,Paterson NJ 49300
741,Hoffman,Jim,2 Apple Road,DesMoines IA 60010
258,Humbug,Bart,666 Scrooge Way,Strasburg PA 10500
234,Huber,Tim,1 Plum Drive,Kalamazoo MI 48001
963,Knoll,Fred,99 Appian Way,DesMoines IA 60020
159,Morgan,Maxwell,5 Jeremiah,Seattle WA 99999
345,Miller,Roderick,23 23rd Street,Grand Rapids MI 49502
123,Mylor,Frank,81 Tuo Drive,Los Angeles CA 99900
369,Michael,Ed,9 Umm Avenue,New York NY 10019
98,Smith,Kane,99 Gem Road,Los Angeles CA 99100
761,Stevens,Steven,10 Apso Lane,Los Angeles CA 92011
```

- If the data document has been successfully converted, run Microsoft Word and load the FORMDATA.DOC file using the Transfer/Load command.

- Enter the following in the first line of the document:

  ```
  no,name,first_name,street,city_state
  ```

- Select the Transfer/Save command. Enter the name DATA1.DOC in the file name: command field. Select Text only in the Format: command field and press the <Enter> key.

Word saves the data file under the name DATA1.DOC. Now you can write the main document of the form letter (the text itself).

- Select the Transfer/Clear/All command to clear the data from memory. Enter the following as the first line of text (include any DOS path if needed):

«DATA data1.doc»

The first character of the line is inserted by pressing the <Ctrl><[> keys; the last character is inserted by pressing <Ctrl><]> keys.

- Enter the remaining text so that your main document looks like this:

```
«DATA data1.doc»
«first_name» «name»                        Customer No.:«no»
«street»
«city_state»

Dear «first_name»,

This is a form letter created using Microsoft Word.

Sincerely,
```

- Select Transfer/Save, enter MAINDOC.DOC as the filename and press the <Enter> key to save the main document.

- Select the Print/Merge command if you wish to print form letters. This command offers you the option of sending the form letters to the printer, or generating a single document file containing all the form letter texts for later printing.

When writing the main document above, be sure that you include the drive specifier and path of the data document if this document lies in any directory other than the current directory.

Note: Microsoft Word will also accept the dB-FORM1.DEL file as it appears with quotation marks as text delimiters.

4.1.7 dBASE Data—IBM DisplayWrite 4

DisplayWrite 4 can use data from dBASE IV as document files, as well as data for form letters.

4.1.7.1 dBASE—DisplayWrite 4 Document

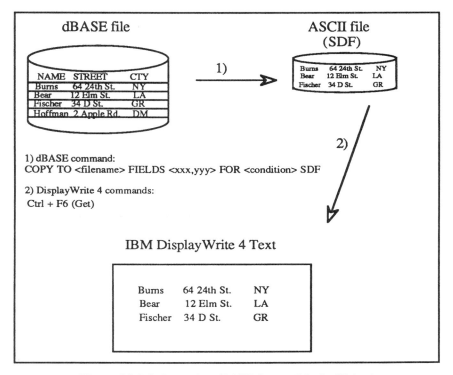

Figure 4.1.7.1: Importing dBASE data to DisplayWrite 4

Create a dBASE ASCII(SDF) file and transfer this data to DisplayWrite 4 as follows:

-     Activate the DATA.DBF database with the USE command.

-     Enter the following command to save a file named DB-DW4.SDF to disk:

```
COPY TO db-dw4.sdf FIELDS name,cty FOR cty="GR" .OR. cty="LA" SDF
```

The file DB-DW4.SDF has the following contents:

```
Bear      LA
Fischer   GR
Miller    GR
Mylor     LA
Smith     GR
Stevens   LA
```

This file can be added to an existing DisplayWrite 4 document using the Get function.

- Create a new document in DisplayWrite 4 named DBTEST.

- Enter the following text:

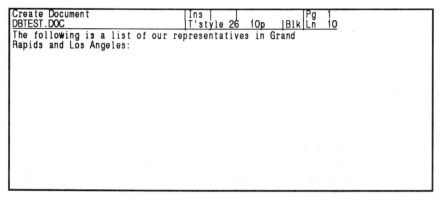

```
Create Document               Ins                    Pg
DBTEST.DOC                    T'style 26  10p  |Blk|Ln  10
The following is a list of our representatives in Grand
Rapids and Los Angeles:
```

- Press the <Enter> key to insert a paragraph after the end of the document.

- Press <Ctrl><F6> to activate the Get function.

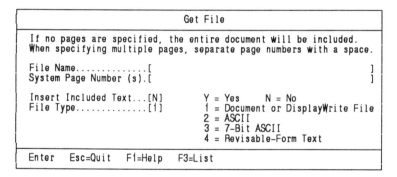

```
                            Get File
If no pages are specified, the entire document will be included.
When specifying multiple pages, separate page numbers with a space.

File Name.............[                                         ]
System Page Number (s).[                                        ]

Insert Included Text...[N]    Y = Yes    N = No
File Type.............[1]     1 = Document or DisplayWrite File
                              2 = ASCII
                              3 = 7-Bit ASCII
                              4 = Revisable-Form Text

Enter    Esc=Quit   F1=Help   F3=List
```

- Enter the name and path of the dBASE ASCII(SDF) file DB-DW4.SDF. Use the <Cursor down> key to move to the File Type field. Press the <2> key to instruct DisplayWrite 4 to accept dBASE data.

- Press the <Enter> key to load the document.

The document should look like this:

```
         Merge Instructions
      ─────────────────────────
      1. Variable
      2. Insert.
      3. Skip to Line Number

      Merge with Data File Only:
      4. Math

      5. If variable empty
      6. If variable not empty
      7. End "If" Test
      ─────────────────────────
         Enter  Esc=Quit  F1=Help
```

- Press the <V> key (Variable).

```
                     Variable
   ────────────────────────────────────────────
   Output Formats are used for 'Merge with Data File' only.

   Variable Name..[              ]

   Output Format...[ ]     Blank = Active Format
                           1 - 4 = Format Number
   ────────────────────────────────────────────
   Enter   Esc=Quit   F1=Help   F3=List
```

- Enter the variable called street. The Output Format field remains empty if it is a non-numerical variable. The Variable field should look like this:

```
                     Variable
   ────────────────────────────────────────────
   Output Formats are used for 'Merge with Data File' only.

   Variable Name..[street        ]

   Output Format...[ ]     Blank = Active Format
                           1 - 4 = Format Number
   ────────────────────────────────────────────
   Enter   Esc=Quit   F1=Help   F3=List
```

- Press the <Enter> key to conclude the input. The variable name is shown on the screen:

```
┌──────────────────────────────────────────────────────────────┐
│ Create Document              │Ins │   │         │Pg │        │
│ SHELL1.DOC                   │T'style 26  10p   │Blk│Ln  10  │
│ !name!                                                        │
│ !street!                                                      │
│                                                               │
│                                                               │
│                                                               │
│                                                               │
│                                                               │
│                                                               │
└──────────────────────────────────────────────────────────────┘
```

- Press the \<Enter> key to move to the next line.

- Press the \<F8> key (Instructions).

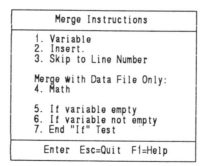

```
┌────────────────────────────────┐
│  1. Begin...                    │
│  2. End...                      │
│                                 │
│  3. Footnote                    │
│  4. Merge Instructions          │
│  5. User-defined Control        │
│  6. Voice note                  │
├────────────────────────────────┤
│    Enter  Esc=Quit  F1=Help     │
└────────────────────────────────┘
```

- Press the \<M> key to select the Merge Instructions.

```
┌────────────────────────────────┐
│       Merge Instructions        │
├────────────────────────────────┤
│  1. Variable                    │
│  2. Insert.                     │
│  3. Skip to Line Number         │
│                                 │
│  Merge with Data File Only:     │
│  4. Math                        │
│                                 │
│  5. If variable empty           │
│  6. If variable not empty       │
│  7. End "If" Test               │
├────────────────────────────────┤
│    Enter  Esc=Quit  F1=Help     │
└────────────────────────────────┘
```

- Press the \<V> key (Variable).

```
┌─────────────────────────────────────────────────────────┐
│                         Variable                         │
├─────────────────────────────────────────────────────────┤
│  Output Formats are used for 'Merge With Data File' only.│
│                                                          │
│  Variable Name..[                   ]                    │
│                                                          │
│  Output Format...[ ]      Blank = Active Format          │
│                           1 - 4 = Format Number          │
├─────────────────────────────────────────────────────────┤
│  Enter   Esc=Quit   F1=Help   F3=List                    │
└─────────────────────────────────────────────────────────┘
```

- Enter the variable called cty. The Output Format field remains empty if it is a non-numerical variable. The Variable field should look like this:

```
┌─────────────────────────────────────────────────────────┐
│                         Variable                         │
├─────────────────────────────────────────────────────────┤
│  Output Formats are used for 'Merge With Data File' only.│
│                                                          │
│  Variable Name..[cty                ]                    │
│                                                          │
│  Output Format...[ ]      Blank = Active Format          │
│                           1 - 4 = Format Number          │
├─────────────────────────────────────────────────────────┤
│  Enter   Esc=Quit   F1=Help   F3=List                    │
└─────────────────────────────────────────────────────────┘
```

- Press the <Enter> key to conclude the input. The variable name is shown on the screen:

```
┌───────────────────────────┬─────────────────────┬───────┐
│Create Document            │Ins                  │Pg   1 │
│SHELL1.DOC                 │T'style 26   10p  |Blk│Ln   10│
│!name!                                                    │
│!street!                                                  │
│!cty!                                                     │
│                                                          │
│                                                          │
│                                                          │
│                                                          │
│                                                          │
│                                                          │
└──────────────────────────────────────────────────────────┘
```

- Press the <Enter> key to move to the next line.

- To edit a variable name, move the cursor to the variable you would like to edit and press <Ctrl><F8> (View/Revise). Edit the name and press the <Enter> key.

- Enter the following text (remember to follow the above instructions for inserting the name variable in the salutation of the document):

```
Create Document            Ins              Pg  1
SHELL1.DOC                 T'style 26  10p  |Blk|Ln  10
!name!
!street!
!cty!

Dear Sales Rep. !name!,

This is a form letter created using IBM DisplayWrite 4.

Sincerely
```

- The Shell document can now be saved (press <F2> and select End and Save).

- Once the Shell document is created, a file description for the data document must be provided. In the main menu of DisplayWrite 4:

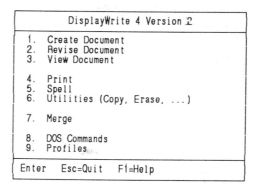

```
DisplayWrite 4 Version 2

1.  Create Document
2.  Revise Document
3.  View Document

4.  Print
5.  Spell
6.  Utilities (Copy, Erase, ...)

7.  Merge

8.  DOS Commands
9.  Profiles

Enter   Esc=Quit   F1=Help
```

- Press the <M> key (Merge).

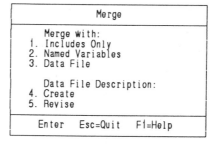

```
Merge

    Merge with:
1.  Includes Only
2.  Named Variables
3.  Data File

    Data File Description:
4.  Create
5.  Revise

    Enter   Esc=Quit   F1=Help
```

- Press the <4> key (Create Data File Description):

```
                 Data File Description

   File Description Name..[                        ]

   Enter    Esc=Quit   F1=Help    F3=List
```

- Enter the name DWFORM for the file description and press the <Enter> key. DisplayWrite 4 automatically adds the extension .DES to the file description name.

- The next menu appears:

```
            Create/Revise Data File Description

      1. Create Field Descriptions

      2. Revise or Display Field Descriptions

      3. Delete Field Descriptions

   Enter  Esc=Quit  F1=Help
```

- Press the <C> key or the <1> key (Create Field Descriptions).

```
                  Field Description

   Field Name..[              ]

   Field Type..[N]          N = Numeric   C = Character

   Length.....[200]    1-17   (Numeric Field Type)
                       1-500  (Character Field Type)

   Enter  Esc=Quit  F1=Help
```

- Enter <name> in the Field Name field. Press the <Cursor down> key or <Tab> key to move to the Field Type field and press the <C> key.

- Press the <Cursor down> key or <Tab> key again to move to the Length field. Delete existing text and enter 10.

```
                  Field Description

   Field Name..[name         ]

   Field Type..[C]          N = Numeric   C = Character

   Length.....[10 ]    1-17   (Numeric Field Type)
                       1-500  (Character Field Type)

   Enter  Esc=Quit  F1=Help
```

- Press the <Enter> key to add this information to the field description.

- Enter <street> in the Field Name field. Press the <Cursor down> key or <Tab> key to move to the Field Type field and press the <C> key.

- Press the <Cursor down> key or <Tab> key again to move to the Length field. Delete existing text and enter 12.

```
┌─────────────────────────────────────────────────────────┐
│                     Field Description                   │
├─────────────────────────────────────────────────────────┤
│  Field Name..street              ]                      │
│                                                         │
│  Field Type..[C]          N = Numeric   C = Character   │
│                                                         │
│  Length.....[12 ]    1-17   (Numeric Field Type)        │
│                      1-500  (Character Field Type)      │
├─────────────────────────────────────────────────────────┤
│  Enter  Esc=Quit  F1=Help                               │
└─────────────────────────────────────────────────────────┘
```

- Press the <Enter> key to add this information to the field description.

- Enter <cty> in the Field Name field. Press the <Cursor down> key or <Tab> key to move to the Field Type field and press the <C> key.

- Press the <Cursor down> key or <Tab> key again to move to the Length field. Delete existing text and enter 4.

```
┌─────────────────────────────────────────────────────────┐
│                     Field Description                   │
├─────────────────────────────────────────────────────────┤
│  Field Name..[cty                ]                      │
│                                                         │
│  Field Type..[C]          N = Numeric   C = Character   │
│                                                         │
│  Length.....[4  ]    1-17   (Numeric Field Type)        │
│                      1-500  (Character Field Type)      │
├─────────────────────────────────────────────────────────┤
│  Enter  Esc=Quit  F1=Help                               │
└─────────────────────────────────────────────────────────┘
```

- Press the <Enter> key to add this information to the field description.

- Press the <Esc> key to move to the preceding menu.

- If you made a mistake, you should be in the Create/Revise Data File Description menu. Press <R> to Revise or Display the descriptions. If there is a problem with one of the descriptions (e.g., typing error), highlight the incorrect word using the direction keys and press the <Enter> key. The Field Description window for that name appears. Make your revision and press <Enter>. Press <Esc> to move to the preceding menu.

- Press the <Esc> key until you are back in DisplayWrite's opening menu:

```
┌─────────────────────────────────────────────┐
│           DisplayWrite 4 Version 2            │
├─────────────────────────────────────────────┤
│   1.  Create Document                         │
│   2.  Revise Document                         │
│   3.  View Document                           │
│                                               │
│   4.  Print                                   │
│   5.  Spell                                   │
│   6.  Utilities (Copy, Erase, ...)            │
│                                               │
│   7.  Merge                                   │
│                                               │
│   8.  DOS Commands                            │
│   9.  Profiles                                │
├─────────────────────────────────────────────┤
│   Enter   Esc=Quit   F1=Help                  │
└─────────────────────────────────────────────┘
```

  •   Press the <M> key or the <7> key (Merge).

```
┌─────────────────────────────────────────────┐
│                    Merge                      │
├─────────────────────────────────────────────┤
│       Merge with:                             │
│   1.  Includes Only                           │
│   2.  Named Variables                         │
│   3.  Data File                               │
│                                               │
│       Data File Description:                  │
│   4.  Create                                  │
│   5.  Revise                                  │
├─────────────────────────────────────────────┤
│       Enter   Esc=Quit   F1=Help              │
└─────────────────────────────────────────────┘
```

  •   Press the <D> key or the <3> key (Data File).

```
┌─────────────────────────────────────────────────────────────┐
│                        Data File                              │
├─────────────────────────────────────────────────────────────┤
│ Data File Name ....[FORM2.DOC                      ]          │
│                                                               │
│ Data File Format.[1]  1 = PDS *          2=WKS,WK1,WRK or WRK*│
│                       3 = Fixed Length   4=BASIC Sequential   │
│                       5 = DIF *          6=SYLK *             │
│                       7 = dBASE II or III*  8=User-supplied   │
│                                                               │
│ * For trademark information and supported versions, position  │
│   the cursor on the Data File format field and select Help.   │
├─────────────────────────────────────────────────────────────┤
│ Enter   Esc=Quit   F1=Help   F3=List                          │
└─────────────────────────────────────────────────────────────┘
```

  •   Enter the name of the data document (in this case, FORM2.DOC). Be
      sure to include the drive specifier and path if needed.

  •   Press the <Cursor down> key or <Tab> key to move to the Data File
      Format field. Press the <4> key (BASIC Sequential). Press the <Enter>
      key. The following appears:

```
┌─────────────────────────────────────────────────────┐
│              Data File Description                    │
├─────────────────────────────────────────────────────┤
│                                                       │
│   File Description Name..[                      ]     │
│                                                       │
├─────────────────────────────────────────────────────┤
│   Enter    Esc=Quit   F1=Help    F3=List              │
└─────────────────────────────────────────────────────┘
```

- Enter the name of the data file description (DWFORM.DES), adding the drive specifier and path if necessary.

- Press the <Enter> key.

```
┌─────────────────────────────────────────────────────────────┐
│              Merge with Data File (1 of 2)                    │
├─────────────────────────────────────────────────────────────┤
│   Shell Document.........[A:SHELL1.DOC                    ]    │
│                                                               │
│   Merged Document.Name...[                                ]    │
│                                                               │
│   Print Merged Document..[Y]      Y = Yes    N = No           │
│                                                               │
│   Cancel on Error........[Y]      Y = Yes    N = No           │
│                                                               │
│   Restart number.........[   ]   (Any valid record number, or none) │
├─────────────────────────────────────────────────────────────┤
│   Enter Esc=Quit. F1=Help  F3=List              PgDn=More Options │
└─────────────────────────────────────────────────────────────┘
```

- Enter the name of the Shell document.

- Turn on the printer and press the <Enter> key.

The following appears when the merging is done.

```
┌─────────────────────────────────────────────────────┐
│   ┌─────────────────────────────────────────┐        │
│   │         Merge With Data File Status       │        │
│   ├─────────────────────────────────────────┤        │
│   │                                           │        │
│   │   To stop Merge Task, press Ctrl+Break.   │        │
│   │                      ─────────            │        │
│   │   Number of Records Merged..3             │        │
│   │                                           │        │
│   │   Number of errors..........             │        │
│   │                                           │        │
│   │   Restart Number............             │        │
│   └─────────────────────────────────────────┘        │
│ > Processing is complete for "$SYSDOC1.$$T"           │
└─────────────────────────────────────────────────────┘
```

4.1.8 dBASE—Aldus PageMaker

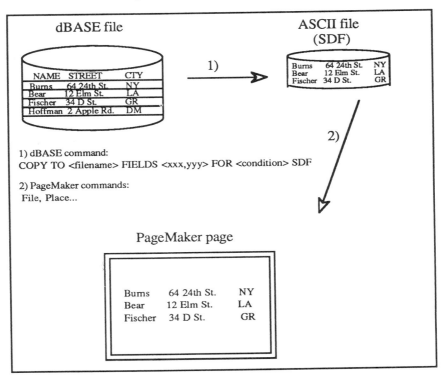

Figure 4.1.8:Importing dBASE data to PageMaker

dBASE files can be positioned directly in PageMaker, provided that you have installed a dBASE import/export filter in PageMaker (see your PageMaker installation information).

Add the worksheet file DATA.DBF to PageMaker as follows:

- Run PageMaker. Lay out a new publication or load an existing publication.

- Select the File menu and the Place... option. Click on the DATA.DBF filename and click OK.

- Once the file is loaded, PageMaker prompts you to enter the fields you want placed. Click on the Add All button and click OK.

The mouse pointer changes to a manual flow text icon.

- Move this pointer to the location at which you want the file to begin. Press and hold the left mouse button and move the pointer down and to the right of the starting point of the pointer. Release the left mouse button. An alternate method is to click once at the desired starting point of the file.

If the file is larger than the amount of space you have created, a plus sign within a semicircle appears at the bottom of the page. This is the bottom windowshade handle. By dragging this handle down, dragging the handles at the edge of each text block, or clicking on the bottom windowshade handle and creating another block for the remaining text, you can insert the remaining text.

You can now edit your data from within PageMaker.

Here's an alternate method, using a dBASE-generated ASCII(SDF) file:

- Run dBASE. Activate the DATA.DBF file with the USE command.

- Enter the following to create a dBASE ASCII(SDF) file named DB-PM.TXT:

```
COPY TO db-pm.txt FIELDS name,cty,sales FOR sales>300 SDF
```

The file DB-PM.TXT has the following contents:

```
Burns          NY          370.00
Bear           LA          378.00
Smith          GR          500.00
```

Add the file to PageMaker as follows:

- Lay out a new publication or load an existing publication.

- Select the File menu and the Place... option. Click on the DB-PM.TXT filename and click OK.

The mouse pointer changes to a manual flow text icon.

- Move this pointer to the location at which you want the file to begin. Press and hold the left mouse button and move the pointer down and to the right of the starting point of the pointer. Release the left mouse button. An alternate method is to click once at the desired starting point of the file.

If the file is larger than the amount of space you have created, a plus sign within a semicircle appears at the bottom of the page. This is the bottom windowshade handle. By dragging this handle down, dragging the handles at the edge of each text block, or clicking on the bottom windowshade handle and creating another block for the remaining text, you can insert the remaining text.

You can now edit your data from within PageMaker.

4.1.9 dBASE—Ventura Publisher

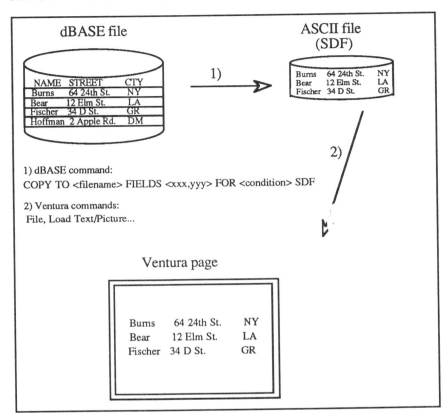

Figure 4.1.9: Importing data in Ventura Publisher

Create a dBASE ASCII(SDF) file from the DATA.DBF file and transfer it to Ventura Publisher as follows:

- Activate the DATA.DBF database with the USE command.

- Enter the following to create an ASCII(SDF) file named DB-VP.DOC:

```
COPY TO db-vp.doc FIELDS name,street,cty,sales FOR cty="GR" .or. cty="LA" SDF
```

131

The file DB-VP.DOC has the following contents:

```
Bear      12 Elm St.     LA     378.00
Fischer   34 D St.       GR     260.00
Miller    123 23rd St.   GR     100.00
Mylor     81 Tuo Dr.     LA     299.00
Smith     99 Gem Rd.     GR     500.00
Stevens   10 Apso Ln.    LA     300.00
```

- Exit dBASE and run Ventura Publisher.

- Click on the Add New Frame addition button. Create a frame within Ventura Publisher.

- Select the File menu and the Load Text/Picture... option.

- Click on the Text button, then the WS 4.0/5.0 button.

- Click on the Directory line and replace the file extension with .*. Click on the bar above the file list.

- Click on the DB-VP.DOC filename and click on the OK button.

The file can now be edited from within Ventura Publisher.

4.2 Microsoft Multiplan

The following Multiplan worksheet named DATA.MP will be used as an example
in much of this section:

```
#1        1           2          3   4      5         6
    1 NAME        STREET         CTY SALES  DATE
    2 Burns       64 24th St.    NY  370.00 01/01/88
    3 Bear        12 Elm St.     LA  378.00 02/01/88
    4 Fischer     34 D St.       GR  260.00 12/31/87
    5 Hoffman     2 Apple Rd.    DM  250.00 03/01/88
    6 Huber       1 Plum Dr.     KZ  190.00 04/01/88
    7 Miller      23 23rd St.    GR  100.00 05/01/88
    8 Mylor       81 Tuo Dr.     LA  299.00 07/01/88
    9 Michael     9 Umm Ave.     NY  150.00 08/01/88
   10 Smith       99 Gem Rd.     GR  500.00 07/20/88
   11 Stevens     10 Apso Ln.    LA  300.00 07/30/88
   12
   13
   14
   15
   16
   17
   18
   19
   20
COMMAND: Alpha Blank Copy Delete Edit Format Goto Help Insert Lock Move
         Name Options Print Quit Run Sort Transfer Value Window Xternal
Select option or type command letter
R1C1     "NAME"              ? 100% free      Multiplan: DATA.MP
```

This worksheet should have the following column widths (set these using the
Format/Width command for each column) and formats (Format/Cells):

Column	Width	Alignment	Format Code
1	Default	Def	Def
2	12	Def	Def
3	4	Def	Def
4	7	Right	Fixed
5	9	Left	–

In addition, make sure that the dates in column 5 are configured as mm/dd/yy.

4.2.1 Multiplan—dBASE IV

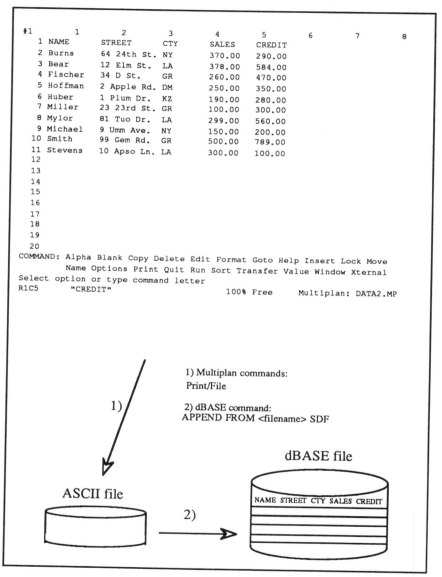

```
#1       1         2        3        4        5        6        7        8
     1 NAME      STREET    CTY     SALES    CREDIT
     2 Burns     64 24th St. NY    370.00   290.00
     3 Bear      12 Elm St.  LA    378.00   584.00
     4 Fischer   34 D St.    GR    260.00   470.00
     5 Hoffman   2 Apple Rd. DM    250.00   350.00
     6 Huber     1 Plum Dr.  KZ    190.00   280.00
     7 Miller    23 23rd St. GR    100.00   300.00
     8 Mylor     81 Tuo Dr.  LA    299.00   560.00
     9 Michael   9 Umm Ave.  NY    150.00   200.00
    10 Smith     99 Gem Rd.  GR    500.00   789.00
    11 Stevens   10 Apso Ln. LA    300.00   100.00
    12
    13
    14
    15
    16
    17
    18
    19
    20
COMMAND: Alpha Blank Copy Delete Edit Format Goto Help Insert Lock Move
         Name Options Print Quit Run Sort Transfer Value Window Xternal
Select option or type command letter
R1C5      "CREDIT"                      100% Free      Multiplan: DATA2.MP
```

1) Multiplan commands:
Print/File

2) dBASE command:
APPEND FROM <filename> SDF

1)

2)

ASCII file

dBASE file

NAME STREET CTY SALES CREDIT

Figure 4.2.1: Importing Multiplan data to dBASE

Multiplan data must be saved as an ASCII file before it can be loaded into dBASE.

•   Select the Print/Options command. Enter the part of the worksheet you want stored as an ASCII file in the area: command field. In this case, select R2C1:R11C5. This area can also be defined using the mouse or the cursor keys. The field names in the first row are not transferred because these are defined in the dBASE structure. The setup: command field must be left empty, since only printer specific control characters can be entered in this command field. The other command fields can remain unchanged because they are not needed for an ASCII file. Press the <Enter> key to exit.

- Select the Print/Margins command. Enter 0 in the left: and top: command fields. Enter a number in the print width: command field that is larger than the record length (at least 42 here). Enter a number that is larger than the maximum number of records in the print length: and page length: command fields. Enter a 0 in the indent: command field. Press the <Enter> key to end.

- Select the Print/File command. Enter the name MP-DB-1.SDF in the PRINT on file: command field and press the <Enter> key.

Multiplan writes the ASCII(SDF) file MP-DB-1.SDF to disk.

- Exit Multiplan and start dBASE IV. Open a new or existing file that has an ASCII structure.

- Enter the total column width of the Multiplan file as the field length. Create a character field with a length of nine characters for the date field.

The following structure should be created:

```
Structure for database: APPEND.DBF
Number of data records:        0
Date of last update: 01/23/90
Field     Field Name  Type       Width  Dec.  Index
   1      NAME        Character    10            N
   2      STREET      Character    12            N
   3      CTY         Character     4            N
   4      SALES       Numeric       7    2       N
   5      DATE        Character     9            N
** TOTAL **                        43
```

- Enter the following command:

```
APPEND FROM mp-db-1.sdf SDF
```

If the records of the ASCII file are successfully copied, the following message appears:

```
xx Records copied
```

- Even though your Multiplan database contained 10 records, the transfer may include an eleventh "garbage" record. If this occurs, use <Ctrl><U> to mark the record for deletion, and use the PACK command to remove the record from the database.

- When the records are copied, use the MODIFY STRUCTURE command to change the date format.

```
Layout   Organize   Append   Go To   Exit                        12:36:52 am
                                                    Bytes remaining:    3954
 ┌──────┬─────────────┬─────────────┬────────┬──────┬───────┐
 │ Num  │ Field Name  │ Field Type  │ Width  │ Dec  │ Index │
 ├──────┼─────────────┼─────────────┼────────┼──────┼───────┤
 │  1   │ NAME        │ Character   │  10    │      │   N   │
 │  2   │ STREET      │ Character   │  12    │      │   N   │
 │  3   │ CTY         │ Character   │   4    │      │   N   │
 │  4   │ SALES       │ Numeric     │   7    │  2   │   N   │
 │  5   │ DATE        │ Date        │   9    │      │   N   │
 │      │             │             │        │      │       │
 └──────┴─────────────┴─────────────┴────────┴──────┴───────┘
Database║A:\APPEND            ║Field 1/10      ║               ║
         Enter the field name. Insert/Delete field:Ctrl-N/Ctrl-U
Field names begin with a letter and may contain letters, digits and underscores
```

Figure 4.2.1a: Modifying structure in dBASE

- Move the cursor to the date field. Enter the <D> key for the Field type. Press <Ctrl><End> to save the new structure. This new file has the following structure:

```
Structure for database: APPEND.DBF
Number of data records:         0
Date of last update: 01/23/90
Field    Field Name  Type       Width   Dec.   Index
    1    NAME        Character     10            N
    2    STREET      Character     12            N
    3    CTY         Character      4            N
    4    SALES       Numeric        6     2      N
    5    DATE        Date           8            N
** TOTAL **                        41
```

The dBASE file has the following contents:

```
Record  NAME       STREET         CTY SALES   DATE
   1    Burns      64 24th St.    NY  370.00  01/01/88
   2    Bear       12 Elm St.     LA  378.00  02/01/88
   3    Fischer    34 D St.       GR  260.00  12/31/87
   4    Hoffman    2 Apple Rd.    DM  250.00  03/01/88
   5    Huber      1 Plum Dr.     KZ  190.00  04/01/88
   6    Miller     23 23rd St.    GR  100.00  05/01/88
   7    Mylor      81 Tuo Dr.     LA  299.00  07/01/88
   8    Michael    9 Umm Ave.     NY  150.00  08/01/88
   9    Smith      99 Gem Rd.     GR  500.00  07/20/88
  10    Stevens    10 Apso Ln.    LA  300.00  07/30/88
```

The file can then be edited from within dBASE.

4.2.2 Multiplan—Microsoft Excel

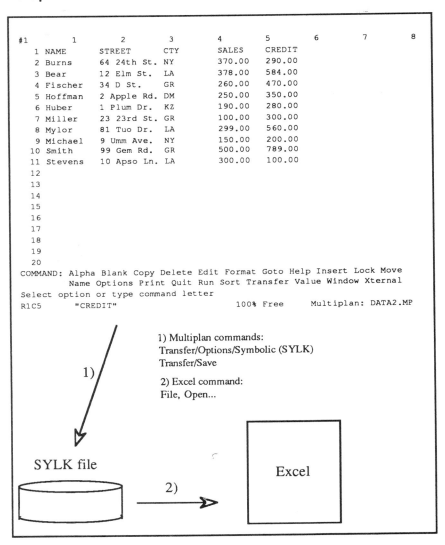

```
#1         1          2          3          4         5        6        7        8
      1 NAME       STREET      CTY      SALES     CREDIT
      2 Burns      64 24th St. NY       370.00    290.00
      3 Bear       12 Elm St.  LA       378.00    584.00
      4 Fischer    34 D St.    GR       260.00    470.00
      5 Hoffman    2 Apple Rd. DM       250.00    350.00
      6 Huber      1 Plum Dr.  KZ       190.00    280.00
      7 Miller     23 23rd St. GR       100.00    300.00
      8 Mylor      81 Tuo Dr.  LA       299.00    560.00
      9 Michael    9 Umm Ave.  NY       150.00    200.00
     10 Smith      99 Gem Rd.  GR       500.00    789.00
     11 Stevens    10 Apso Ln. LA       300.00    100.00
     12
     13
     14
     15
     16
     17
     18
     19
     20
COMMAND: Alpha Blank Copy Delete Edit Format Goto Help Insert Lock Move
        Name Options Print Quit Run Sort Transfer Value Window Xternal
Select option or type command letter
R1C5      "CREDIT"                        100% Free      Multiplan: DATA2.MP
```

1) Multiplan commands:
Transfer/Options/Symbolic (SYLK)
Transfer/Save

2) Excel command:
File, Open...

1)

SYLK file

2)

Excel

Figure 4.2.2: Importing data to Excel

Data from Multiplan can only be transferred to Microsoft Excel in SYLK format.

```
#1        1         2       3    4      5         6
    1 NAME      STREET      CTY SALES  DATE
    2 Burns     64 24th St. NY  370.00 01/01/88
    3 Bear      12 Elm St.  LA  378.00 02/01/88
    4 Fischer   34 D St.    GR  260.00 12/31/87
    5 Hoffman   2 Apple Rd. DM  250.00 03/01/88
    6 Huber     1 Plum Dr.  KZ  190.00 04/01/88
    7 Miller    23 23rd St. GR  100.00 05/01/88
    8 Mylor     81 Tuo Dr.  LA  299.00 07/01/88
    9 Michael   9 Umm Ave.  NY  150.00 08/01/88
   10 Smith     99 Gem Rd.  GR  500.00 07/20/88
   11 Stevens   10 Apso Ln. LA  300.00 07/30/88
   12
   13
   14
   15
   16
   17
   18
   19
   20
COMMAND: Alpha Blank Copy Delete Edit Format Goto Help Insert Lock Move
         Name Options Print Quit Run Sort Transfer Value Window Xternal
Select option or type command letter
R1C1    "NAME"              ? 100% free    Multiplan: DATA.MP
```

- Select the Transfer/Options command. Select the Symbolic option in the mode: command field, then press the <Enter> key.

- Select Transfer/Save, enter the filename MP-EX.SLK and press the <Enter> key to save the file.

- Exit Multiplan.

The saved SYLK file can then be loaded directly into Excel.

- Run Excel.

- Start Microsoft Excel.

- Select the File menu and click on the Open... option. A window appears, listing a set of files. In addition, you'll see a text box listing a file wildcard of *.XL*. Change this wildcard to read *.*, press the <Enter> key and watch the change.

- Select the desired path from the Directories window.

- Select the filename MP-EX.SLK and either press <Enter> or click on the OK button to load the file.

- Select the cells containing the date fields.

- Convert the date field to the proper date format using the Format Number command.

The file can then be edited from within Excel. When you save this file from Excel, Excel maintains the original SYLK file and generates its own Excel file as well.

4.2.3 Multiplan—Microsoft Chart

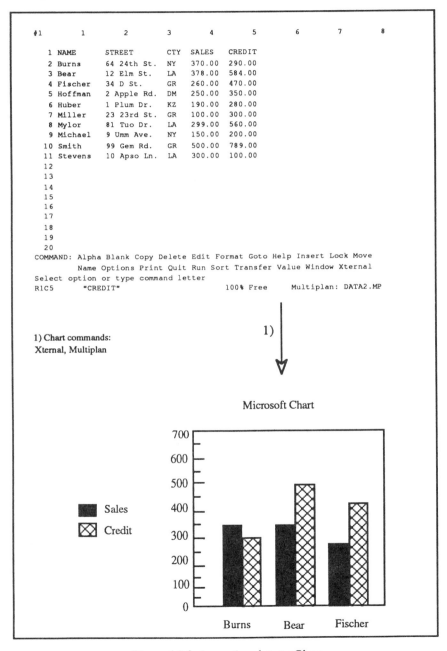

```
#1      1          2          3      4        5         6        7        8

  1  NAME       STREET      CTY   SALES    CREDIT
  2  Burns      64 24th St.  NY   370.00   290.00
  3  Bear       12 Elm St.   LA   378.00   584.00
  4  Fischer    34 D St.     GR   260.00   470.00
  5  Hoffman    2 Apple Rd.  DM   250.00   350.00
  6  Huber      1 Plum Dr.   KZ   190.00   280.00
  7  Miller     23 23rd St.  GR   100.00   300.00
  8  Mylor      81 Tuo Dr.   LA   299.00   560.00
  9  Michael    9 Umm Ave.   NY   150.00   200.00
 10  Smith      99 Gem Rd.   GR   500.00   789.00
 11  Stevens    10 Apso Ln.  LA   300.00   100.00
 12
 13
 14
 15
 16
 17
 18
 19
 20
COMMAND: Alpha Blank Copy Delete Edit Format Goto Help Insert Lock Move
         Name Options Print Quit Run Sort Transfer Value Window Xternal
Select option or type command letter
R1C5      "CREDIT"                     100% Free    Multiplan: DATA2.MP
```

1) Chart commands:
Xternal, Multiplan

1)

Microsoft Chart

Figure 4.2.3: Importing data to Chart

The following Multiplan worksheet DATA2.MP is used for this example:

```
#1       1        2        3   4      5        6        7        8
     1 NAME     STREET      CTY SALES  CREDIT
     2 Burns    64 24th St. NY  370.00 290.00
     3 Bear     12 Elm St.  LA  378.00 584.00
     4 Fischer  34 D St.    GR  260.00 470.00
     5 Hoffman  2 Apple Rd. DM  250.00 350.00
     6 Huber    1 Plum Dr.  KZ  190.00 280.00
     7 Miller   23 23rd St. GR  100.00 300.00
     8 Mylor    81 Tuo Dr.  LA  299.00 560.00
     9 Michael  9 Umm Ave.  NY  150.00 200.00
    10 Smith    99 Gem Rd.  GR  500.00 789.00
    11 Stevens  10 Apso Ln. LA  300.00 100.00
    12
    13
    14
    15
    16
    17
    18
    19
    20
COMMAND: Alpha Blank Copy Delete Edit Format Goto Help Insert Lock Move
         Name Options Print Quit Run Sort Transfer Value Window Xternal
Select option or type command letter
R1C1     "NAME"              ? 100% free      Multiplan: DATA2.MP
```

Microsoft Chart can read Multiplan files without modification.

Do the following to display all representatives in GR (Grand Rapids):

•   Select the Xternal Multiplan command in Chart.

•   Enter DATA2.MP in the filename: command field. Press the <Tab> key to move to the linked: command field. Press the <Y> key (Yes). This updates chart data every time you update the Multiplan worksheet and run Chart.

•   Press the <Tab> key to move to the named area or reference: command field. Enter the following to display all data pertaining to GR:

R4C4:5,R7C4:5,R10C4:5

•   Press the <Tab> key to move on to the orient series by: command field. Here you can select column or row orientation. Press <R> (Rows) and press the <Tab> key to move on to the series name(s) from: field. Press <1> and press the <Tab> key to move on the categories from: command field.

•   Press <1> and press the <Tab> key to move on to the category type: command field. Press <T> then press the <Enter> key.

The list contains the following entry:

Incl.(*)	Name	Source of data	Type	# pts.
1 *	Fischer	Linked: data2.mp:R4C4:5	Text	2
2 *	Miller	Linked: data2.mp:R7C4:5	Text	2
3 *	Smith	Linked: data2.mp:R10C4:5	Text	2

The graphic created by Chart has the following structure:

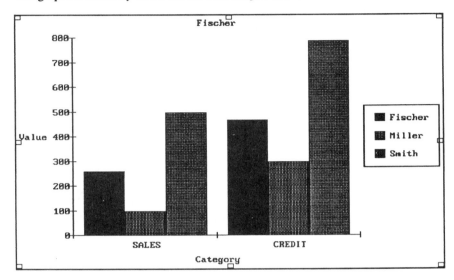

Figure 4.2.3a: Chart graphic created from Multiplan data

- Select the Xternal Multiplan command in Chart.

- Enter DATA2.MP in the filename: command field. Press the <Tab> key to move to the linked: command field. Press the <Y> key (Yes). This updates chart data every time you update the Multiplan worksheet and run Chart.

- Press the <Tab> key to move to the named area or reference: command field. Enter the following to display all data pertaining to GR:

  R4C4:5,R7C4:5,R10C4:5

- Press the <Tab> key to move on to the orient series by: command field. Here you can select column or row orientation. Press <C> (Columns) and press the <Tab> key to move on to the series name(s) from: field. Press <1> and press the <Tab> key to move on the categories from: command field. Press the <1> key.

- Press the <Tab> key to move on to the category type: command field. Press <T> then press the <Enter> key.

The list contains the following entry:

Incl. (*)	Name	Source of data	Type	# pts.
1 *	SALES	Linked:data2.mp:R4,7,10C4	Text	3
2 *	CREDIT	Linked:data2.mp:R4,7,10C5	Text	3

The graphic created by Chart has the following structure:

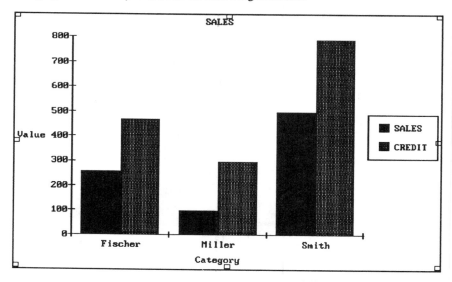

Figure 4.2.3b: Chart graphic created from Multiplan data

You can then save the chart data using the Transfer/Save command.

4.2.4 Multiplan—Lotus 1-2-3

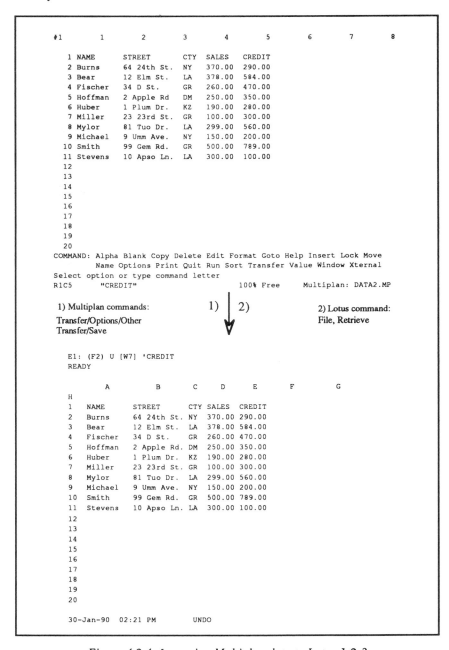

Figure 4.2.4: Importing Multiplan data to Lotus 1-2-3

Multiplan files can be saved directly in a format recognized by Lotus 1-2-3. The DATA.MP worksheet (see Section 4.2) will be used for this example.

Remember two items when exchanging data between Multiplan and Lotus 1-2-3:

1)   Multiplan macros are not interchangeable in Lotus 1-2-3 format. Lotus 1-2-3 interprets Multiplan macros as text, rather than as macros.

2)   Multiplan formulas containing the following functions are deleted when saved in Lotus format, but the values in the cells using these formulas are transferred regardless:

```
DELTA, FEST, INDEX, LENGTH, QIKV, ROUND, COLUMN, SEARCH, SECTION, SIGN, WÄHRUNG,
VALUE, REPEAT, WEEKDAY, COUNTER, LINE, ZZR
```

Transfer the Multiplan file to Lotus 1-2-3 format as follows:

•   Select Transfer/Options. Select the Other option from the mode: command field and press the <Enter> key.

•   Select the Transfer/Save command. Enter the filename MP-LO-1.WK1. Press the <Enter> key to save the file.

•   Exit Multiplan. Run Lotus 1-2-3. Select / File Retrieve to load the worksheet.

•   The dates will appear as date numbers. Select / Range Format Date and select Long Intn'l. Press the <Enter> key to accept this.

```
A1:  'Burns                                                              READY
          A         B         C    D       E        F        G        H
1    NAME      STREET       CTY  SALES   DATE
2    Burns     64 24th St.  NY   370.00  01/01/88
3    Bear      12 Elm St.   LA   378.00  02/01/88
4    Fischer   34 D St.     GR   260.00  12/31/87
5    Hoffman   2 Apple Rd.  DM   250.00  03/01/88
6    Huber     1 Plum Dr.   KZ   190.00  04/01/88
7    Miller    23 23rd St.  GR   100.00  05/01/88
8    Mylor     81 Tuo Dr.   LA   299.00  07/01/88
9    Michael   9 Umm Ave.   NY   150.00  08/01/88
10   Smith     99 Gem Rd.   GR   500.00  07/20/88
11   Stevens   10 Apso Ln.  LA   300.00  07/30/88
12
13
14
15
16
17
18
19
20
23-Jan-89   08:55 AM             UNDO
```

4.2.5 Multiplan—Lotus Freelance Plus

Data from Lotus 1-2-3, Multiplan, Excel and dBASE can be shown as graphics. In addition, data from most other applications can be displayed as text charts by Freelance. The DATA2.MP worksheet (see Section 4.2.3) will be used for this example.

4.2.5.1 Multiplan—Freelance Graphics

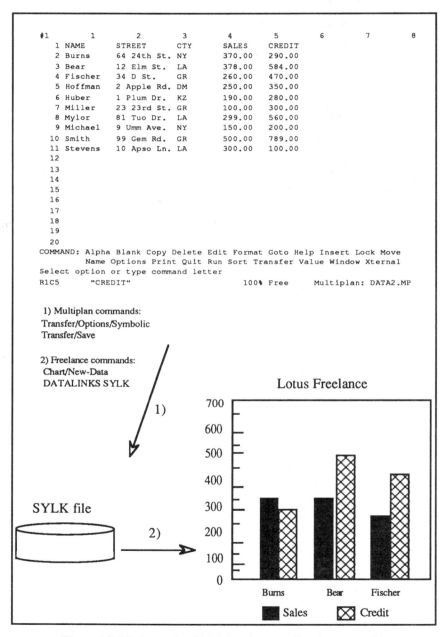

```
#1          1           2        3        4         5        6        7        8
       1 NAME        STREET     CTY     SALES     CREDIT
       2 Burns       64 24th St. NY     370.00    290.00
       3 Bear        12 Elm St.  LA     378.00    584.00
       4 Fischer     34 D St.    GR     260.00    470.00
       5 Hoffman     2 Apple Rd. DM     250.00    350.00
       6 Huber       1 Plum Dr.  KZ     190.00    280.00
       7 Miller      23 23rd St. GR     100.00    300.00
       8 Mylor       81 Tuo Dr.  LA     299.00    560.00
       9 Michael     9 Umm Ave.  NY     150.00    200.00
      10 Smith       99 Gem Rd.  GR     500.00    789.00
      11 Stevens     10 Apso Ln. LA     300.00    100.00
      12
      13
      14
      15
      16
      17
      18
      19
      20
COMMAND: Alpha Blank Copy Delete Edit Format Goto Help Insert Lock Move
         Name Options Print Quit Run Sort Transfer Value Window Xternal
Select option or type command letter
R1C5      "CREDIT"                       100% Free      Multiplan: DATA2.MP
```

1) Multiplan commands:
Transfer/Options/Symbolic
Transfer/Save

2) Freelance commands:
Chart/New-Data
DATALINKS SYLK

1)

SYLK file

2)

Lotus Freelance

Sales   Credit

Figure 4.2.5.1: Importing Multiplan data to a Freelance graphic

Save the Multiplan file DATA2.MP in SYLK format and convert to Freelance graphics as follows:

- Select the Transfer/Options command in Multiplan. Select the Symbolic option from the mode: command field and press the <Enter> key.

- Select the Transfer/Save command, enter the filename MP-FL-1.SLK and press the <Enter> key to save.

- Quit Multiplan and run Freelance. Select the Charts and Drawings menu of Freelance.

- Select the Chart New-Data command.

- The cursor should be in the Chart type item. Press the <Tab> key to move to the DATALINKS bar. Press <Space> to see the Datalinks menu.

- The cursor should be in the File type: item. Press <Space> to see a list of file types available. Select the SYLK option and press the <Enter> key.

- Press the <Tab> key or the <Cursor down> key to move to the File path: item if needed. Press <Space> to display a list of the current level's directories. Select the proper drive specifier and path and press the <Enter> key. Continue this instruction as needed until you reach the directory containing the MP-FL-1.SLK file.

- Move the cursor down to the File name: item using the <Tab> key or the <Cursor down> key. Enter the name MP-FL-1.SLK in this line.

- Move the cursor down to the Type of import: item. This item should read Specified Ranges.

- Leave the Headings:, Notes:, Legends: and axis Title: items blank.

- Move the cursor to the Cluster Labels: item and enter A2..A11 (this corresponds to Multiplan's R2C1:R11C1).

- Move the cursor to the Bar 1 Values: item and enter D2..D11 (this corresponds to Multiplan's R2C4:R11C4).

- Move the cursor to the Bar 2 Values: item and enter E2..E11 (this corresponds to Multiplan's R2C5:R11C5).

- Press the <End> key to move to the DONE bar. Press <Enter> to accept the above data. If Freelance asks if you want to update data, press the <Y> key.

- Press the <F10> key for the menu. Press the <G> key (Go) to generate the chart. If a confirmation message appears, press the <Y> key to go on.

- Freelance may ask you to adjust the chart size or shape. For now, just press the keys required to draw the chart (usually <Enter>).

- Press the <Enter> key to accept the chart.

The chart can now be edited from within Freelance.

When importing SYLK files to Freelance, you must remember that Freelance reads ranges in Lotus syntax rather than Multiplan syntax. For example, if you wanted Freelance to read the Multiplan range R1C1:R10C16, you would have to enter the values A1..P10. The Multiplan worksheet columns must be converted to Lotus syntax. The line numbers stay the same. The column numbers are converted to the letters of the alphabet. Multiplan columns 1-26 become A-Z, columns 27-53 become AA-AZ, 54-80 become BA-BZ and so on.

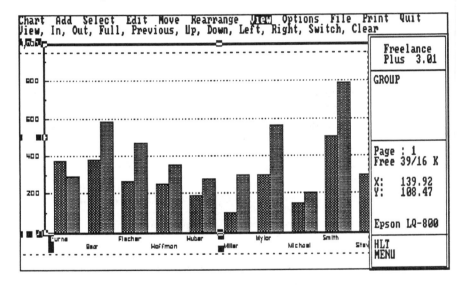

Figure 4.2.5.1a: Freelance graphic from Multiplan data

4.2.6.2 Multiplan (ASCII)—Microsoft Word

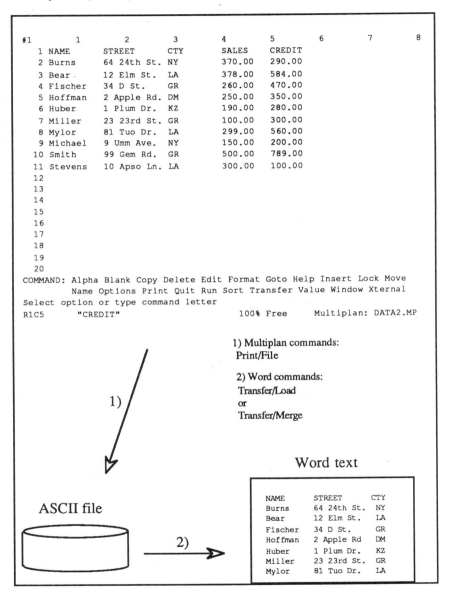

```
#1        1           2         3       4        5       6       7       8
       1 NAME       STREET     CTY    SALES    CREDIT
       2 Burns      64 24th St. NY    370.00   290.00
       3 Bear       12 Elm St.  LA    378.00   584.00
       4 Fischer    34 D St.    GR    260.00   470.00
       5 Hoffman    2 Apple Rd. DM    250.00   350.00
       6 Huber      1 Plum Dr.  KZ    190.00   280.00
       7 Miller     23 23rd St. GR    100.00   300.00
       8 Mylor      81 Tuo Dr.  LA    299.00   560.00
       9 Michael    9 Umm Ave.  NY    150.00   200.00
      10 Smith      99 Gem Rd.  GR    500.00   789.00
      11 Stevens    10 Apso Ln. LA    300.00   100.00
      12
      13
      14
      15
      16
      17
      18
      19
      20
COMMAND: Alpha Blank Copy Delete Edit Format Goto Help Insert Lock Move
        Name Options Print Quit Run Sort Transfer Value Window Xternal
Select option or type command letter
R1C5      "CREDIT"                 100% Free     Multiplan: DATA2.MP
```

1) Multiplan commands:
Print/File

2) Word commands:
Transfer/Load
or
Transfer/Merge

Word text

```
NAME       STREET      CTY
Burns      64 24th St. NY
Bear       12 Elm St.  LA
Fischer    34 D St.    GR
Hoffman    2 Apple Rd  DM
Huber      1 Plum Dr.  KZ
Miller     23 23rd St. GR
Mylor      81 Tuo Dr.  LA
```

ASCII file

Figure 4.2.6.2: Importing Multiplan ASCII data to Word

Save a Multiplan worksheet as an ASCII file and transfer it to Word as follows:

- Load the DATA2.MP worksheet into Multiplan using the Transfer/Load command.

- Select the Print/Options command. Enter the part of the worksheet you want stored as an ASCII file in the area: command field, or define the area using the mouse or the cursor keys (in this case, R1C1:R1C11). The setup: command field must be left empty, since only printer specific control characters can be entered in this command field. The other command fields can remain unchanged because they are not needed for an ASCII file. Press the <Enter> key to exit.

- Select the Print/Margins command. Enter 0 in the left: and top: command fields. Enter a number in the print width: command field that exceeds the record length. Enter a number that is larger than the maximum number of records in the print length: and page length: command fields (at least 12). Enter a 0 in the indent: command field. Press the <Enter> key to end.

- Select the Print/File command. Enter the filename MP-WO.DOC (with drive specifier and path as needed) in the file: command field and press the <Enter> key.

- Exit Multiplan.

- Run Word and select the Transfer/Load command. Enter the filename (with drive specifier and path if needed) and press the <Enter> key.

The data can then be formatted or edited from within Word.

4.2.7 Multiplan—IBM DisplayWrite 4

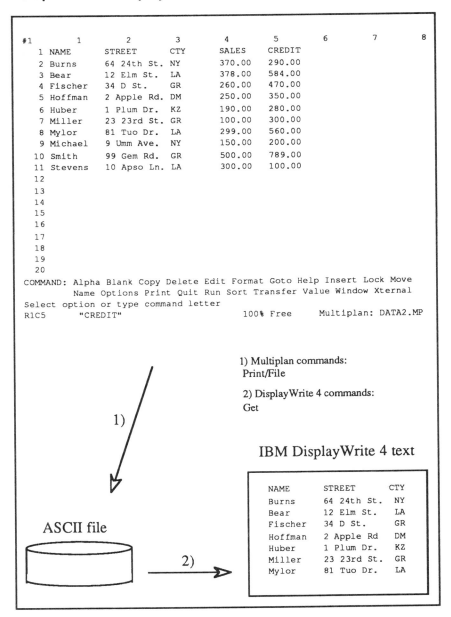

```
#1        1          2         3        4         5          6        7         8
   1 NAME       STREET      CTY      SALES     CREDIT
   2 Burns      64 24th St. NY       370.00    290.00
   3 Bear       12 Elm St.  LA       378.00    584.00
   4 Fischer    34 D St.    GR       260.00    470.00
   5 Hoffman    2 Apple Rd. DM       250.00    350.00
   6 Huber      1 Plum Dr.  KZ       190.00    280.00
   7 Miller     23 23rd St. GR       100.00    300.00
   8 Mylor      81 Tuo Dr.  LA       299.00    560.00
   9 Michael    9 Umm Ave.  NY       150.00    200.00
  10 Smith      99 Gem Rd.  GR       500.00    789.00
  11 Stevens    10 Apso Ln. LA       300.00    100.00
  12
  13
  14
  15
  16
  17
  18
  19
  20
COMMAND: Alpha Blank Copy Delete Edit Format Goto Help Insert Lock Move
         Name Options Print Quit Run Sort Transfer Value Window Xternal
Select option or type command letter
R1C5      "CREDIT"                    100% Free      Multiplan: DATA2.MP
```

1) Multiplan commands:
Print/File

2) DisplayWrite 4 commands:
Get

IBM DisplayWrite 4 text

1)

ASCII file

2)

```
NAME       STREET        CTY
Burns      64 24th St.   NY
Bear       12 Elm St.    LA
Fischer    34 D St.      GR
Hoffman    2 Apple Rd    DM
Huber      1 Plum Dr.    KZ
Miller     23 23rd St.   GR
Mylor      81 Tuo Dr.    LA
```

Figure 4.2.7: Importing data to DisplayWrite 4

Save Multiplan data as an ASCII file and transfer it to DisplayWrite 4 as follows:

- Select the Print/Options command. Enter the part of the worksheet you want stored as an ASCII file in the area: command field, or define the area using the mouse or the cursor keys. The setup: command field must be left empty, since only printer specific control characters can be entered in this command field. The other command fields can remain unchanged because they are not needed for an ASCII file. Press the <Enter> key to exit.

- Select the Print/Margins command. Enter 0 in the left: and top: command fields. Enter the record length in the print width: command field. Enter a number that is larger than the maximum number of records in the print length: and page length: command fields. Enter a 0 in the indent: command field. Press the <Enter> key to end.

- Select the Print/File command. Enter the filename (with drive specifier and path as needed) in the file: command field and press the <Enter> key.

- Exit Multiplan and run DisplayWrite 4.

- Create a new document named MPTEST.DOC.

- Select the Get function by pressing <Ctrl><F6>.

```
┌─────────────────────────────────────────────────────────────────┐
│                          Get File                               │
├─────────────────────────────────────────────────────────────────┤
│ If no pages are specified, the entire document will be included. │
│ When specifying multiple pages, separate page numbers with a space.│
│                                                                   │
│ File Name..............[ MP-DW.DOC                            ]   │
│ System Page Number (s).[                                      ]   │
│                                                                   │
│ Insert Included Text...[N]    Y = Yes    N = No                  │
│ File Type..............[2]    1 = Document or DisplayWrite File  │
│                               2 = ASCII                          │
│                               3 = 7-Bit ASCII                    │
│                               4 = Revisable-Form Text            │
├─────────────────────────────────────────────────────────────────┤
│ Enter    Esc=Quit   F1=Help   F3=List                           │
└─────────────────────────────────────────────────────────────────┘
```

- Enter the name of the ASCII file in this menu. Use the <Cursor down> key or <Tab> key to move to the File Type field. Press the <2> key to load an ASCII file.

- Press the <Enter> key to load the file into the existing document.

- Press the <F2> key to save the document.

```
Create Document                  Ins                    Pg
MPTEST.DOC                       T'style 26   10p   Blk Ln   10
NAME     STREET      CTY SALES CREDIT
Burns    64 24th St. NY  370.00 290.00
Bear     12 Elm St.  LA  378.00 584.00
Fischer  34 D St.    GR  260.00 470.00
Hoffman  2 Apple Rd. DM  250.00 350.00
Huber    1 Plum Dr.  KZ  190.00 280.00
Miller   23 23rd St. GR  100.00 300.00
Mylor    81 Tuo Dr.  LA  299.00 560.00
Michael  9 Umm Ave.  NY  150.00 200.00
Smith    99 Gem Rd.  GR  500.00 789.00
Stevens  10 Apso Ln. LA  300.00 100.00
```

The data can be formatted or edited from within DisplayWrite 4.

4.2.8 Multiplan—Aldus PageMaker

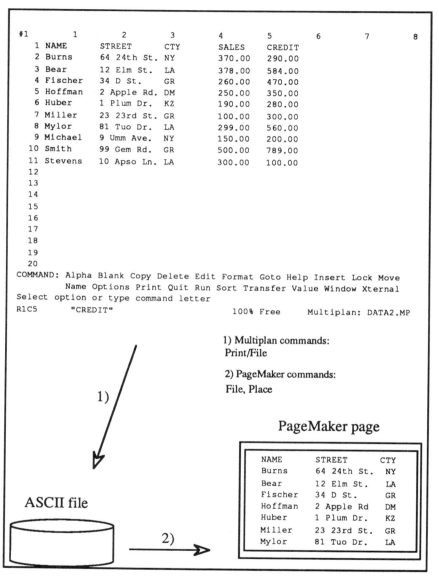

Figure 4.2.8: Importing Multiplan data to PageMaker

Save Multiplan data as an ASCII file named MP-PM.TXT and transfer it to PageMaker as follows:

- Select the Print/Options command. Enter the part of the worksheet you want stored as an ASCII file in the area: command field, or define the area using the mouse or the cursor keys. The setup: command field must be left empty, since only printer specific control characters can be entered in this command field. The other command fields can remain unchanged because they are not needed for an ASCII file. Press the <Enter> key to exit.

- Select the Print/Margins command. Enter 0 in the left: and top: command fields. Enter the record length in the print width: command field. Enter a number that is larger than the maximum number of records in the print length: and page length: command fields. Enter a 0 in the indent: command field. Press the <Enter> key to end.

- Select the Print/File command. Enter the filename MP-PM.TXT in the file: command field and press the <Enter> key.

- Exit Multiplan and run PageMaker.

- Lay out a new publication or load an existing publication.

- Select the File menu and the Place... option. Click on the MP-PM.TXT filename and click OK.

- Once the file is loaded, PageMaker prompts you to enter the fields you want placed. Click on the Add All button and click OK.

The mouse pointer changes to a manual flow text icon.

- Move this pointer to the location at which you want the file to begin. Press and hold the left mouse button and move the pointer down and to the right of the starting point of the pointer. Release the left mouse button. An alternate method is to click once at the desired starting point of the file.

If the file is larger than the amount of space you have created, a plus sign within a semicircle appears at the bottom of the page. This is the bottom windowshade handle. By dragging this handle down, dragging the handles at the edge of each text block, or clicking on the bottom windowshade handle and creating another block for the remaining text, you can insert the remaining text.

You can now edit your data from within PageMaker.

4.2.9 Multiplan—Ventura Publisher

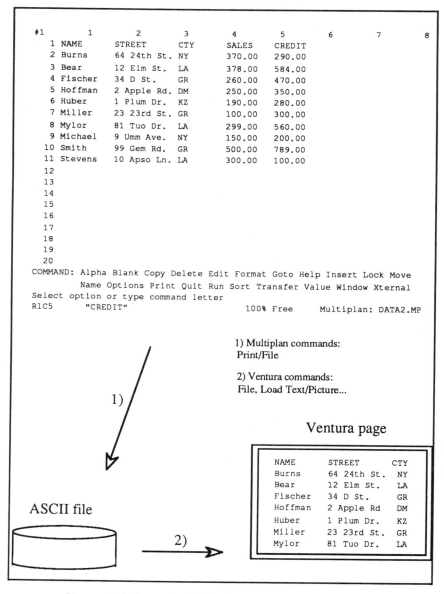

Figure 4.2.9: Importing Multiplan data to Ventura Publisher

Save the Multiplan DATA2.MP worksheet as an ASCII file and transfer it to Ventura Publisher as follows:

- Load the DATA2.MP worksheet into Multiplan. Select the Print/Options command. Enter the part of the worksheet you want stored as an ASCII file in the area: command field, or define the area using the mouse or the cursor keys (in this case, R2C1:R11C5). The setup: command field must be left empty, since only printer specific control characters can be entered in this command field. The other command fields can remain unchanged because they are not needed for an ASCII file. Press the <Enter> key to exit.

- Select the Print/Margins command. Enter 0 in the left: and top: command fields. Enter the record length in the print width: command field (try 50). Enter a number that is larger than the maximum number of records in the print length: and page length: command fields (a minimum of 12 for each). Enter a 0 in the indent: command field. Press the <Enter> key to end.

- Select the Print/File command. Enter the filename MP-VP.DOC (with drive specifier and path if needed) in the file: command field and press the <Enter> key.

- Exit Multiplan and run Ventura Publisher.

- Click on the Add New Frame addition button. Create a frame within Ventura Publisher.

- Select the File menu and the Load Text/Picture... option.

- Click on the Text button, then the WS 4.0/5.0 button.

- Click on the Directory line, and replace the file extension characters with .*. Click on the bar above the list of files.

- Click on the MP-VP.DOC filename and click on the OK button.

The file can now be edited from within Ventura Publisher.

4.3 Microsoft Excel

The following Excel worksheet will be used in many examples in this section:

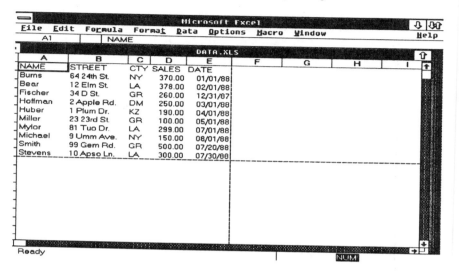

4.3.1 Excel—dBASE IV

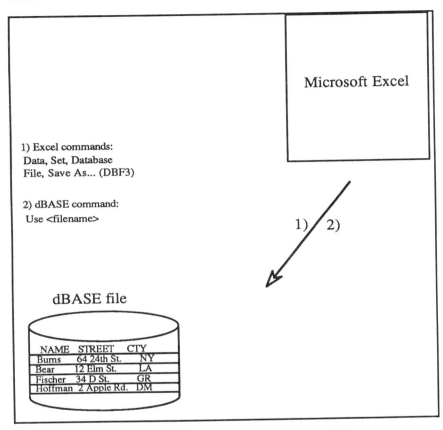

Figure 4.3.1: Importing Excel data to dBASE

Excel can create files that can be directly read by dBASE IV.

- Select the worksheet cells to be exported to dBASE. Include the column headings in the selection (dBASE uses these as field names for your data). Select the Data Set Database command.

- Select the File Save As... command. Enter the filename without a file extension in the Save Worksheet as: command field and click on the Options button. Select DBF 3 and click OK to save the file. Excel automatically adds a .DBF extension to the filename.

- Exit Excel and start dBASE.

The data can now be used and edited from within dBASE.

4.3.2 Excel—Microsoft Multiplan

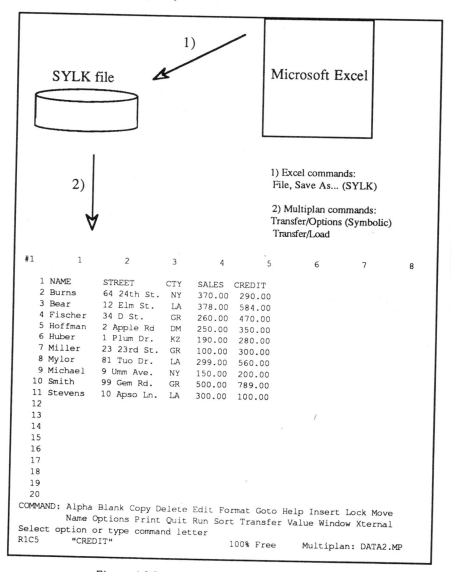

Figure 4.3.2: Importing Excel data to Multiplan

Excel data must be converted to SYLK file format before it can be loaded into Multiplan. Convert the Excel worksheet and load it into Multiplan as follows:

• Select the File Save As... command.

- Enter the filename without a file extension in the Save Worksheet as: command field and click on the Options button.

- Select SYLK and click OK to save the file. Excel automatically adds a .SLK extension to the filename.

- Exit Excel and run Multiplan.

- Select the Transfer/Options command. Select Symbolic in the mode: command field and press the <Enter> key.

- Select the Transfer/Load command. Enter the filename and press the <Enter> key to load the file.

Because of differences in the way Excel and Multiplan store dates internally, date data loses its format during translation and reverts to a basic date number.

- Use the Format/Time-Date command to change the date formats.

Some columns may need width adjustment after the transfer.

- Use the Format/Width command to change column widths.

The data can then be edited from within Multiplan.

4.3.3 Excel—Lotus 1-2-3

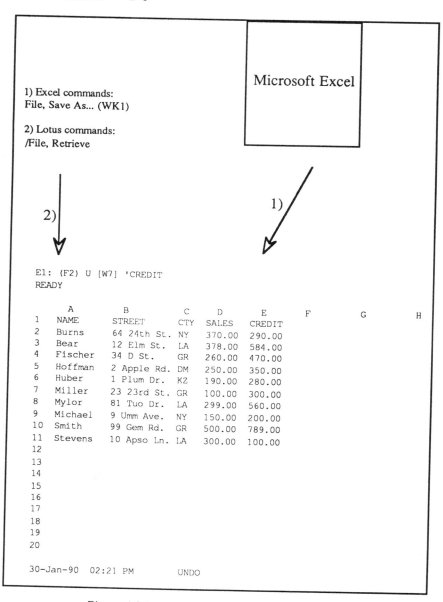

1) Excel commands:
File, Save As... (WK1)

2) Lotus commands:
/File, Retrieve

Microsoft Excel

2)

1)

E1: (F2) U [W7] 'CREDIT
READY

	A	B	C	D	E	F	G	H
1	NAME	STREET	CTY	SALES	CREDIT			
2	Burns	64 24th St.	NY	370.00	290.00			
3	Bear	12 Elm St.	LA	378.00	584.00			
4	Fischer	34 D St.	GR	260.00	470.00			
5	Hoffman	2 Apple Rd.	DM	250.00	350.00			
6	Huber	1 Plum Dr.	KZ	190.00	280.00			
7	Miller	23 23rd St.	GR	100.00	300.00			
8	Mylor	81 Tuo Dr.	LA	299.00	560.00			
9	Michael	9 Umm Ave.	NY	150.00	200.00			
10	Smith	99 Gem Rd.	GR	500.00	789.00			
11	Stevens	10 Apso Ln.	LA	300.00	100.00			
12								
13								
14								
15								
16								
17								
18								
19								
20								

30-Jan-90 02:21 PM   UNDO

Figure 4.3.3: Importing Excel data to Lotus 1-2-3

Excel can save files in WK1 format for direct transfer to Lotus 1-2-3.

• Select the File Save As... command.

•   Enter the filename without a file extension in the Save Worksheet as: command field and click on the Options button.

•   Select WK1 and click OK to save the file. Excel automatically adds a .WK1 extension to the filename.

•   Exit Excel and start Lotus 1-2-3. Select the / File Retrieve command to load the file into 1-2-3.

The file can then be edited from within Lotus 1-2-3.

Note: Because of date handling differences between the two packages, you will need to reformat the cells containing date codes with the Lotus 1-2-3 / Worksheet Range Format Date command sequence.

4.3.4 Excel—Microsoft Chart

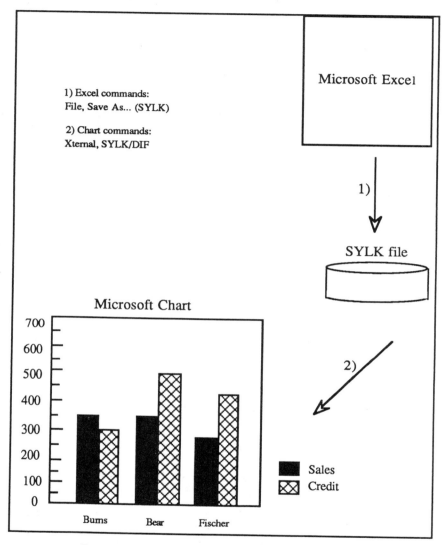

Figure 4.3.4: Importing Excel data to Microsoft Chart

An Excel worksheet must be saved as a SYLK file before it can be accessed by Microsoft Chart.

The following Excel worksheet called DATA2.XLS will be used in this example. DATA2.XLS contains the following information:

```
NAME     STREET       CITY  SALES   CREDIT
Burns    64 24th St.  NY    370.00  290.00
Bear     12 Elm St.   LA    378.00  584.00
Fischer  34 D St.     GR    260.00  470.00
Hoffman  2 Apple Rd.  DM    250.00  350.00
Huber    1 Plum Dr.   KZ    190.00  280.00
Miller   23 23rd St.  GR    100.00  300.00
Mylor    81 Tuo Dr.   LA    299.00  560.00
Michael  9 Umm Ave.   NY    150.00  200.00
Smith    99 Gem Rd.   LA    500.00  789.00
Stevens  10 Apso Ln.  LA    300.00  100.00
```

- Select the File Save As... command.

- Enter the filename EX-CH-1 without a file extension in the Save Worksheet as: command field and click on the Options button.

- Select SYLK and click OK to save the file. Excel automatically adds a .SLK extension to the filename.

- Exit Excel and run Microsoft Chart.

- Select the Xternal SYLK/DIF command.

- Enter EX-CH.SLK in the filename: command field. Press the <Tab> key to move to the linked: command field. Press the <Y> key to instruct Chart not to update the chart when the worksheet is updated.

- Press the <Tab> key to move to the selected rows: command field. Enter 2,4.

- Press the <Tab> key to move to the selected columns: command field. Enter 4,5.

- Press the <Tab> key to move to the orient series by: command field.

This command field allows you to orient your chart by rows or columns. To create a row-oriented chart:

- Press the <R> key (Rows).

- Press the <Tab> key to move to the series name(s) from: command field. Enter 1.

- Press the <Tab> key to move to the categories from: command field. Enter 1.

- Press the <Tab> key to move to the category type: command field. Press the <T> key (Text) and press the <Enter> key.

The list screen displays the following entries:

Incl.(*)	Name	Source of data	Type	# pts.
1	Burns	Linked: a:ex-ch.slk:R2C4:5	Text	2
2	Bear	Linked: a:ex-ch.slk:R3C4:5	Text	2

- Press the <C> key. The graphic created by Chart has the following structure:

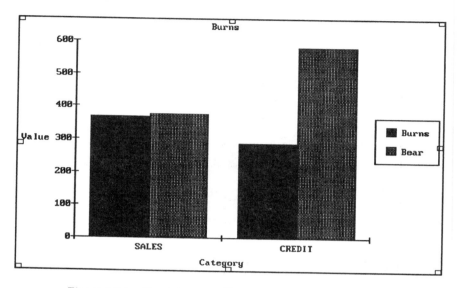

Figure 4.3.4a: Excel data as a Chart graphic (row orientation)

To create a column-oriented chart:

- Press the <C> key (Columns).

- Press the <Tab> key to move to the series name(s) from: command field. Enter 1.

- Press the <Tab> key to move to the categories from: command field. Enter 1.

- Press the <Tab> key to move to the category type: command field. Press the <T> key (Text) and press the <Enter> key.

The list screen displays the following entries:

Incl.(*)	Name	Source of data	Type	# pts.
1	SALES	Linked: a:ex-ch.slk:R2:3C4	Text	2
2	CREDIT	Linked: a:ex-ch.slk:R2:3C5	Text	2

- Press the <C> key. The graphic created by Chart has the following structure:

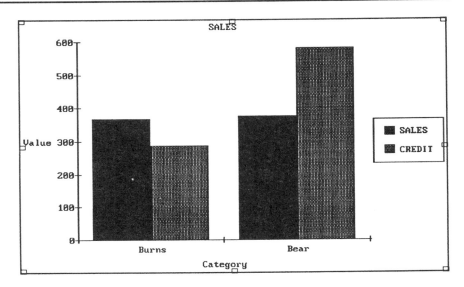

Figure 4.3.4b: Excel data as a Chart graphic (column orientation)

4.3.5 Excel—Lotus Freelance Plus

Data from other programs can be shown as text graphics in Freelance. In addition, data from Lotus 1-2-3, Multiplan, Excel and dBASE can be shown as chart graphics.

4.3.5.1 Excel—Freelance Chart

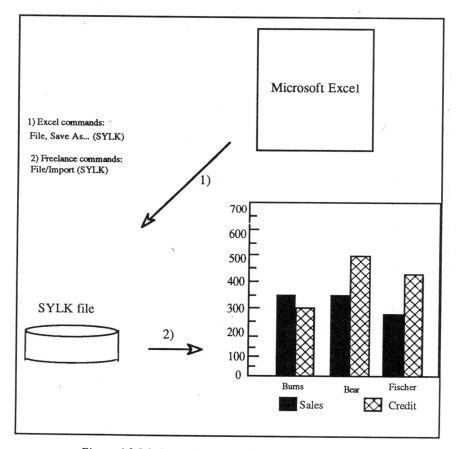

Figure 4.3.5.1: Importing Excel data as a Freelance chart

Excel data must be converted to SYLK file format before it can be accessed by Freelance. Convert the Excel worksheet DATA2.XLS and load it into Freelance as follows:

- Select the File Save As... command.

- Enter the filename EX-FL without a file extension in the Save Worksheet as: command field and click on the Options button.

- Select SYLK and click OK to save the file. Excel automatically adds a .SLK extension to the filename.

- Exit Excel and run Freelance. Select the Charts and Drawings command.

- Select the Chart New-Data command. The Chart Type: field should list a chart type of Bar - Vertical. Press the <Tab> key or <Cursor right> key to move to the DATALINKS bar. Press <Space>.

- The cursor should be in the File type: field. Press <Space> to see a list of file types. Use the <Cursor up> and <Cursor down> keys to highlight the SYLK item and press the <Enter> key.

- Press the <Tab> key or the <Cursor down> key to move to the File path: field. Enter the proper file path and press the <Enter> key.

- Enter the name EX-FL.SLK in the File name: field and press the <Enter> key.

- Leave the Type of import: field set at Specified Ranges.

- Leave the Headings:, Notes:, Legends: and axis Title: fields blank.

- Move the cursor to the Cluster Labels: field. Enter A2..A11 and press the <Enter> key.

- Move the cursor to the Bar 1 Values: field. Enter D2..D11 and press the <Enter> key.

- Move the cursor to the Bar 2 Values: field. Enter E2..E11 and press the <F10> key. If Freelance asks you whether you want to update the chart, just press the <Y> key.

- Press the <G> key (Go) to generate the chart screen. Press <Enter> to accept the current chart dimensions and draw the chart.

4.3.5.2 Excel—Freelance Text Chart

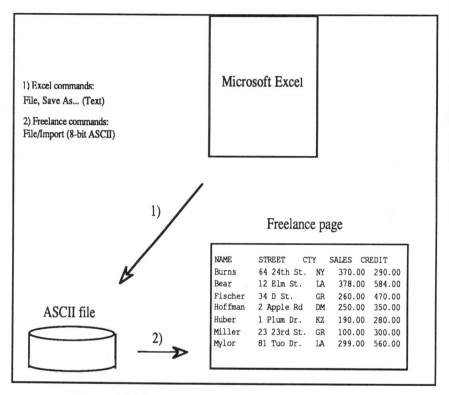

Figure 4.3.5.2: Importing data to a Freelance text graphic

Excel data must be saved as an ASCII file before it can be interpreted by Freelance as a text graphic. Convert the DATA.XLS file to ASCII format as follows:

- Run Excel. Select the File Open... command. Click on the name DATA.XLS and click on OK to load.

- Select the File Save As... command.

- Enter the filename EX-TXT in the Save Worksheet as: command field and click on the Options button.

- Select Text and click OK to save the file. Excel automatically adds a file extension of .TXT.

- Exit Excel.

The file EX-TXT.TXT has the following contents:

```
NAME     STREET    CTY SALES    DATE
Burns    64 24th St. NY 370.00  01/01/88
Bear     12 Elm St.  LA 378.00  02/01/88
Fischer  34 D St.    GR 260.00  12/31/87
Hoffman  2 Apple Rd. DM 250.00  03/01/88
Huber    1 Plum Dr.  KZ 190.00  04/01/88
Miller   23 23rd St. GR 100.00  05/01/88
Mylor    81 Tuo Dr.  LA 299.00  07/01/88
Michael  9 Umm Ave.  NY 150.00  08/01/88
Smith    99 Gem Rd.  GR 500.00  07/20/88
Stevens  10 Apso Ln. LA 300.00  07/30/88
```

- Run Freelance and Select the File Import command.

- Press <Space> to see a list of file types. Select the 8-bit ASCII item and press the <Tab> key or the <Cursor down> key to move to the Name field.

- Enter the filename EX-TXT.TXT.

- Press the <F10> key.

You can now edit the data as a text chart.

Note: Excel saves text files under a default file extension of .TXT, but Freelance defaults to a file extension of .ASC for ASCII files. If you move the cursor to the Name field and press <Space> in Freelance, Freelance will only search for files with extensions of .ASC. Before running Freelance, you may want to rename the .TXT file extension to .ASC to help you find the file quickly.

4.3.6 Excel—Microsoft Word

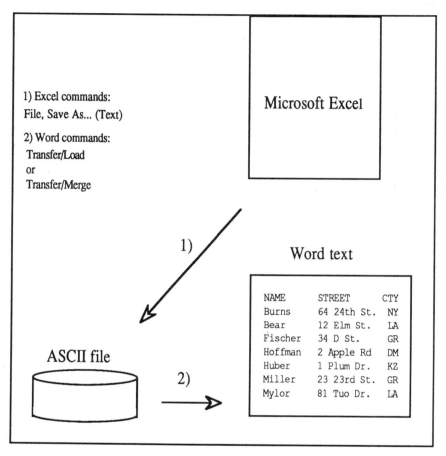

Figure 4.3.6: Importing Excel data to Word

Excel data must be converted to ASCII format before it can be loaded into Word. The EX-TXT.TXT file created in Section 4.3.5.2 will be used for this example (see Section 4.3.5.2 for instructions on creating an ASCII text file).

- Run Word and select the Transfer/Load command. Enter the name EX-TXT.TXT in the file name: command field and press the <Enter> key to load the file.

Note: When searching for files, Word defaults to an extension of .DOC for its files. To make searching for and loading files easier, you may want to rename your .TXT files with extensions of .DOC before loading them into Word.

4.3.7 Excel—IBM DisplayWrite 4

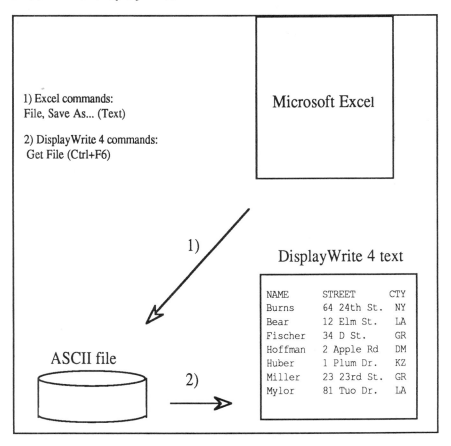

1) Excel commands:
File, Save As... (Text)

2) DisplayWrite 4 commands:
 Get File (Ctrl+F6)

Microsoft Excel

1)

DisplayWrite 4 text

ASCII file

2)

```
NAME        STREET        CTY
Burns       64 24th St.   NY
Bear        12 Elm St.    LA
Fischer     34 D St.      GR
Hoffman     2 Apple Rd    DM
Huber       1 Plum Dr.    KZ
Miller      23 23rd St.   GR
Mylor       81 Tuo Dr.    LA
```

Figure 4.3.7: Importing Excel data to DisplayWrite 4

DisplayWrite 4 accepts data from Excel that has been saved as ASCII text. The EX-TXT.TXT file created in Section 4.3.5.2 will be used for this example (see Section 4.3.5.2 for instructions on creating an ASCII text file).

•   Run DisplayWrite 4.

•   Create a new DisplayWrite 4 document or call an existing one. Move the cursor to the location where you want the ASCII file to begin.

•   Select the Get function by pressing <Ctrl><F6>.

```
┌──────────────────────────────────────────────────────────────┐
│                           Get File                             │
├──────────────────────────────────────────────────────────────┤
│ If no pages are specified, the entire document will be included.│
│ When specifying multiple pages, separate page numbers with a space.│
│                                                                │
│ File Name.............[                                       ]│
│ System Page Number (s).[                                      ]│
│                                                                │
│ Insert Included Text...[N]    Y = Yes      N = No             │
│ File Type.............[2]      1 = Document or DisplayWrite File│
│                               2 = ASCII                        │
│                               3 = 7-Bit ASCII                  │
│                               4 = Revisable-Form Text          │
├──────────────────────────────────────────────────────────────┤
│ Enter    Esc=Quit    F1=Help    F3=List                        │
└──────────────────────────────────────────────────────────────┘
```

- Enter the filename EX-TXT.TXT in the File Name field. Press the <Cursor Down> key to move the cursor to the File Type line.

- Press the <2> key (ASCII) and press the <Enter> key to load the ASCII text.

Multiple-page documents may need to be paginated then saved.

4.3.8 Excel—Aldus PageMaker

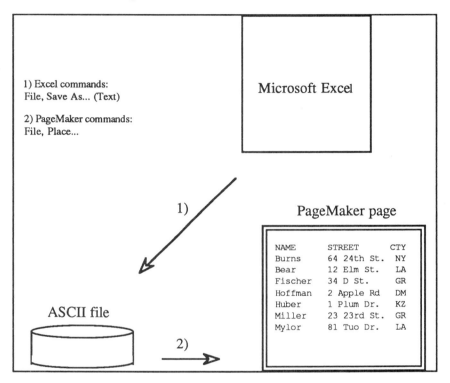

1) Excel commands:
File, Save As... (Text)

2) PageMaker commands:
File, Place...

Microsoft Excel

1)

PageMaker page

NAME	STREET	CTY
Burns	64 24th St.	NY
Bear	12 Elm St.	LA
Fischer	34 D St.	GR
Hoffman	2 Apple Rd	DM
Huber	1 Plum Dr.	KZ
Miller	23 23rd St.	GR
Mylor	81 Tuo Dr.	LA

ASCII file

2)

Figure 4.3.8: Importing Excel data to PageMaker

The Windows Clipboard allows you to easily transfer data from Excel to Aldus PageMaker.

Windows must be used to call both Excel and PageMaker.

- Invoke Excel from Windows.

- Select the data and select the Edit Copy command to place the data in the clipboard.

- Press <Alt><Esc> to invoke the Windows screen.

- Call PageMaker from the Windows screen.

- Press <Alt><Space> to activate the Clipboard.

- Press <Alt><Esc> to invoke the PageMaker screen. Select the Edit Paste command to paste the data into PageMaker.

The data can now be edited from within PageMaker.

An alternate method is to use the File Save As... command to save the file as Text, then load it into PageMaker as you would any ASCII text file.

4.3.9 Excel—Ventura Publisher

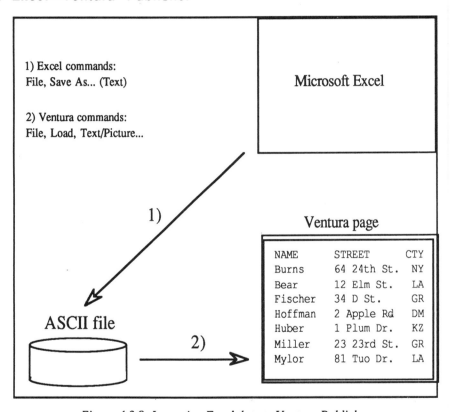

Figure 4.3.9: Importing Excel data to Ventura Publisher

Ventura Publisher accepts Excel data in ASCII format. The EX-TXT.TXT file created in Section 4.3.5.2 will be used for this example.

- Run Ventura Publisher from DOS or from Windows (depending on your system's memory capacity).

- Select the File menu and the Load Text/Picture... option.

- Click on the Text button, then on the WS 4.0/5.0 button when it appears in the lower half of the dialog box. Click on the OK button.

• An ITEM SELECTOR box appears. Click on the Directory: line and change the file wildcard from *.WS* to *.*. Click on the top bar of the file list.

• Look in the box for the filename. Click on the filename EX-TXT.TXT and click on the OK button.

The file can then be edited from within Ventura Publisher.

4.4 Lotus 1-2-3

The following Lotus worksheet named DATA.WK1 will be used as an example in much of this section:

```
A1: U 'NAME                                                           READY


          A          B          C    D       E         F      G      H
 1   NAME        STREET       CTY  SALES    DATE
 2   Burns       64 24th St.  NY   370.00   01/01/88
 3   Bear        12 Elm St.   LA   378.00   02/01/88
 4   Fischer     34 D St.     GR   260.00   12/31/87
 5   Hoffman     2 Apple Rd.  DM   250.00   03/01/88
 6   Huber       1 Plum Dr.   KZ   190.00   04/01/88
 7   Miller      23 23rd St.  GR   100.00   05/01/88
 8   Mylor       81 Tuo Dr.   LA   299.00   07/01/88
 9   Michael     9 Umm Ave.   NY   150.00   08/01/88
10   Smith       99 Gem Rd.   GR   500.00   07/20/88
11   Stevens     10 Apso Ln.  LA   300.00   07/30/88
12
13
14
15
16
17
18
19
20
23-Jan-89   08:55 AM            UNDO
```

4.4.1 Lotus 1-2-3—dBASE

You can transfer data between Lotus and dBASE in two ways:

1)   Save the dBASE data as an ASCII file.

2)   Convert the Lotus 1-2-3 file to a dBASE file using the Translate program.

4.4.1.1 Lotus 1-2-3 (ASCII)—dBASE IV

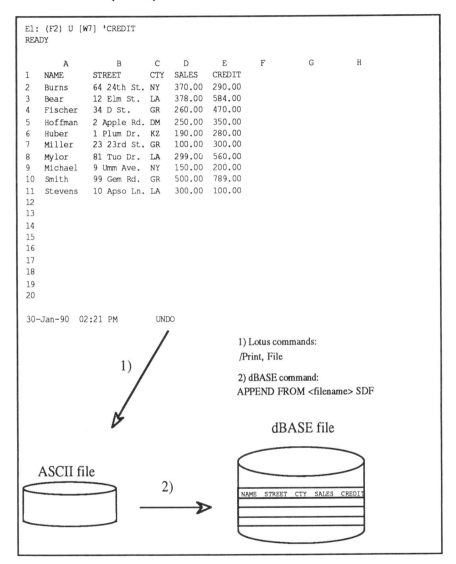

```
E1: (F2) U [W7] 'CREDIT
READY

        A           B        C      D       E       F       G        H
1   NAME        STREET      CTY   SALES   CREDIT
2   Burns       64 24th St. NY    370.00  290.00
3   Bear        12 Elm St.  LA    378.00  584.00
4   Fischer     34 D St.    GR    260.00  470.00
5   Hoffman     2 Apple Rd. DM    250.00  350.00
6   Huber       1 Plum Dr.  KZ    190.00  280.00
7   Miller      23 23rd St. GR    100.00  300.00
8   Mylor       81 Tuo Dr.  LA    299.00  560.00
9   Michael     9 Umm Ave.  NY    150.00  200.00
10  Smith       99 Gem Rd.  GR    500.00  789.00
11  Stevens     10 Apso Ln. LA    300.00  100.00
12
13
14
15
16
17
18
19
20

30-Jan-90  02:21 PM         UNDO
```

1) Lotus commands:
/Print, File

2) dBASE command:
APPEND FROM <filename> SDF

dBASE file

ASCII file

NAME STREET CTY SALES CREDIT

Figure 4.4.1.1: Importing Lotus 1-2-3 ASCII data to dBASE

- Select the / Print File command. Enter the filename LOT-DB.SDF (including a drive specifier and path if needed). Press the <Enter> key.

- 1-2-3 then displays a menu listing the parameters of the worksheet about to be saved to disk. Press the <R> key to select the Range menu. Select the range from A2 to E11 using either keyboard coordinate entry or the cursor keys. Press the <Enter> key.

- 1-2-3 displays the menu of worksheet parameters again. Press the <O> key to invoke the Options menu. Press the <M> key to select Margins. Set the left and top margins to zero (0), the bottom margin to a number greater than the number of rows used in the worksheet (at least 10) and the right margin to 45 (the total length of a row). Press the <Enter> key.

- Press the <P> key to invoke the Pg-Length menu. Enter a page length larger than the maximum number of rows being transferred (in this case, a minimum of 12). Press the <Enter> key.

- Press the <O> key to move to the Other menu. Press the <U> key (Unformatted).

- Press the <Q> key to return to the Print menu. Press the <A> key (Align) to align the system to the "top of the page." Press the <G> key (Go) to save the data to the file.

- Press the <Q> key to return to the worksheet.

- Exit 1-2-3 and start dBASE IV.

- Create a new database named APPEND.DBF containing the following structure:

```
Structure for database: APPEND.DBF
Number of data records:        0
Date of last update: 01/23/90
Field    Field Name  Type        Width  Dec.  Index
  1      NAME        Character     10           N
  2      STREET      Character     12           N
  3      CTY         Character      4           N
  4      SALES       Numeric        7     2     N
  5      DATE        Character      9           N
** TOTAL **                        43
```

- Enter the following command in dBASE:

```
APPEND FROM lot-db1.sdf SDF
```

If the records of the file are successfully copied, the following message appears:

```
10 Records copied
```

- Call the MODIFY STRUCTURE command.

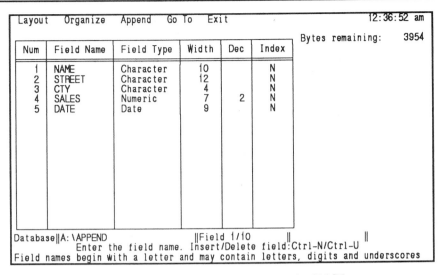

```
 Layout   Organize    Append    Go To    Exit              12:36:52 am
                                                    Bytes remaining:    3954
  ┌─────┬────────────┬────────────┬───────┬─────┬────────┐
  │ Num │ Field Name │ Field Type │ Width │ Dec │ Index  │
  ├─────┼────────────┼────────────┼───────┼─────┼────────┤
  │  1  │ NAME       │ Character  │  10   │     │  N     │
  │  2  │ STREET     │ Character  │  12   │     │  N     │
  │  3  │ CTY        │ Character  │   4   │     │  N     │
  │  4  │ SALES      │ Numeric    │   7   │  2  │  N     │
  │  5  │ DATE       │ Date       │   9   │     │  N     │
  │     │            │            │       │     │        │
  │     │            │            │       │     │        │
  │     │            │            │       │     │        │
  └─────┴────────────┴────────────┴───────┴─────┴────────┘
 Database‖A:\APPEND            ‖Field 1/10      ‖             ‖
         Enter the field name. Insert/Delete field:Ctrl-N/Ctrl-U
 Field names begin with a letter and may contain letters, digits and underscores
```

Figure 4.4.1.1a: Modifying structure in dBASE

•   Move the cursor to the Width parameter of the Sales field. Change the 7 to a 6. Move the cursor to the Type parameter for the Date field. Enter the <D> key to change the field to a Date type. Press the <Tab> key to move to the Width parameter of the Date field. Change the 9 to an 8 and press <Ctrl><End> to save the new structure.

This new file has the following structure:

```
 Structure for database: APPEND.DBF
 Number of data records:        10
 Date of last update: 01/23/90
 Field    Field Name   Type        Width    Dec.   Index
    1      NAME         Character     10             N
    2      STREET       Character     12             N
    3      CTY          Character      4             N
    4      SALES        Numeric        6      2      N
    5      DATE         Date           8             N
 ** TOTAL **                          41
```

The dBASE file now has the following contents:

```
 Record  NAME      STREET        CTY SALES   DATE
    1     Burns     64 24th St.   NY  370.00  01/01/88
    2     Bear      12 Elm St.    LA  378.00  02/01/88
    3     Fischer   34 D St.      GR  260.00  12/31/87
    4     Hoffman   2 Apple Rd.   DM  250.00  03/01/88
    5     Huber     1 Plum Dr.    KZ  190.00  04/01/88
    6     Miller    23 23rd St.   GR  100.00  05/01/88
    7     Mylor     81 Tuo Dr.    LA  299.00  07/01/88
    8     Michael   9 Umm Ave.    NY  150.00  08/01/88
    9     Smith     99 Gem Rd.    GR  500.00  07/20/88
   10     Stevens   10 Apso Ln.   LA  300.00  07/30/88
```

4.4.1.2 Lotus 1-2-3—Translate—dBASE IV

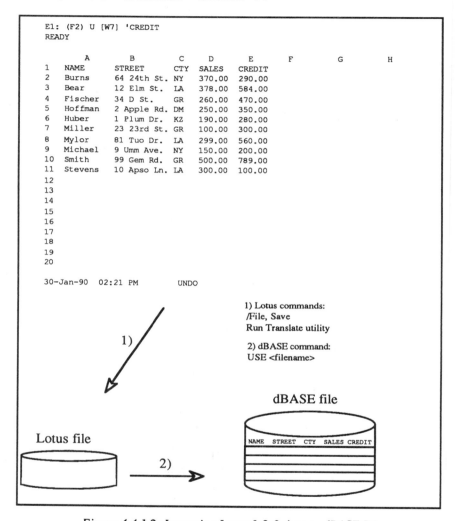

```
E1: (F2) U [W7] 'CREDIT
READY

         A          B          C     D        E        F          G          H
 1  NAME       STREET         CTY   SALES    CREDIT
 2  Burns      64 24th St.    NY    370.00   290.00
 3  Bear       12 Elm St.     LA    378.00   584.00
 4  Fischer    34 D St.       GR    260.00   470.00
 5  Hoffman    2 Apple Rd.    DM    250.00   350.00
 6  Huber      1 Plum Dr.     KZ    190.00   280.00
 7  Miller     23 23rd St.    GR    100.00   300.00
 8  Mylor      81 Tuo Dr.     LA    299.00   560.00
 9  Michael    9 Umm Ave.     NY    150.00   200.00
10  Smith      99 Gem Rd.     GR    500.00   789.00
11  Stevens    10 Apso Ln.    LA    300.00   100.00
12
13
14
15
16
17
18
19
20

30-Jan-90   02:21 PM           UNDO
```

1) Lotus commands:
/File, Save
Run Translate utility

2) dBASE command:
USE <filename>

dBASE file

Lotus file

Figure 4.4.1.2: Importing Lotus 1-2-3 data to dBASE IV

Lotus files can be converted to dBASE file with the Translate program supplied by
Lotus. If a name for an area is given in a Lotus file, just this renamed area can be
converted by the Translate program to a dBASE file.

The Lotus file or the area for conversion must meet the following criteria:

* The worksheet or range must be laid out as an organized database
  worksheet.

- The first line of the file or range must consist of field names. These field names must be label cells that begin with a letter.

- The second line must contain the first actual record of the database. Each field or cell in this line must contain data or be formatted.

- The columns must be wide enough to display the data.

- Exponential format may not be used.

- The data records must consist of 1 to 128 fields. Each field is assigned a field type. The field types in the first record of the worksheet or range correspond to the field types in each dBASE data set.

- The format of each field in the first record applies to the entire database, regardless of the contents of the records that follow.

- Field names must meet the requirements for names in dBASE.

- Numbers within fields must be valid dBASE numbers.

- Numeric columns can be up to 19 characters in length.

- All cells in the active worksheet or range (including empty records) are converted.

The Lotus worksheet DATA.WK1 used above can be converted to the dBASE format with the Translate program.

```
A1: U 'NAME                                                              READY

         A           B          C    D       E        F      G      H
1   NAME        STREET       CTY  SALES   DATE
2   Burns       64 24th St.  NY   370.00  01/01/88
3   Bear        12 Elm St.   LA   378.00  02/01/88
4   Fischer     34 D St.     GR   260.00  12/31/87
5   Hoffman     2 Apple Rd.  DM   250.00  03/01/88
6   Huber       1 Plum Dr.   KZ   190.00  04/01/88
7   Miller      23 23rd St.  GR   100.00  05/01/88
8   Mylor       81 Tuo Dr.   LA   299.00  07/01/88
9   Michael     9 Umm Ave.   NY   150.00  08/01/88
10  Smith       99 Gem Rd.   GR   500.00  07/20/88
11  Stevens     10 Apso Ln.  LA   300.00  07/30/88
12
13
14
15
16
17
18
19
20
23-Jan-89   08:55 AM        UNDO
```

The entire Translate operation is menu driven.

- Start the 1-2-3 Access System utility.

- Select Translate from the main menu.

- You can convert an entire file or a range if you wish. For now, convert the entire worksheet. Select the type and the name of the source file (DATA.WK1) and the target file (LOT-DB .DBF). The target file should be saved in dBASE III or dBASE IV format, depending on what your version of the Translate utility lists in the menu. You can enter the source filename as the target filename, provided you assign a different extension to the filename.

Note: Be sure to give the target file a file extension of .DBF.

- The percentage of the conversion is displayed on the screen. The Translate program informs the user of whether the file conversion was successful or not.

- Press the <Esc> key to exit the Translate program. Select Exit to return to DOS.

- Run dBASE and USE the database. The file has the following structure:

```
Structure for database: LOT-DB.DBF
Number of data records:        10
Date of last update: 01/24/90
Field     Field Name  Type        Width   Dec.   Index
  1       NAME        Character      10             N
  2       STREET      Character      12             N
  3       CTY         Character       4             N
  4       SALES       Numeric         7     2       N
  5       DATE        Date            8             N
**  TOTAL  **                        42
```

The dBASE file LOT-DB.DBF has the following contents:

```
Record   NAME      STREET        CTY SALES   DATE
   1     Burns     64 24th St.   NY  370.00  01/01/88
   2     Bear      12 Elm St.    LA  378.00  02/01/88
   3     Fischer   34 D St.      GR  260.00  12/31/87
   4     Hoffman   2 Apple Rd.   DM  250.00  03/01/88
   5     Huber     1 Plum Dr.    KZ  190.00  04/01/88
   6     Miller    23 23rd St.   GR  100.00  05/01/88
   7     Mylor     81 Tuo Dr.    LA  299.00  07/01/88
   8     Michael   9 Umm Ave.    NY  150.00  08/01/88
   9     Smith     99 Gem Rd.    GR  500.00  07/20/88
  10     Stevens   10 Apso Ln.   LA  300.00  07/30/88
```

This file can then be edited from within dBASE.

4.4.2 Lotus 1-2-3—Microsoft Chart

The following Lotus worksheet named DATA2.WK1 is used as an example:

```
A1: U 'NAME                                              READY

        A         B          C    D       E       F     G      H
 1  NAME      STREET        CTY SALES   CREDIT
 2  Burns     64 24th St.   NY  370.00  290.00
 3  Bear      12 Elm St.    LA  378.00  584.00
 4  Fischer   34 D St.      GR  260.00  470.00
 5  Hoffman   2 Apple Rd.   DM  250.00  350.00
 6  Huber     1 Plum Dr.    KZ  190.00  280.00
 7  Miller    23 23rd St.   GR  100.00  300.00
 8  Mylor     81 Tuo Dr.    LA  299.00  560.00
 9  Michael   9 Umm Ave.    NY  150.00  200.00
10  Smith     99 Gem Rd.    GR  500.00  789.00
11  Stevens   10 Apso Ln.   LA  300.00  100.00
12
13
14
15
16
17
18
19
20
23-Jan-89   08:55 AM           UNDO
```

Data can be imported from a Lotus worksheet or a Lotus chart to Chart.

4.4.2.1 Lotus 1-2-3 Worksheet—Microsoft Chart

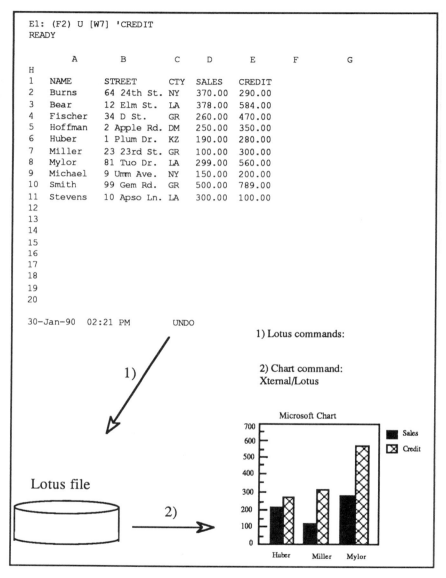

```
E1: (F2) U [W7] 'CREDIT
READY


          A          B          C     D       E        F        G
H
1    NAME       STREET       CTY   SALES   CREDIT
2    Burns      64 24th St.  NY    370.00  290.00
3    Bear       12 Elm St.   LA    378.00  584.00
4    Fischer    34 D St.     GR    260.00  470.00
5    Hoffman    2 Apple Rd.  DM    250.00  350.00
6    Huber      1 Plum Dr.   KZ    190.00  280.00
7    Miller     23 23rd St.  GR    100.00  300.00
8    Mylor      81 Tuo Dr.   LA    299.00  560.00
9    Michael    9 Umm Ave.   NY    150.00  200.00
10   Smith      99 Gem Rd.   GR    500.00  789.00
11   Stevens    10 Apso Ln.  LA    300.00  100.00
12
13
14
15
16
17
18
19
20

30-Jan-90  02:21 PM         UNDO
```

1) Lotus commands:

2) Chart command:
Xternal/Lotus

Lotus file

Figure 4.4.2.1: Importing Lotus 1-2-3 data to Chart

Transfer the 1-2-3 worksheet to Chart and read only certain elements of the worksheet as follows:

- Select the Xternal Lotus command in Chart. Enter the name DATA2.WK1 in the filename: command field (including drive specifier and path if needed).

- Press the <Tab> key to move to the linked: command field. Press the <Y> key (Yes) and press the <Tab> key to move to the type: field. The Worksheet option should be selected; if not, press the <W> key.

- Press the <Tab> key to move to the named area or reference: command field. Enter the following to display data for personnel in GR (Grand Rapids) only:

```
R4C4:5,R7C4:5,R10C4:5
```

- Press the <Tab> key to move to the orient series by: command field.

You can either orient the series by rows or columns. If you wish to orient the series by rows, do the following:

- Press the <R> key (Rows) for row orientation.

- Press the <Tab> key until the cursor reaches the series name(s) from: command field. Press the <1> key.

- Press the <Tab> key to move to the categories from: command field. Press the <1> key. The category type: command field should be set at Text.

- Press the <Enter> key to load.

- The List screen contains the following entries:

```
Incl.(*) Name      Source of data         Type       # pts.
1        Fischer   Linked: a:\data2.wk1:R4C4:5 Text    2
2        Miller    Linked: a:\data2.wk1 R7C4:5 Text    2
3        Smith     Linked: a:\data2.wk1 R10C4: Text    2
```

- Press the <C> key. The graphic created by Chart has the following structure:

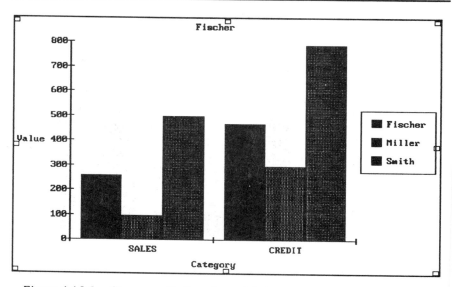

Figure 4.4.2.1a: Chart graphic from Lotus 1-2-3 worksheet data (row orientation)

If you wish to orient the series by columns, do the following:

- Press the <C> key (Columns) for column orientation.

- Press the <Tab> key until the cursor reaches the series name(s) from: command field. Press the <1> key.

- Press the <Tab> key to move to the categories from: command field. Press the <1> key. The category type: command field should be set at T.

- Press the <Enter> key to load.

- The List screen contains the following entries:

```
Incl.(*) Name        Source of data      Type   # pts.
1        SALES       Linked: a:\data2.wk1:R4,7,1  Text 3
2        CREDIT      Linked: a:\data2.wk1:R4,7,1  Text 3
```

- Press the <C> key. The graphic created by Chart has the following structure:

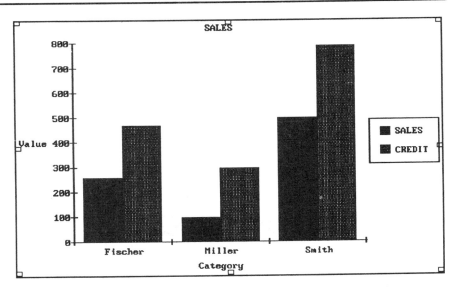

Figure 4.4.2.1b: Chart graphic from Lotus 1-2-3 worksheet data
(column orientation)

4.4.2.2 Lotus 1-2-3 Graph—Microsoft Chart

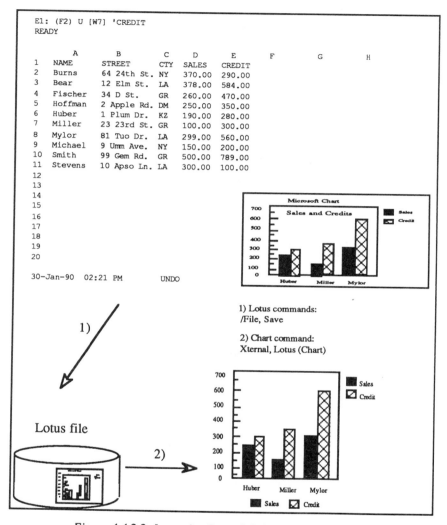

Figure 4.4.2.2: Importing Lotus 1-2-3 chart data to Chart

- Load the DATA2.WK1 worksheet file in 1-2-3. Select the / File Save command and save this worksheet under the name LO-CH-GR.WK1.

- Select the / Graph command. Configure the Graph Settings window so that it looks like this:

4.4.4 Lotus 1-2-3—Microsoft Excel

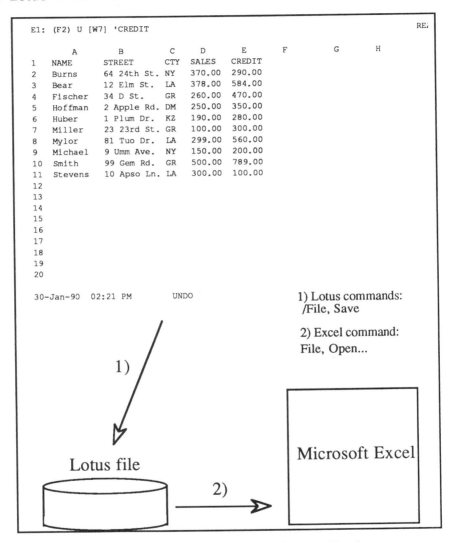

```
E1: (F2) U [W7] 'CREDIT                                                    RE
                A         B        C      D       E      F       G       H
         1   NAME      STREET      CTY  SALES   CREDIT
         2   Burns     64 24th St. NY   370.00  290.00
         3   Bear      12 Elm St.  LA   378.00  584.00
         4   Fischer   34 D St.    GR   260.00  470.00
         5   Hoffman   2 Apple Rd. DM   250.00  350.00
         6   Huber     1 Plum Dr.  KZ   190.00  280.00
         7   Miller    23 23rd St. GR   100.00  300.00
         8   Mylor     81 Tuo Dr.  LA   299.00  560.00
         9   Michael   9 Umm Ave.  NY   150.00  200.00
        10   Smith     99 Gem Rd.  GR   500.00  789.00
        11   Stevens   10 Apso Ln. LA   300.00  100.00
        12
        13
        14
        15
        16
        17
        18
        19
        20

        30-Jan-90  02:21 PM          UNDO
```

1) Lotus commands:
/File, Save

2) Excel command:
File, Open...

1)

Lotus file

2)

Microsoft Excel

Figure 4.4.4: Importing Lotus 1-2-3 data to Excel

A Lotus 1-2-3 worksheet file can be loaded directly into Excel:

•   Run Microsoft Excel.

•   Select the File menu and click on the Open... option. A window appears, listing a set of files. In addition, you'll see a text box listing a file wildcard of *.XL*. Change this wildcard to read *.*, press the <Enter> key and watch the change.

- Select the desired path from the Directories window.

- Select the filename DATA2.WK1 and either press <Enter> or click on the OK button to load the file.

The file type and percent of conversion are shown in the upper right corner.

- Select the File/Save As... option.

- Select the Options... button and select Normal.

- Change the file extension to .XLS. Click on OK to save the file as an Excel worksheet file.

4.4.5 Lotus 1-2-3—Lotus Freelance Plus

Data from other programs can be shown as text graphics in Freelance. In addition, data from Lotus 1-2-3 can be shown as presentation graphics.

The DATA2.WK1 worksheet from Section 4.4.2 will be used for this example.

4.4.5.1 Lotus 1-2-3 Worksheet—Freelance Chart

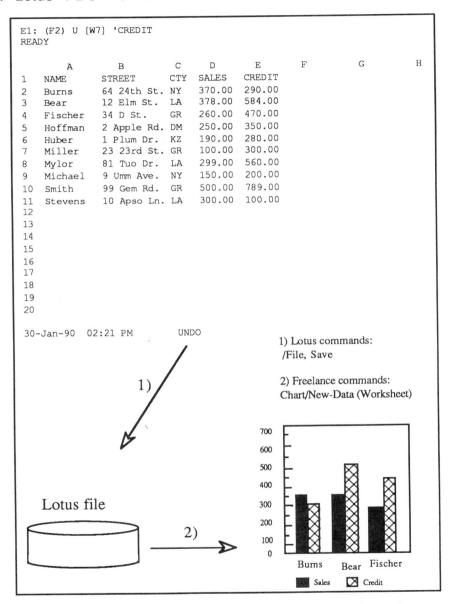

```
E1: (F2)  U  [W7]  'CREDIT
READY

          A          B          C     D        E        F        G          H
 1   NAME       STREET        CTY   SALES   CREDIT
 2   Burns      64 24th St.   NY    370.00  290.00
 3   Bear       12 Elm St.    LA    378.00  584.00
 4   Fischer    34 D St.      GR    260.00  470.00
 5   Hoffman    2 Apple Rd.   DM    250.00  350.00
 6   Huber      1 Plum Dr.    KZ    190.00  280.00
 7   Miller     23 23rd St.   GR    100.00  300.00
 8   Mylor      81 Tuo Dr.    LA    299.00  560.00
 9   Michael    9 Umm Ave.    NY    150.00  200.00
10   Smith      99 Gem Rd.    GR    500.00  789.00
11   Stevens    10 Apso Ln.   LA    300.00  100.00
12
13
14
15
16
17
18
19
20

30-Jan-90  02:21 PM          UNDO
```

1) Lotus commands:
/File, Save

2) Freelance commands:
Chart/New-Data (Worksheet)

1)

2)

Lotus file

Figure 4.4.5.1: Importing Lotus 1-2-3 worksheet data to a Freelance chart

Data can be read directly from a Lotus 1-2-3 file in Freelance. It can then be converted to a Freelance chart.

- Load Freelance and select the Charts and Drawings command.

- Select the Chart New-Data command. The cursor should be in the Chart type: field. Press <Space> to see a list of file types accessible from Freelance. Select the Bar - Vertical item and press the <Enter> key.

- Press the <Tab> or <Cursor right> key to move to the DATALINKS bar. Press <Space> to display the Datalinks menu.

- The cursor should be in the File type: item. Press <Space> to see a list of file types available. Select the Worksheet option and press the <Enter> key.

- Press the <Tab> key or the <Cursor down> key to move to the File path: item. Enter the proper drive specifier and path.

- Move the cursor down to the File name: item using the <Tab> key or the <Cursor down> key. Enter the name DATA2.WK1 in this line.

- The default name in the Type of import: item should read Specified Ranges.

- Leave the Headings:, Notes:, Legends: and axis Title: items blank.

- Move the cursor to the Cluster Labels: item and enter A2..A11.

- Move the cursor to the Bar 1 Values: item and enter D2..D11.

- Move the cursor to the Bar 2 Values: item and enter E2..E11.

- Press the <End> key to move to the DONE bar. Press <Enter> to accept the above data. If a confirmation message appears, press the <Y> key.

- Press <Ctrl><PgDn> twice. The top bar should read Form 3 of 3. Move the cursor to the Legend: field beneath the number 1 and enter SALES. Press the <Cursor right> key to move to the Legend: field beneath the number 2 and enter CREDITS.

- Press the <F10> key for the menu. Press the <G> key (Go) to generate the chart. Freelance may ask you to adjust the chart size or shape. For now, just press the keys required to draw the chart (usually <Enter>).

- Press the <Enter> key to accept the chart.

- Select the File Save Both command. Enter the name LOT-FL-GR for the drawing file, the proper path for the drawing file, and the proper path for the chart file. Press the <F10> key to save this data.

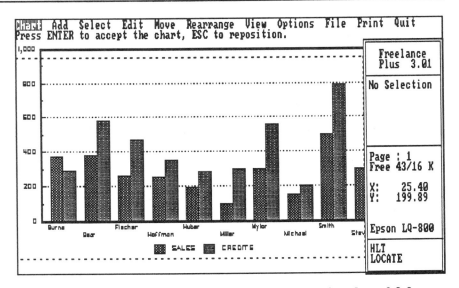

Figure 4.4.5.1a: Freelance chart using worksheet data from Lotus 1-2-3

4.4.5.2 Lotus 1-2-3 Chart—Lotus Freelance Chart

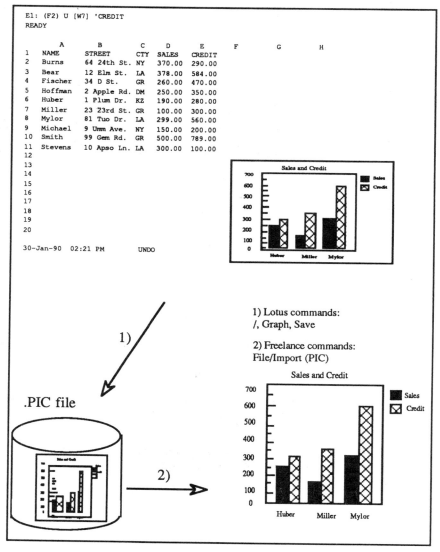

Figure 4.4.5.2: Importing Lotus 1-2-3 chart data to a Freelance chart

Lotus 1-2-3 charts can be imported to Freelance directly as long as they are saved as PIC files. The Lotus charts are transferred complete with titles, axis titles and labels.

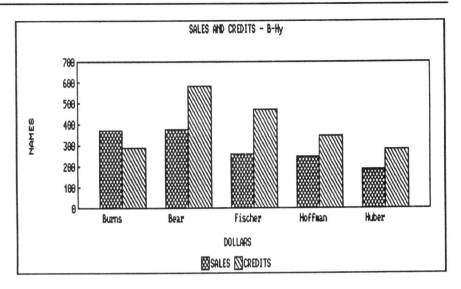

Figure 4.4.5.2a: Saved Lotus chart

- Copy the LO-CH-GR.PIC file as follows from the DOS prompt:

```
copy lo-ch-gr.pic lo-fl-gr.pic
```

- Run Freelance and select the Charts and Drawings command.

- Select the File Import command. The cursor will appear in the File type: item. Press <Space> to display a number of choices. Use the cursor keys to highlight the PIC item and press the <Enter> key.

- Select the path and filename and press the <F10> key to load and display the graphic. A Lotus graphic file is loaded with the PIC option and then translated into the Freelance format.

Note: The RAW PIC option should be used only if Freelance has problems loading a PIC file through normal means.

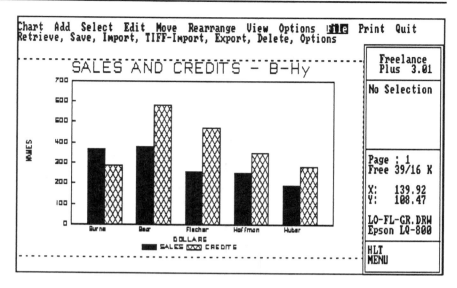

Figure 4.4.5.2b: Freelance chart from an existing Lotus chart

The imported graphic can now be edited from within Freelance.

4.4.5.3 Lotus 1-2-3 Worksheet—Freelance Text Chart

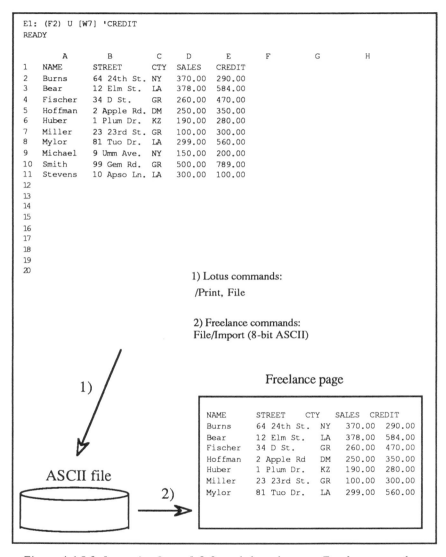

Figure 4.4.5.3: Importing Lotus 1-2-3 worksheet data to a Freelance text chart

Lotus 1-2-3 data saved in ASCII format can be loaded into Freelance as a text chart.

- Load the DATA2.WK1 worksheet using the / File Retrieve command.

- Select the / Print File command. Enter the filename LOT-FL.ASC (including a drive specifier and path if needed). Press the <Enter> key.

- 1-2-3 then displays a menu listing the parameters of the worksheet about to be saved to disk. Press the <R> key to select the Range menu. Select the range from A2 to E9 using either keyboard coordinate entry or the cursor keys. Press the <Enter> key.

- 1-2-3 displays the menu of worksheet parameters again. Press the <O> key to invoke the Options menu. Press the <M> key to select Margins. Set the left and top margins to zero (0), the bottom margin to a number greater than the number of rows used in the worksheet (at least 10) and the right margin to 45 (the total length of a row). Press the <Enter> key.

- Press the <P> key to invoke the Pg-Length menu. Enter a page length larger than the maximum number of rows being transferred (in this case, a minimum of 12). Press the <Enter> key.

- Press the <O> key to move to the Other menu. Press the <U> key (Unformatted).

- Press the <Q> key to return to the Print menu. Press the <A> key (Align) to align the system to the "top of the page." Press the <G> key (Go) to save the data to the file.

- Press the <Q> key to return to the worksheet.

- Quit Lotus 1-2-3 and run Freelance. Select the Charts and Drawings command.

- Select the File Import command. The cursor will be in the File type: item. Press <Space> to display a list of file types. Highlight the 8-bit ASCII option and press the <Enter> key. Enter the proper name and disk path and press the <F10> key to load the data as a text chart.

This data can now be edited from within Freelance as a text chart.

4.4.6 Lotus 1-2-3—Microsoft Word

Lotus 1-2-3 worksheets can be loaded directly or after conversion to an ASCII file into Word.

The DATA2.WK1 worksheet will be used as our example in this section.

4.4.6.1 Lotus 1-2-3—Microsoft Word

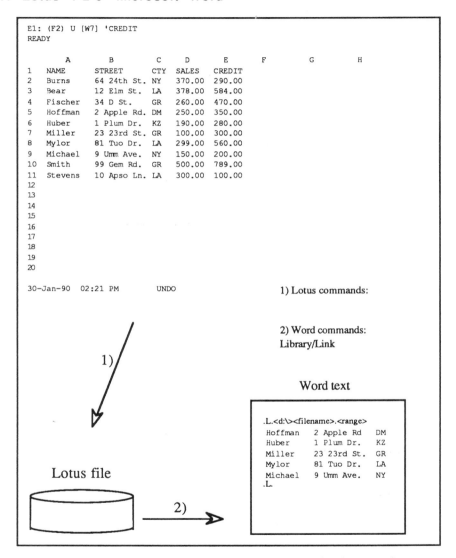

```
E1: (F2) U [W7] 'CREDIT
READY

          A         B         C     D      E       F       G         H
 1    NAME      STREET      CTY   SALES  CREDIT
 2    Burns     64 24th St. NY    370.00 290.00
 3    Bear      12 Elm St.  LA    378.00 584.00
 4    Fischer   34 D St.    GR    260.00 470.00
 5    Hoffman   2 Apple Rd. DM    250.00 350.00
 6    Huber     1 Plum Dr.  KZ    190.00 280.00
 7    Miller    23 23rd St. GR    100.00 300.00
 8    Mylor     81 Tuo Dr.  LA    299.00 560.00
 9    Michael   9 Umm Ave.  NY    150.00 200.00
10    Smith     99 Gem Rd.  GR    500.00 789.00
11    Stevens   10 Apso Ln. LA    300.00 100.00
12
13
14
15
16
17
18
19
20

30-Jan-90  02:21 PM          UNDO
```

1) Lotus commands:

2) Word commands:
Library/Link

Word text

```
.L.<d:\><filename>.<range>
Hoffman    2 Apple Rd    DM
Huber      1 Plum Dr.    KZ
Miller     23 23rd St.   GR
Mylor      81 Tuo Dr.    LA
Michael    9 Umm Ave.    NY
.L.
```

Lotus file

1)

2)

Figure 4.4.6.1: Importing Lotus 1-2-3 data to Word (Library/Link)

A spreadsheet created in Lotus can be integrated completely or partially into Word. The data from this table can be updated at any time.

•   Open an existing Word document or start a new one.

- Move the cursor to the location in the Word document at which you want the worksheet data to begin.

- Select the Library/Link/Spreadsheet command. Enter the filename DATA2.WK1 (with drive specifier and path if needed), or press the <F1> key to see a list of available files in the current drive, and highlight the desired filename. Press <Enter> to insert the worksheet data.

The Word document version of the Lotus 1-2-3 data may look like this (your Word screen may look different):

```
.L. DATA2.WK1,
NAME→       STREET→        CTY→SALES→ CREDIT
Burns→      64 24th St.→       NY→ 370.00→ 290.00
Bear→       12 Elm St.→        LA→ 378.00→ 584.00
Fischer→ 34 D St.→             GR→ 260.00→ 470.00
Hoffman→ 2 Apple Rd.→          DM→ 250.00→ 350.00
Huber→      1 Plum Dr.→        KZ→ 190.00→ 280.00
Miller→ 23 23rd St.→           GR→ 100.00→ 300.00
Mylor→      81 Tuo Dr.→        LA→ 299.00→ 560.00
Michael→ 9 Umm Ave.→           NY→ 150.00→ 200.00
Smith→      99 Gem Rd.→        GR→ 500.00→ 789.00
Stevens→ 10 Apso Ln.→          LA→ 300.00→ 100.00
.L.
```

The .L. codes at the first and last line of the inserted data are formatted as hidden text. These .L. codes allow you to still edit the file from within 1-2-3. Deleting these .L. codes while in Word makes the worksheet data a Word file. That is, you cannot access this data from 1-2-3 again unless you convert it. The right arrows following each entry represent tabs.

This data can be updated at any time as follows:

- Select the desired area by pressing <F10>, or the entire document by pressing <Shift><F10>. If you aren't sure which portion of a document is spreadsheet data, select the Options command and select (Yes) in the show hidden text command field to make the .L. codes visible.

- Select the Library/Link/Spreadsheet command and press the <Enter> key without changing any command fields.

Word then highlights the area that needs updating and prompts the user for confirmation of the update.

- Press the <Y> key to update the information, or the <N> key to abort.

4.4.6.2   Lotus 1-2-3—ASCII—Word

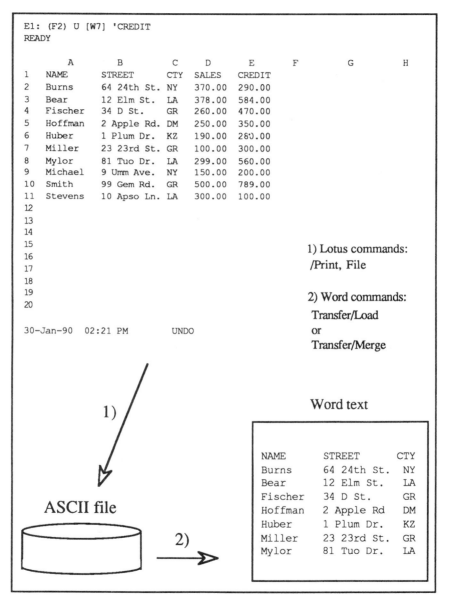

```
E1: (F2) U [W7] 'CREDIT
READY

        A           B          C      D       E        F        G        H
1   NAME        STREET       CTY   SALES    CREDIT
2   Burns       64 24th St.  NY    370.00   290.00
3   Bear        12 Elm St.   LA    378.00   584.00
4   Fischer     34 D St.     GR    260.00   470.00
5   Hoffman     2 Apple Rd.  DM    250.00   350.00
6   Huber       1 Plum Dr.   KZ    190.00   280.00
7   Miller      23 23rd St.  GR    100.00   300.00
8   Mylor       81 Tuo Dr.   LA    299.00   560.00
9   Michael     9 Umm Ave.   NY    150.00   200.00
10  Smith       99 Gem Rd.   GR    500.00   789.00
11  Stevens     10 Apso Ln.  LA    300.00   100.00
12
13
14
15
16
17
18
19
20

30-Jan-90   02:21 PM         UNDO
```

1) Lotus commands:
/Print, File

2) Word commands:
Transfer/Load
or
Transfer/Merge

1)

ASCII file

2)

Word text

```
NAME        STREET       CTY
Burns       64 24th St.  NY
Bear        12 Elm St.   LA
Fischer     34 D St.     GR
Hoffman     2 Apple Rd   DM
Huber       1 Plum Dr.   KZ
Miller      23 23rd St.  GR
Mylor       81 Tuo Dr.   LA
```

Figure 4.4.6.2: Importing Lotus 1-2-3 data to Word (ASCII)

Lotus-1-2-3 data can be saved in ASCII format and the resulting ASCII file loaded into Word.

- Load the DATA2.WK1 worksheet using the / File Retrieve command.

- Select the / Print File command. Enter the filename LOT-WO.ASC (including a drive specifier and path if needed). Press the <Enter> key.

- 1-2-3 then displays a menu listing the parameters of the worksheet about to be saved to disk. Press the <R> key to select the Range menu. Select the range from A1 to E11 using either keyboard coordinate entry or the cursor keys. Press the <Enter> key.

- 1-2-3 displays the menu of worksheet parameters again. Press the <O> key to invoke the Options menu. Press the <M> key to select Margins. Set the left and top margins to zero (0), the bottom margin to a number greater than the number of rows used in the worksheet (at least 12) and the right margin to 45 (the total length of a row). Press the <Enter> key.

- Press the <P> key to invoke the Pg-Length menu. Enter a page length larger than the maximum number of rows being transferred (in this case, a minimum of 12). Press the <Enter> key.

- Press the <O> key to move to the Other menu. Press the <U> key (Unformatted).

- Press the <Q> key to return to the Print menu. Press the <A> key (Align) to align the system to the "top of the page." Press the <G> key (Go) to save the data to the file.

- Press the <Q> key to return to the worksheet.

- Quit Lotus 1-2-3 and run Word.

You can now load this file into Word using the Transfer Load command.

4.4.7 Lotus 1-2-3—IBM DisplayWrite 4

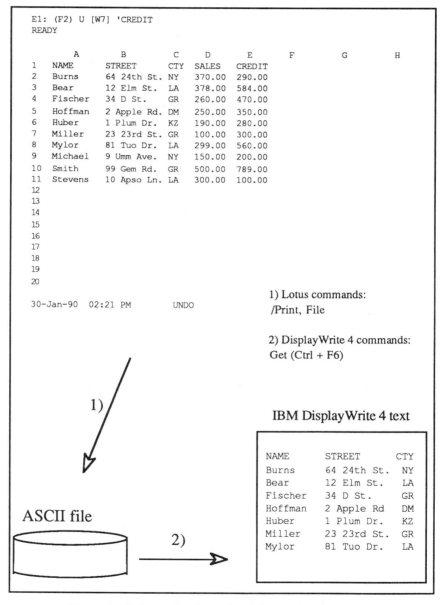

```
E1: (F2) U [W7] 'CREDIT
READY

          A          B         C      D        E        F        G        H
  1   NAME       STREET      CTY   SALES    CREDIT
  2   Burns      64 24th St. NY    370.00   290.00
  3   Bear       12 Elm St.  LA    378.00   584.00
  4   Fischer    34 D St.    GR    260.00   470.00
  5   Hoffman    2 Apple Rd. DM    250.00   350.00
  6   Huber      1 Plum Dr.  KZ    190.00   280.00
  7   Miller     23 23rd St. GR    100.00   300.00
  8   Mylor      81 Tuo Dr.  LA    299.00   560.00
  9   Michael    9 Umm Ave.  NY    150.00   200.00
 10   Smith      99 Gem Rd.  GR    500.00   789.00
 11   Stevens    10 Apso Ln. LA    300.00   100.00
 12
 13
 14
 15
 16
 17
 18
 19
 20

30-Jan-90  02:21 PM          UNDO
```

1) Lotus commands:
/Print, File

2) DisplayWrite 4 commands:
Get (Ctrl + F6)

1)

ASCII file

2)

IBM DisplayWrite 4 text

```
NAME       STREET        CTY
Burns      64 24th St.   NY
Bear       12 Elm St.    LA
Fischer    34 D St.      GR
Hoffman    2 Apple Rd    DM
Huber      1 Plum Dr.    KZ
Miller     23 23rd St.   GR
Mylor      81 Tuo Dr.    LA
```

Figure 4.4.7: Importing Lotus 1-2-3 data to DisplayWrite 4

Lotus 1-2-3 files are saved in ASCII format. These ASCII files are integrated into
DisplayWrite 4 with the Get command.

- Select the / File Retrieve command and load the DATA.WK1 worksheet.

- Select the / Print File command. Enter the filename LOT-DW.DOC (including a drive specifier and path if needed). Press the <Enter> key.

- 1-2-3 then displays a menu listing the parameters of the worksheet about to be saved to disk. Press the <R> key to select the Range menu. Select the range from A2 to E11 using either keyboard coordinate entry or the cursor keys. Press the <Enter> key.

- 1-2-3 displays the menu of worksheet parameters again. Press the <O> key to invoke the Options menu. Press the <M> key to select Margins. Set the left and top margins to zero (0), the bottom margin to a number greater than the number of rows used in the worksheet (at least 10) and the right margin to 45 (the total length of a row). Press the <Enter> key.

- Press the <P> key to invoke the Pg-Length menu. Enter a page length larger than the maximum number of rows being transferred (in this case, a minimum of 12). Press the <Enter> key.

- Press the <O> key to move to the Other menu. Press the <U> key (Unformatted).

- Press the <Q> key to return to the Print menu. Press the <A> key (Align) to align the system to the "top of the page." Press the <G> key (Go) to save the data to the file.

- Press the <Q> key to return to the worksheet.

- Quit 1-2-3 and start DisplayWrite 4.

- Create a new document or get an existing one. Place the cursor at the point where you would like the ASCII file added.

- Select the Get function by pressing <Ctrl><F6>.

```
┌─────────────────────────────────────────────────────────────────┐
│                              Get File                             │
├─────────────────────────────────────────────────────────────────┤
│  If no pages are specified, the entire document will be included. │
│  When specifying multiple pages, separate page numbers with a space. │
│                                                                   │
│  File Name.............[                                        ] │
│  System Page Number (s).[                                       ] │
│                                                                   │
│  Insert Included Text...[N]     Y = Yes    N = No                 │
│  File Type.............[2]      1 = Document or DisplayWrite File  │
│                                 2 = ASCII                         │
│                                 3 = 7-Bit ASCII                   │
│                                 4 = Revisable-Form Text           │
├─────────────────────────────────────────────────────────────────┤
│  Enter   Esc=Quit   F1=Help   F3=List                            │
└─────────────────────────────────────────────────────────────────┘
```

- Enter the name of the ASCII file in the File Name field.

•   Press the <Tab> key or the <Cursor down> key to move down to the File Type field. Press the <2> key (ASCII), then press the <Enter> key to load the file.

4.4.8 Lotus 1-2-3—Aldus PageMaker

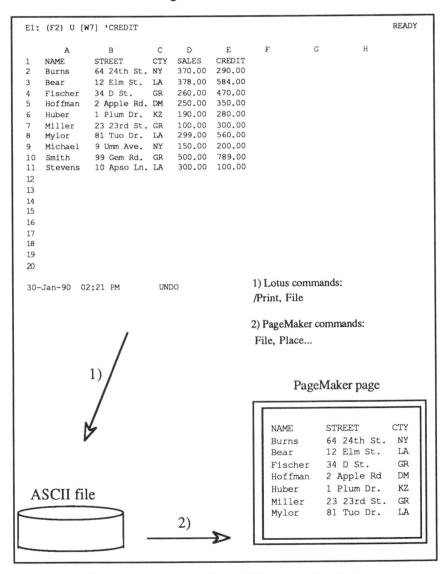

Figure 4.4.8: Importing Lotus 1-2-3 data to PageMaker

Lotus 1-2-3 worksheet files can be positioned directly in Pagemaker, provided that you have installed a Lotus 1-2-3 import/export filter in PageMaker (see your PageMaker installation information).

Add the worksheet file DATA.WK1 to PageMaker as follows:

- Run PageMaker.

- Lay out a new publication or load an existing publication.

- Select the File menu and the Place... option. Click on the DATA.WK1 filename and click OK.

- Once the file is loaded, PageMaker prompts you to enter the range you want placed. Click OK to place all the worksheet data.

The mouse pointer changes to a manual flow text icon.

- Move this pointer to the location at which you want the file to begin. Press and hold the left mouse button and move the pointer down and to the right of the starting point of the pointer. Release the left mouse button. An alternate method is to click once at the desired starting point of the file.

If the file is larger than the amount of space you have created, a plus sign within a semicircle appears at the bottom of the page. This is the bottom windowshade handle. By dragging this handle down, dragging the handles at the edge of each text block, or clicking on the bottom windowshade handle and creating another block for the remaining text, you can insert the remaining text.

You can now edit your data from within PageMaker.

4.4.9 Lotus 1-2-3—Ventura Publisher

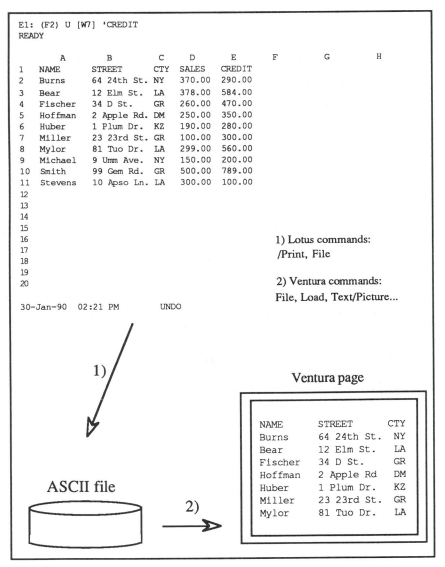

```
E1: (F2) U [W7] 'CREDIT
READY

          A        B          C     D       E        F        G        H
  1  NAME       STREET       CTY   SALES   CREDIT
  2  Burns      64 24th St.  NY    370.00  290.00
  3  Bear       12 Elm St.   LA    378.00  584.00
  4  Fischer    34 D St.     GR    260.00  470.00
  5  Hoffman    2 Apple Rd.  DM    250.00  350.00
  6  Huber      1 Plum Dr.   KZ    190.00  280.00
  7  Miller     23 23rd St.  GR    100.00  300.00
  8  Mylor      81 Tuo Dr.   LA    299.00  560.00
  9  Michael    9 Umm Ave.   NY    150.00  200.00
 10  Smith      99 Gem Rd.   GR    500.00  789.00
 11  Stevens    10 Apso Ln.  LA    300.00  100.00
 12
 13
 14
 15
 16
 17
 18
 19
 20

 30-Jan-90  02:21 PM            UNDO
```

1) Lotus commands:
/Print, File

2) Ventura commands:
File, Load, Text/Picture...

1)

ASCII file

2)

Ventura page

```
NAME         STREET         CTY
Burns        64 24th St.    NY
Bear         12 Elm St.     LA
Fischer      34 D St.       GR
Hoffman      2 Apple Rd     DM
Huber        1 Plum Dr.     KZ
Miller       23 23rd St.    GR
Mylor        81 Tuo Dr.     LA
```

Figure 4.4.9 Importing Lotus 1-2-3 data to Ventura Publisher

Lotus 1-2-3 data is saved in ASCII format and can then be loaded in Ventura Publisher.

• Select the / File Retrieve command and load the DATA2.WK1 worksheet file.

- Select the / Print File command. Enter the filename LOT-VP.DOC (including a drive specifier and path if needed). Press the <Enter> key.

- 1-2-3 then displays a menu listing the parameters of the worksheet about to be saved to disk. Press the <R> key to select the Range menu. Select the range from A2 to E11 using either keyboard coordinate entry or the cursor keys. Press the <Enter> key.

- 1-2-3 displays the menu of worksheet parameters again. Press the <O> key to invoke the Options menu. Press the <M> key to select Margins. Set the left and top margins to zero (0), the bottom margin to a number greater than the number of rows used in the worksheet (at least 10) and the right margin to 45 (the total length of a row). Press the <Enter> key.

- Press the <P> key to invoke the Pg-Length menu. Enter a page length larger than the maximum number of rows being transferred (in this case, a minimum of 12). Press the <Enter> key.

- Press the <O> key to move to the Other menu. Press the <U> key (Unformatted).

- Press the <Q> key to return to the Print menu. Press the <A> key (Align) to align the system to the "top of the page." Press the <G> key (Go) to save the data to the file.

- Press the <Q> key to return to the worksheet.

- Quit 1-2-3 and start Ventura Publisher.

- Click on the Add New Frame addition button. Create a frame within Ventura Publisher.

- Select the File menu and the Load Text/Picture... option. Click on the Text button and the WS 4.0/5.0 button. Click on OK.

- Click on the Directory line and replace the file extension characters with .*. Click on the bar above the file list box.

- Click on the LOT-VP.DOC filename when it appears in the ITEM SELECTOR box and click on OK.

The file can then be edited from within Ventura Publisher.

4.5   Microsoft Word

The following Word document named DATA.DOC will serve as an example:

```
Burns    64 24th St.  NY 370.00 01/01/88
Bear     12 Elm St.   LA 378.00 02/01/88
Fischer  34 D St.     GR 260.00 12/31/87
Hoffman  2 Apple Rd.  DM 250.00 03/01/88
Huber    1 Plum Dr.   KZ 190.00 04/01/88
Miller   23 23rd St.  GR 100.00 05/01/88
Mylor    81 Tuo Dr.   LA 299.00 07/01/88
Michael  9 Umm Ave.   NY 150.00 08/01/88
Smith    99 Gem Rd.   GR 500.00 07/20/88
Stevens  10 Apso Ln.  LA 300.00 07/30/88
```

Word 4.0

Use the following method to save a document in ASCII format in Word 4.0:

•   Select the text to be saved.

•   Select the Format/Division/Margins command.

•   Enter the value 0 in the top:, bottom:, left: and right: command fields.

•   Enter the record length in the width: command field. This can be entered in inches. In the example the record length is 42 characters, so enter 4.2 in.

•   Press the <Enter> key to execute.

•   Select the Print/Options command.

•   Select the PLAIN printer driver in the printer: command field.

•   Move to the range: command field and press the <S> key (Select).

•   Press the <Enter> key.

•   Select the Print/File command. Enter the filename of the ASCI file (with the correct drive specifier and path if needed). Press the <Enter> key.

Word 5.0

Use the following method to save a document in ASCII format in Word 5.0:

•   Select the Transfer/Save command. Enter the filename and press the <Tab> key to move to the format: command field.

•   Select the Text-with-line-breaks item and press the <Enter> key.

Portions of files can be selected for saving in ASCII format, or files can be printed to disk as described above for Word 4.0.

4.5.1 Word—dBASE IV

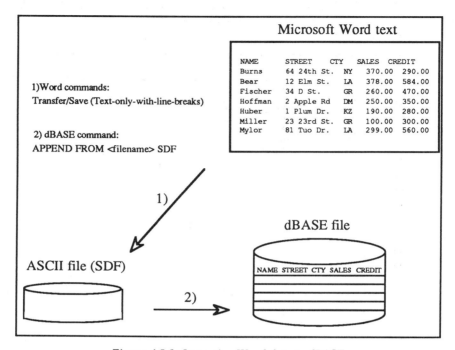

Figure 4.5.1: Importing Word data to dBASE

- Save the DATA.DOC file as an ASCII file named ASCII.DOC using the instructions described above.

- Create a new file in dBASE named WO-DB.DBF. Define this database with the following structure (notice that the DATE field is assigned a Character field type):

```
Structure for database: WO-DB.DBF
Number of data records:      0
Date of last update: 01/29/90
Field    Field Name  Type      Width   Dec.   Index
   1       NAME      Character    10            N
   2       STREET    Character    12            N
   3       CTY       Character     4            N
   4       SALES     Numeric       7      2     N
   5       DATE      Character     8            N
** TOTAL **                       42
```

- Enter the following command from the dot prompt of dBASE:

```
APPEND FROM ascii.doc SDF
```

Once the records have been copied over to the database file, dBASE displays:

```
10 records added
```

The DATE field type is currently a Character field type. To convert this to a Date field type, enter the MODIFY STRUCTURE command in dBASE. The following screen appears:

```
 Layout   Organize   Append  Go To   Exit                        12:36:52 am
                                                        ┌Bytes remaining:   3954
   ┌─────┬────────────┬────────────┬───────┬──────┬───────┐
   │ Num │ Field Name │ Field Type │ Width │ Dec  │ Index │
   ├─────┼────────────┼────────────┼───────┼──────┼───────┤
   │  1  │ NAME       │ Character  │  10   │      │   N   │
   │  2  │ STREET     │ Character  │  12   │      │   N   │
   │  3  │ CTY        │ Character  │   4   │      │   N   │
   │  4  │ SALES      │ Numeric    │   7   │  2   │   N   │
   │  5  │ DATE       │ Character  │   8   │      │   N   │
   │     │            │            │       │      │       │
   │     │            │            │       │      │       │
   │     │            │            │       │      │       │
   │     │            │            │       │      │       │
   └─────┴────────────┴────────────┴───────┴──────┴───────┘
 Database║A:WO-DB              ║Field 1/5        ║     :Ctrl-N/Ctrl-U
          Enter the field name.  Insert/Delete field:Ctrl-N/Ctrl-U
 Field names begin with a letter and may contain letters, digits and underscores
```

Figure 4.5.1a: Modifying structure in dBASE

•   Move the cursor to the Width column of the SALES field. Change the 7 to a 6.

•   Move the cursor to the Field type column of the Date field. Press the \<D\> key to change the field type to Date. Press \<Ctrl\>\<End\> to save the new structure.

```
┌──────────────────────────────────────────────────┐
│ Structure for database: WO-DB.DBF                 │
│ Number of data records:      10                   │
│ Date of last update: 01/29/90                     │
│ Field    Field Name  Type       Width  Dec.  Index│
│   1       NAME        Character    10           N  │
│   2       STREET      Character    12           N  │
│   3       CTY         Character     4           N  │
│   4       SALES       Numeric       6    2      N  │
│   5       DATE        Date          8           N  │
│ ** TOTAL **                        41              │
└──────────────────────────────────────────────────┘
```

The data can now be edited from within dBASE.

4.5.2 Word—Microsoft Multiplan

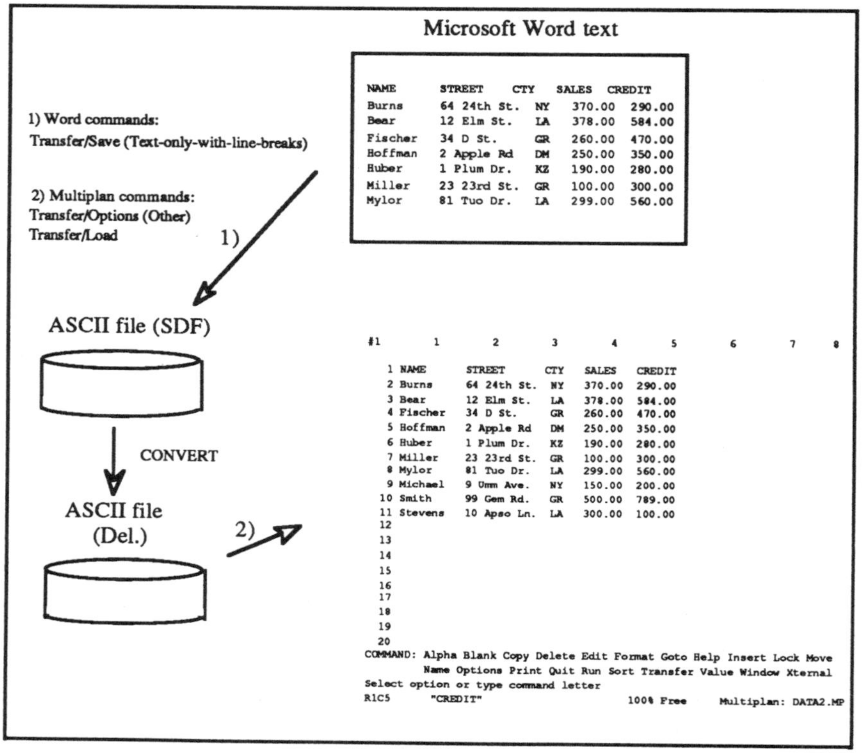

Figure 4.5.2: *Importing Word data to Multiplan*

The ASCII.DOC file created in the preceding section can be converted to a format readable by Multiplan.

This is done using the CONVERT program, found on the companion disk for this book, and printed in the Appendix as a Turbo Pascal source code.

- Start the CONVERT utility from the DOS prompt. The program prompts the user for the name of the source file. Enter the source filename and press the <Enter> key.

- The CONVERT utility then prompts the user for the ASCII format of the source file: Press the <S> key (SDF).

- Next the program prompts the user for the number of fields in each record (press the <5> key, then the <Enter> key).

- The program then prompts the user for the length of each field. Enter the following for each field:

Field 1: 10
Field 2: 12
Field 3: 4
Field 4: 6
Field 5: 11

- CONVERT displays a test record. Press the <Y> key to accept this record layout or the <N> key to try again.

- The program prompts the user for the name of the target file. Enter the target filename (in this case, WO-MP.DEL) and press the <Enter> key. If CONVERT finds an existing file of the same name, it will ask if you want to overwrite the existing file with the new data. Press the <Y> key to overwrite the existing file, or the <N> key to end the program.

- The CONVERT utility then determines that the target file is in DELIMITED format. The program prompts the user for the field separator character (press the <,> key) and the text delimiter (press the <"> key).

- CONVERT prompts the user for each field type: press <T> for the first three fields, <N> for the fourth field and <D> for the last field.

CONVERT then converts the file to the proper format.

The target file WO-MP.DEL has the following structure:

```
"Burns","64 24th St.","NY",370.00,01/01/88
"Bear","12 Elm St.","LA",378.00,02/01/88
"Fischer","34 D St.","GR",260.00,12/31/87
"Hoffman","2 Apple Rd.","DM",250.00,03/01/88
"Huber","1 Plum Dr.","KZ",190.00,04/01/88
"Miller","23 23rd St.","GR",100.00,05/01/88
"Mylor","81 Tuo Dr.","LA",299.00,07/01/88
"Michael","9 Umm Ave.","NY",150.00,08/01/88
"Smith","99 Gem Rd.","GR",500.00,07/20/88
"Stevens","10 Apso Ln.","LA",300.00,07/30/88
```

- Run Multiplan and select the Transfer/Options command.

- Select the Other option and press the <Enter> key.

- Select the Transfer/Import command.

- Enter the filename WO-MP.DEL in the file name: command field. Press the <Tab> key.

- The at: command field should contain the starting point of the range into which the ASCII file should be transferred. Enter the upper left corner of the range (R1C1). Press the <Tab> key.

- The cursor should be in the numbers: command field. Press the <Y> key (Yes) to accept numeric and alphanumeric data and press the <Tab> key.

- The query: command field controls whether Multiplan should prompt the user for overwriting data. Press the <N> key, then press the <Tab> key.

- The delimiters: command field determines which ASCII character should be considered as the field separator. The defaults are the space and the Tab character (^s,^t). Press the <,> key, then press the <Enter> key.

The data transfers into Multiplan. The worksheet looks like this:

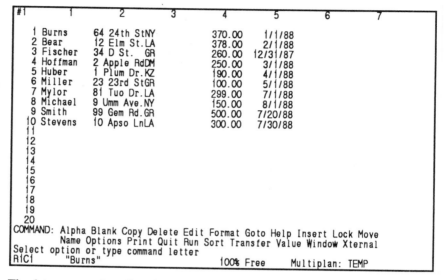

The data can now be edited from within Multiplan.

4.5.3 Word—Microsoft Excel

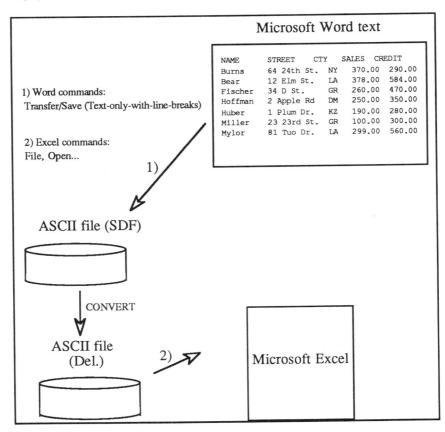

Microsoft Word text

```
NAME        STREET       CTY   SALES   CREDIT
Burns       64 24th St.  NY    370.00  290.00
Bear        12 Elm St.   LA    378.00  584.00
Fischer     34 D St.     GR    260.00  470.00
Hoffman     2 Apple Rd   DM    250.00  350.00
Huber       1 Plum Dr.   KZ    190.00  280.00
Miller      23 23rd St.  GR    100.00  300.00
Mylor       81 Tuo Dr.   LA    299.00  560.00
```

1) Word commands:
Transfer/Save (Text-only-with-line-breaks)

2) Excel commands:
File, Open...

ASCII file (SDF)

CONVERT

ASCII file
(Del.)

Microsoft Excel

Figure 4.5.3: Importing Word data to Excel

Excel will read ASCII data from Microsoft Word that has been converted to DELIMITED format with commas, and assigned a file extension of .CSV.

- Create a file named DATA2.DOC in Word, containing the following information:

```
NAME       STREET        CTY SALES  CREDIT
Burns      64 24th St.   NY  370.00 290.00
Bear       12 Elm St.    LA  378.00 584.00
Fischer    34 D St.      GR  260.00 470.00
Hoffman    2 Apple Rd.   DM  250.00 350.00
Huber      1 Plum Dr.    KZ  190.00 280.00
Miller     23 23rd St.   GR  100.00 300.00
Mylor      81 Tuo Dr.    LA  299.00 560.00
Michael    9 Umm Ave.    NY  150.00 200.00
Smith      99 Gem Rd.    GR  500.00 789.00
Stevens    10 Apso Ln.   LA  300.00 100.00
```

- Save it to disk as an ASCII (Text-only-with-line-breaks) file named ASCII2.DOC and quit Word.

Now the file has to be converted to a format that Excel can read.

- Start the CONVERT utility from the DOS prompt. The program prompts the user for the name of the source file. Enter the source filename ASCII2.DOC and press the <Enter> key.

- The CONVERT utility then prompts the user for the ASCII format of the source file: Press the <S> key (SDF).

- Next the program prompts the user for the number of fields in each record (press the <5> key, then the <Enter> key).

- The program then prompts the user for the length of each field. Enter the following for each field:

Field 1: 10
Field 2: 12
Field 3: 4
Field 4: 6
Field 5: 7

- CONVERT displays a test record. Press the <Y> key to accept this record layout or the <N> key to try again.

- The program prompts the user for the name of the target file. Enter the target filename WO-EXC.CSV and press the <Enter> key. If CONVERT finds an existing file of the same name, it will ask if you want to overwrite the existing file with the new data. Press the <Y> key to overwrite the existing file, or the <N> key to end the program.

- The CONVERT utility then determines that the target file is in DELIMITED format. The program prompts the user for the field separator character (press the <,> key) and the text delimiter (press <Space>).

- CONVERT prompts the user for each field type: press <T> for all five fields.

CONVERT then converts the file to the proper format.

The file WO-EXC.CSV has the following contents:

```
NAME , STREET , CTY , SALES , CREDIT
Burns , 64 24th St. , NY ,370.00,290.00
Bear , 12 Elm St. , LA ,378.00,584.00
Fischer , 34 D St. , GR ,260.00,470.00
Hoffman , 2 Apple Rd. , DM ,250.00,350.00
Huber , 1 Plum Dr. , KZ ,190.00,280.00
Miller , 23 23rd St. , GR , 00.00,300.00
Mylor , 81 Tuo Dr. , LA ,299.00,560.00
Michael , 9 Umm Ave. , NY ,150.00,200.00
Smith , 99 Gem Rd. , GR ,500.00,789.00
Stevens , 10 Apso Ln. , LA ,300.00,100.00
```

- Start Microsoft Excel.

- Select the File menu and click on the Open... option. A window appears, listing a set of files. In addition, you'll see a text box listing a file wildcard of *.XL*. Change this wildcard to read *.*, press the <Enter> key and watch the change.

- Select the desired path from the Directories window.

- Select the filename WO-EXC.CSV and either press <Enter> or click on the OK button to load the file.

Excel loads the worksheet, but now the numeric formats for the SALES and CREDIT columns are incorrect. This occurs because we formatted these columns as text to compensate for the titles.

- Select all the numbers in the SALES column. Select the Format/Number... command, select the format you want for the numbers (0.00) and click on the OK button.

- Select all the numbers in the CREDIT column. Select the Format/Number... command, select the format you want for the numbers (0.00) and click on the OK button.

The file can now be edited from within Excel.

4.5.4 Word—Microsoft Chart

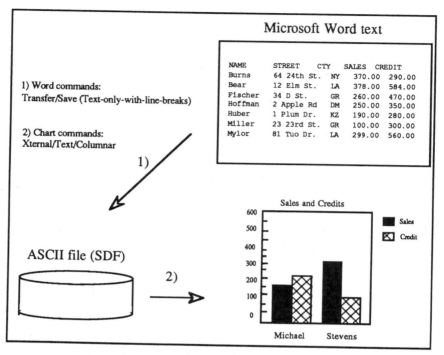

Figure 4.5.4: Importing Word data to Microsoft Chart

The DATA2.DOC file created in Section 4.5.3 will be used in this example:

```
NAME      STREET       CTY SALES  CREDIT
Burns     64 24th St.  NY  370.00 290.00
Bear      12 Elm St.   LA  378.00 584.00
Fischer   34 D St.     GR  260.00 470.00
Hoffman   2 Apple Rd.  DM  250.00 350.00
Huber     1 Plum Dr.   KZ  190.00 280.00
Miller    23 23rd St.  GR  100.00 300.00
Mylor     81 Tuo Dr.   LA  299.00 560.00
Michael   9 Umm Ave.   NY  150.00 200.00
Smith     99 Gem Rd.   GR  500.00 789.00
Stevens   10 Apso Ln.  LA  300.00 100.00
```

•   Save it to disk as an ASCII (Text-only-with-line-breaks) file named ASCII2.DOC and quit Word.

•   Run Chart. Select the Xternal/Text/Columnar command.

•   Enter the name ASCII2.DOC in the filename: command field. Press the <Tab> key to move to the linked: command field. Press the <Y> key, then press the <Tab> key to move to the selected rows: command field.

- Enter 3,6 in the selected rows: command field and press the <Tab> key to move to the selected columns: command field.

- Enter 4,5 in the selected columns: command field and press the <Tab> key to move to the orient series by: command field.

The orient series by: command field allows chart orientation by rows or columns. We'll now take you through each configuration.

If you prefer to orient the chart by rows, do the following:

- Press the <R> key (Rows), then press the <Tab> key to move on to the column width: command field. Enter 10,12,4,7,6 and press the <Tab> key.

- Enter 1 in the series name(s) from: command field. Press the <Tab> key to move to the categories from: command field. Enter 1 and press the <Tab> key.

- Press <T> to select Text in the category type: command field and press the <Enter> key.

The list screen displays the following:

```
Incl.(*) Name      Source of data            Type   # pts.
1    *   Bear      Linked: a:\ascii2.doc:R3C4:5   Text     2
2    *   Huber     Linked: a:\ascii2.doc R6C4:5   Text     2
```

- Press the <C> key to invoke the Chart command. The graphic created by Chart has the following structure:

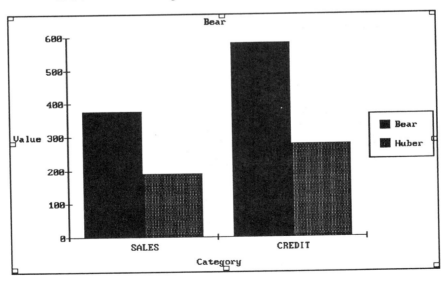

Figure 4.5.4a: Chart graphic from Word ASCII data (row orientation)

You can now edit the headings within Chart.

- Save this data under the title WO-CH-RO.CHA using the Transfer/Save command.

If you prefer to orient the chart by columns, do the following:

- Press the <C> key (Columns), then press the <Tab> key to move to the column width: command field. Enter 10,12,4,7,6 and press the <Tab> key.

- Enter 1 in the series name(s) from: command field. Press the <Tab> key to move to the categories from: command field. Enter 1 and press the <Tab> key.

- Press <T> to select Text in the category type: command field and press the <Enter> key.

The list screen displays the following:

```
Incl.(*) Name      Source of data                 Type    # pts.
1    *    SALES     Linked: a:\ascii2.doc:R3,6C4   Text    2
2    *    CREDIT    Linked: a:\ascii2.doc R3,6C5   Text    2
```

- The graphic created by Chart has the following structure:

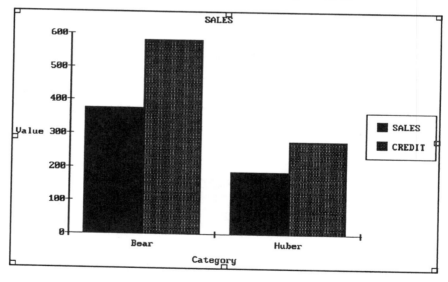

Figure 4.5.4b: Chart graphic from Word ASCII data (column orientation)

- Save this data under the title WO-CH-CO.CHA using the Transfer/Save command.

You can now edit the headings within Chart.

4.5.5 Word—Lotus Freelance Plus Text Charts

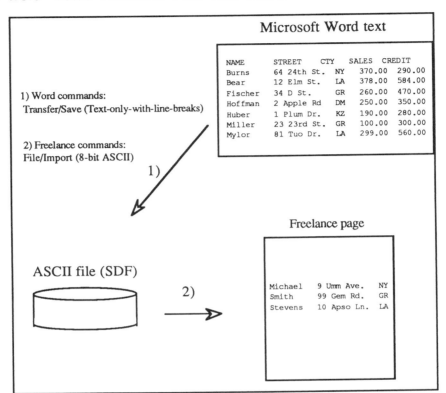

Figure 4.5.5: Importing Word data to a Freelance text chart

The ASCII2.DOC file created in Section 4.5.3 will be used in this example.

- Run Lotus Freelance and select the Charts and Drawings command.

- Select the File Import command. The cursor will be in the File type: item. Press <Space> to display a list of file types. Highlight the 8-bit ASCII option and press the <Enter> key. Move the cursor to the Path: item and select the correct path (press <Space> to see a list of paths) and press the <Enter> key.

- Move to the File name: item. Enter the filename ASCII2.DOC and press the <F10> key to load the data as a text chart.

This data can now be edited from within Freelance as a text chart.

4.5.6 Word—Lotus 1-2-3

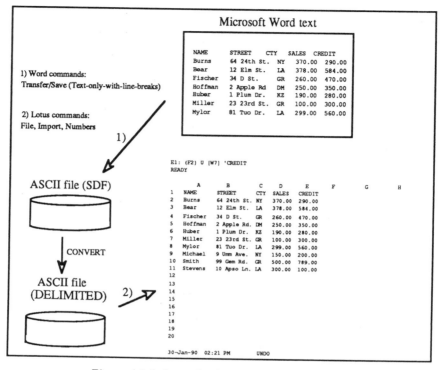

Figure 4.5.6: Importing Word data to Lotus 1-2-3

The ASCII.DOC file created in Section 4.5.1 will be used for this example. This file must be converted to a file format readable by Lotus 1-2-3 before it can be loaded into Lotus 1-2-3.

- Start the CONVERT utility from the DOS prompt. The program prompts the user for the name of the source file. Enter the source filename ASCII.DOC and press the <Enter> key.

- The CONVERT utility then prompts the user for the ASCII format of the source file: Press the <S> key (SDF).

- Next the program prompts the user for the number of fields in each record (press the <5> key, then the <Enter> key).

- The program then prompts the user for the length of each field. Enter the following for each field:

Field 1: 10
Field 2: 12

Field 3: 4
Field 4: 6
Field 5: 11

- CONVERT displays a test record. Press the <Y> key to accept this record layout or the <N> key to try again.

- The program prompts the user for the name of the target file. Enter the target filename (in this case, WO-LOT.DEL) and press the <Enter> key. If CONVERT finds an existing file of the same name, it will ask if you want to overwrite the existing file with the new data. Press the <Y> key to overwrite the existing file, or the <N> key to end the program.

- The CONVERT utility then determines that the target file is in DELIMITED format. The program prompts the user for the field separator character (press the <,> key) and the text delimiter (press the <"> key).

- CONVERT prompts the user for each field type: press <T> for the first three fields, <N> for the fourth field and <T> for the last field.

CONVERT then converts the file to the proper format.

The target file WO-LOT.DEL has the following contents:

```
"Burns","64 24th St.","NY",370.00,"01/01/88"
"Bear","12 Elm St.","LA",378.00,"02/01/88"
"Fischer","34 D St.","GR",260.00,"12/31/87"
"Hoffman","2 Apple Rd.","DM",250.00,"03/01/88"
"Huber","1 Plum Dr.","KZ",190.00,"04/01/88"
"Miller","23 23rd St.","GR",100.00,05/01/88"
"Mylor","81 Tuo Dr.","LA",299.00,07/01/88"
"Michael","9 Umm Ave.","NY",150.00,08/01/88"
"Smith","99 Gem Rd.","GR",500.00,07/20/88"
"Stevens","10 Apso Ln.","LA",300.00,07/30/88"
```

- Run Lotus 1-2-3 and select the / File Import Numbers command. Press the <Esc> key until the Enter name of file to import: file is empty.

- Enter the filename WO-LOT.DEL and press the <Enter> key.

Lotus 1-2-3 loads the file, but some formats need specification.

- Make sure that the cell pointer is in cell A1, then select the / Worksheet Insert Row command. Press the <Enter> key to insert a row at the top of the worksheet.

- Enter NAME in cell A1, STREET in cell B1, CITY in cell C1, SALES in cell D1 and DATE in cell E1.

- Move the cell pointer to cell C1 and select the / Worksheet Column Set-Width command. Enter the number 4 and press the <Enter> key.

- Keeping the cell pointer at cell C1, select the / Range Label Center command. Select the entire range of values in column C and press the <Enter> key.

- Move the cell pointer to cell D1 and select the / Range Label Center command. Select the entire range of values in column D and press the <Enter> key.

- Keeping the cell pointer in cell D1, select the / Range Format Fixed command. Press the <2> key, then the <Enter> key.

- Move the cell pointer to cell E1. Select the / Worksheet Column Set-Width command. Enter the number 11 and press the <Enter> key.

- Select the / File Save command and save the file under the name WO-LOT.WK1.

The file and date formats can now be edited from within Lotus 1-2-3.

```
A1:  'NAME                                                        READY

        A          B       C      D        E        F      G      H
 1   NAME       STREET     CITY  SALES    DATE
 2   Burns      64 24th S  NY    370.00  01/01/1988
 3   Bear       12 Elm St  LA    378.00  02/01/1988
 4   Fischer    34 D St.   GR    260.00  12/31/1987
 5   Hoffman    2 Apple R  DM    250.00  03/01/1988
 6   Huber      1 Plum Dr  KZ    190.00  04/01/1988
 7   Miller     23 23rd S  GR    100.00  05/01/1988
 8   Mylor      81 Tuo Dr  LA    299.00  07/01/1988
 9   Michael    9 Umm Ave  NY    150.00  08/01/1988
10   Smith      99 Gem Rd  GR    500.00  07/20/1988
11   Stevens    10 Apso L  LA    300.00  07/30/1988
12
13
14
15
16
17
18
19
20
30-Jan-90   03:43 PM            UNDO
```

4.5.7 Word—DisplayWrite 4

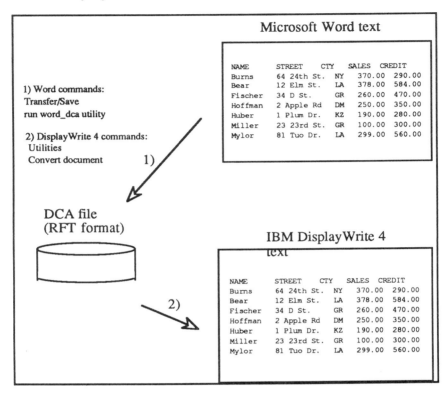

1) Word commands:
Transfer/Save
run word_dca utility

2) DisplayWrite 4 commands:
Utilities
Convert document

DCA file
(RFT format)

Microsoft Word text

NAME	STREET	CTY	SALES	CREDIT
Burns	64 24th St.	NY	370.00	290.00
Bear	12 Elm St.	LA	378.00	584.00
Fischer	34 D St.	GR	260.00	470.00
Hoffman	2 Apple Rd	DM	250.00	350.00
Huber	1 Plum Dr.	KZ	190.00	280.00
Miller	23 23rd St.	GR	100.00	300.00
Mylor	81 Tuo Dr.	LA	299.00	560.00

IBM DisplayWrite 4 text

NAME	STREET	CTY	SALES	CREDIT
Burns	64 24th St.	NY	370.00	290.00
Bear	12 Elm St.	LA	378.00	584.00
Fischer	34 D St.	GR	260.00	470.00
Hoffman	2 Apple Rd	DM	250.00	350.00
Huber	1 Plum Dr.	KZ	190.00	280.00
Miller	23 23rd St.	GR	100.00	300.00
Mylor	81 Tuo Dr.	LA	299.00	560.00

Figure 4.5.7: Importing Word data to IBM DisplayWrite 4

The DATA.DOC file created at the beginning of this section will be used for this example.

Some items must be considered when converting a text from Word format to DisplayWrite 4 format:

Characters

Italic characters are converted to DCA-RFT standard text.
Hidden text is converted to standard text.
DCA-RFT allows spacings of 5.0, 8.55, 10.0, 12.0, 15.0 and 17.1 characters per inch, as well as proportional text.
All spacing is rounded to the nearest DCA-RFT measurement.

Paragraphs

Justified and centered paragraphs are converted to left justified paragraphs.

Left and right indents are converted into page margins.

Hanging indents are not supported in DCA-RFT format. Tabs and spaces are used to approximate the format.

DCA-RFT ignores Word's Keep together and Keep follow commands.

Adjacent columns are changed to consecutive paragraphs on the same page. The original paragraph indenting is retained.

Divisions

Newspaper-style columns are changed to consecutive paragraphs on the same page. The columns are arranged left justified.

The measurement for the top page margin must be entered when printing. The bottom page margin is converted to the correct location.

Page numbering not generated in a header or footer is ignored.

Other

Normal and protected hyphens change to non-breaking hyphens.

Glossary entries such as timeprint or dateprint are ignored.

Tab fill characters are not converted.

Numbered footnotes are changed to a system footnote.

Form letters are not supported.

Indices and tables of contents are not supported.

Any special control characters are converted to normal text.

Style sheets and glossary files are not converted.

After converting a text to DisplayWrite 4, paginate the document.

Convert the document as follows:

- Save the document in Word by normal means (Transfer/Save).

- Quit Word and run the WORD_DCA utility from the DOS prompt.

The WORD_DCA utility displays the following menu:

```
WORD_DCA 5.0 - DCA RFT File Conversion Utility for Microsoft (R) Word 5.0
Copyright (C) Systems Compatibility Corp., 1988-1989. All rights reserved.


                          - INTERACTIVE MODE -
Select Conversion Type:
A = Microsoft Word to DCA/RFT
B = DCA/RFT to Microsoft Word
Enter A or B ==>
```

- Press the <A> key. The program displays the following:

```
Enter the Input File List
==>
```

- Enter the name of the source file (DATA.DOC) and press the <Enter>
  key. The program displays the following:

```
Enter the Output File List (or Output Directory)
==>
```

- Enter the name of the target file (WO-DW.DOC) and press the <Enter>
  key. WORD_DCA converts the file and the utility ends.

- When the conversion is done, run DisplayWrite 4:

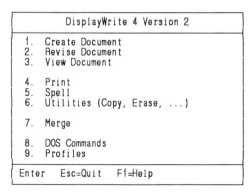

```
              DisplayWrite 4 Version 2
   1.  Create Document
   2.  Revise Document
   3.  View Document

   4.  Print
   5.  Spell
   6.  Utilities (Copy, Erase, ...)

   7.  Merge

   8.  DOS Commands
   9.  Profiles

   Enter   Esc=Quit   F1=Help
```

- Select option 6 (Utilities):

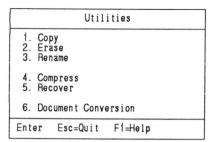

- From Utilities select option 6 (Document Conversion). The following menu appears:

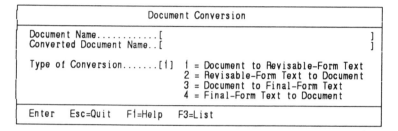

- Enter the name WO-DW.DOC in the Document Name command field. Press the <Cursor down> key to move to the Converted Document Name command field and enter the name DW-RFT.DOC, including the drive specifier and path if necessary.

- Press the <Cursor down> key to move to the next command field and press the <2> key. Press the <Enter> key to complete the task.

When the conversion is done, the text can be loaded into DisplayWrite 4 with the Revise Document option of the DisplayWrite 4 main menu.

4.5.8 Word—Aldus PageMaker

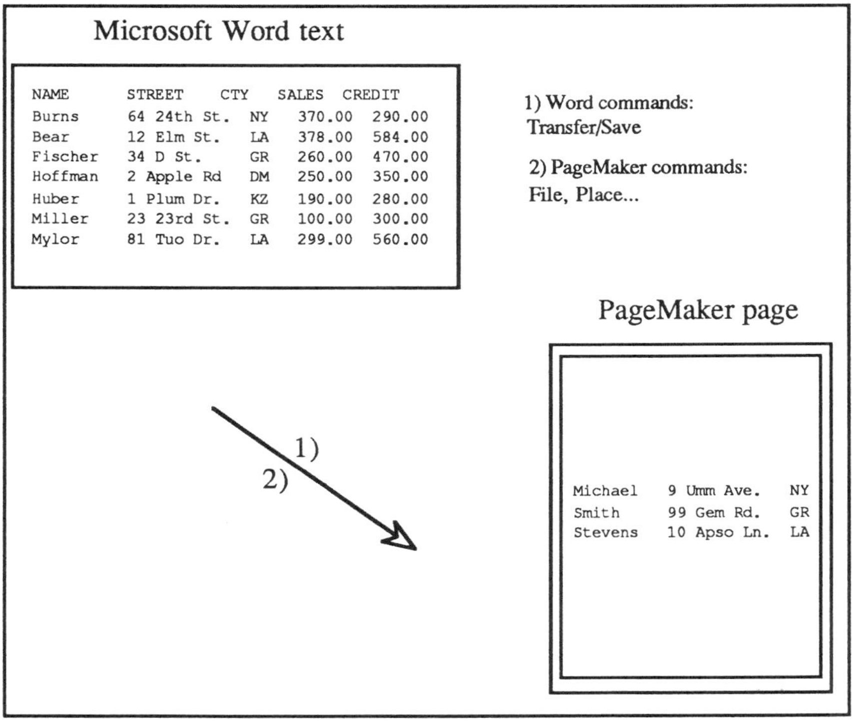

Microsoft Word text

```
NAME       STREET      CTY   SALES   CREDIT
Burns      64 24th St.  NY   370.00  290.00
Bear       12 Elm St.   LA   378.00  584.00
Fischer    34 D St.     GR   260.00  470.00
Hoffman    2 Apple Rd   DM   250.00  350.00
Huber      1 Plum Dr.   KZ   190.00  280.00
Miller     23 23rd St.  GR   100.00  300.00
Mylor      81 Tuo Dr.   LA   299.00  560.00
```

1) Word commands:
Transfer/Save

2) PageMaker commands:
File, Place...

PageMaker page

```
Michael    9 Umm Ave.   NY
Smith      99 Gem Rd.   GR
Stevens    10 Apso Ln.  LA
```

1)
2)

Figure 4.5.8: Importing Word data to PageMaker

Word files can be directly placed in PageMaker, provided that you have installed a Word import/export filter in PageMaker (see your PageMaker installation information).

Add the DATA.DOC Word file to PageMaker as follows:

- Lay out a new publication or load an existing publication.

- Select the File menu and the Place... option. Click on the DATA.DOC filename and click OK.

Once the file is loaded, the mouse pointer changes to a manual flow text icon.

- Move this pointer to the location at which you want the file to begin. Press and hold the left mouse button and move the pointer down and to the right of the starting point of the pointer. Release the left mouse button. An alternate method is to click once at the desired starting point of the file.

If the file is larger than the amount of space you have created, a plus sign within a semicircle appears at the bottom of the page. This is the bottom windowshade handle. By dragging this handle down, dragging the handles at the edge of each text block, or clicking on the bottom windowshade handle and creating another block for the remaining text, you can insert the remaining text.

You can now edit your data from within PageMaker.

4.5.9 Chart/Freelance Graphics—Word

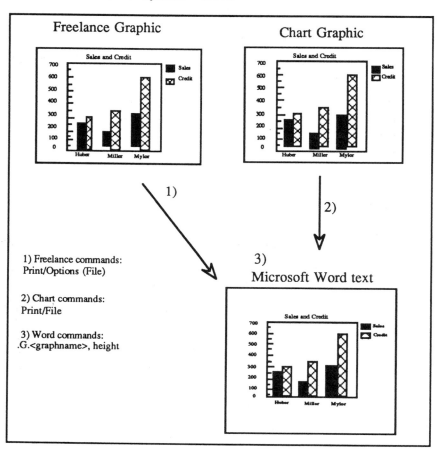

Figure 4.5.9: Importing chart data to Word

Data can be printed direct to a file in Microsoft Chart using the Print/File command. This print file can then be inserted in a Word document, provided the Word document is a single-column format.

*   Run Chart. Load the WO-CH-RO.CHA file created in Section 4.5.4.

- Select the Print/Setup command. Make sure that you select the same printer type as you use in Microsoft Word (i.e., if you plan on printing a Word document containing a Chart graphic on a specific laser printer, select this laser printer now in Chart). After selecting the printer type, press the <Enter> key.

- Select the Print/File command. Enter the name CH-WO.PRN in the name: command field and press the <Enter> key.

- Quit Chart and run Word. Load the Chart file using the Library/Link/Graphics command. Enter the name CH-WO.PRN in the filename: command field.

- Select the print file option in the file format: command field.

- For now, leave the alignment, width and height at default values and press the <Enter> key.

Word loads the file and displays the following data at the current cursor location:

```
.G. A:CH-WO.PRN;6";6";print file
```

You can now print the graphic using the Print/Printer command.

Freelance charts must be printed as files before they can be loaded into Word.

Note: Freelance print files use much more disk memory than equivalent Freelance chart files! The companion diskette for this book does not contain the Freelance print file for this section because of disk space limitations. When you generate a Freelance print file from a chart, make sure the diskette has enough free memory available.

- Run Freelance and select the Devices and Fonts Setup command. From the menu that appears, select the printers you plan to use with Freelance if you haven't already done so. In particular, select the printer device driver identical (or as close as possible) to the printer type you plan to use with Word. Press <F10> and follow any instructions that Freelance displays on the screen.

- Select the Charts and Drawings command.

- Select the File Retrieve Chart command. Enter the filename DB-FL-1.CH1 (this file was generated in Section 4.1.5.1).

- Press the <F10> key to load the file.

- Select the Go command to draw the chart on the screen. Press <Enter> to create the chart. Once the drawing finishes, press <Enter> to accept the chart.

- When the main menu appears, select the Print Options command.

- The cursor should be in the Device: item. Press <Space> to see printer options. Highlight the option closest to your printer. Press the <Enter> key.

- Move the cursor to the Read options from: item and press <Space>. Select the current settings option and press the <Enter> key.

- Move the cursor to the Output mode: item and press <Space>. Highlight the word File and press the <Enter> key.

- Enter the proper path in the File path: item, and enter the name FL-WO in the File name: item (Freelance inserts the correct extension). Press the <Enter> key.

- Press the <F10> key. When the main menu appears, select the Print Go command. Follow instructions as they appear on the screen.

- Quit Freelance and run Word. Load the Chart file using the Library/Link/Graphics command. Enter the name FL-WO.EXT (using whatever extension Freelance assigned the file) in the filename: command field.

- Select the print file option in the file format: command field.

- For now, leave the alignment, width and height at default values and press the <Enter> key.

Word loads the file and displays the following or similar data at the current cursor location:

```
.G. A:FL-WO.ELQ;6";6";print file
```

You can now print the graphic using the Print/Printer command.

Some print files may have formfeeds inserted, which can cause printing problems. You can remove the formfeeds by loading a print file using Transfer/Load, searching for the formfeeds (those single dotted lines runnning across the screen) and deleting them, then saving the file back out.

4.5.10   Word—Ventura Publisher

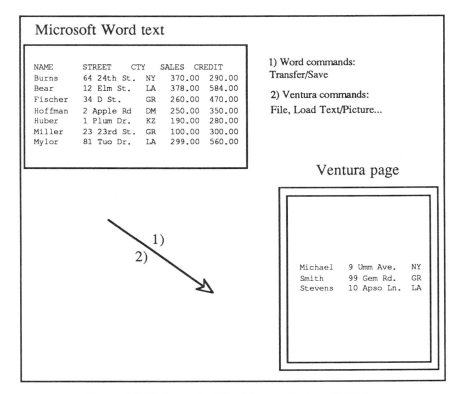

Microsoft Word text

NAME	STREET	CTY	SALES	CREDIT
Burns	64 24th St.	NY	370.00	290.00
Bear	12 Elm St.	LA	378.00	584.00
Fischer	34 D St.	GR	260.00	470.00
Hoffman	2 Apple Rd	DM	250.00	350.00
Huber	1 Plum Dr.	KZ	190.00	280.00
Miller	23 23rd St.	GR	100.00	300.00
Mylor	81 Tuo Dr.	LA	299.00	560.00

1) Word commands:
Transfer/Save

2) Ventura commands:
File, Load Text/Picture...

Ventura page

Michael	9 Umm Ave.	NY
Smith	99 Gem Rd.	GR
Stevens	10 Apso Ln.	LA

Figure 4.5.10: Importing Word data to Ventura Publisher

The DATA.DOC document created at the beginning of this section will be used in this example.

Microsoft Word files can be loaded directly into Ventura Publisher without modifications. Unlike standard ASCII files, which require the addition of paragraph markers, Ventura Publisher reads Word files as they come from Word.

•   Run Ventura Publisher. Click on the Add New Frame addition button and add a frame using the mouse.

•   Select the File menu and the Load Text/Picture... option. Click on the Text button and the MS-Word button, then click on the OK button.

•   When the ITEM SELECTOR box appears, click on the DATA.DOC filename and click on the OK button.

The file can now be edited from within Ventura Publisher.

4.6 IBM DisplayWrite 4

When transferring data from DisplayWrite 4, the data must first be saved in ASCII format. Changing a disk to ASCII format removes control characters governing fonts, bold print, justification, etc. Saving in ASCII format can be done with the Notepad.

Much of this section uses the following document named DATA2.DOC:

```
NAME        STREET        CTY  SALES   CREDIT
Burns       64 24th St.   NY   370.00  290.00
Bear        12 Elm St.    LA   378.00  584.00
Fischer     34 D St.      GR   260.00  470.00
Hoffman     2 Apple Rd.   DM   250.00  350.00
Huber       1 Plum Dr.    KZ   190.00  280.00
Miller      23 23rd St.   GR   100.00  300.00
Mylor       81 Tuo Dr.    LA   299.00  560.00
Michael     9 Umm Ave.    NY   150.00  200.00
Smith       99 Gem Rd.    GR   500.00  789.00
Stevens     10 Apso Ln.   LA   300.00  100.00
```

- Start DisplayWrite 4 and press the <R> key (Revise Document). When the Revise Document window appears, enter the DATA2.DOC filename (including path and drive specifier if needed) and press the <Enter> key.

- Move the cursor to the beginning of the text that should be saved in ASCII format (in this case, keep the cursor at the beginning of the file).

- Press <Ctrl><F4> to invoke the Notepad function.

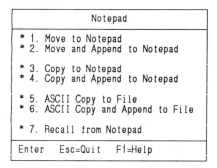

```
                    Notepad
───────────────────────────────────────────
 * 1. Move to Notepad
 * 2. Move and Append to Notepad

 * 3. Copy to Notepad
 * 4. Copy and Append to Notepad

 * 5. ASCII Copy to File
 * 6. ASCII Copy and Append to File

 * 7. Recall from Notepad
───────────────────────────────────────────
 Enter   Esc=Quit   F1=Help
```

- Press the <A> key (ASCII Copy to File). DisplayWrite 4 prompts you to move the cursor to the end of the block you want transferred (select all the text in the DATA2.DOC file for now). Press the <Enter> key once you have selected the text.

The following window appears:

```
┌──────────────────────────────────────────────┐
│               ASCII Copy to File               │
│                                                │
│   File Name..[                            ]    │
│                                                │
├──────────────────────────────────────────────┤
│   Enter   Esc=Quit   F1=Help   F3=List         │
└──────────────────────────────────────────────┘
```

•   Enter the name ASCII2.ASC in the File Name field. If you omit the file extension, DisplayWrite 4 automatically appends a file extension of .ASC.

•   Press the <Enter> key.

4.6.1 DisplayWrite 4—dBASE IV

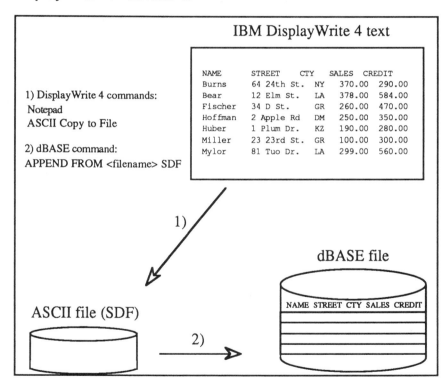

Figure 4.6.1: Importing DisplayWrite 4 data to dBASE

When transferring data from DisplayWrite 4 to dBASE, follow the procedure listed above with one exception: Do not select the field names in the DisplayWrite 4 document—you'll create these field names in dBASE.

- Start DisplayWrite 4 and press the <R> key (Revise Document). When the Revise Document window appears, enter the DATA2.DOC filename (including path and drive specifier if needed) and press the <Enter> key.

- Move the cursor to the beginning of the second line of text.

- Press <Ctrl><F4> to invoke the Notepad function.

```
┌─────────────────────────────────────────────────┐
│                    Notepad                      │
├─────────────────────────────────────────────────┤
│ * 1. Move  to Notepad                           │
│ * 2. Move  and Append  to Notepad               │
│                                                 │
│ * 3. Copy  to Notepad                           │
│ * 4. Copy  and Append  to Notepad               │
│                                                 │
│ * 5. ASCII Copy  to File                        │
│ * 6. ASCII Copy  and Append  to File            │
│                                                 │
│ * 7. Recall  from Notepad                       │
├─────────────────────────────────────────────────┤
│ Enter   Esc=Quit   F1=Help                      │
└─────────────────────────────────────────────────┘
```

- Press the <A> key (ASCII Copy to File). DisplayWrite 4 prompts you to move the cursor to the end of the block you want transferred. Move the cursor to the last line of the document. Press the <Enter> key once you have selected the text.

The following window appears:

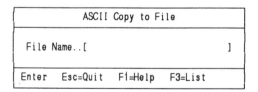

```
┌─────────────────────────────────────────────────┐
│               ASCII  Copy  to File              │
│                                                 │
│  File Name.. [                         ]        │
│                                                 │
├─────────────────────────────────────────────────┤
│ Enter   Esc=Quit   F1=Help   F3=List            │
└─────────────────────────────────────────────────┘
```

- Enter the name DW-DB in the File Name field. If you omit the file extension, DisplayWrite 4 automatically appends a file extension of .ASC.

- Press the <Enter> key.

- Quit DisplayWrite 4 and run dBASE. You must create a new file in dBASE. Create a file named DW4-DB.DBF with the following structure:

```
Structure for database: DW4-DB.DBF
Number of data records:        0
Date of last update: 01/31/90
Field    Field Name  Type        Width   Dec.   Index
    1      NAME       Character     10            N
    2      STREET     Character     12            N
    3      CTY        Character      4            N
    4      SALES      Numeric        7     2      N
    5      CREDIT     Numeric        7     2      N
** TOTAL **                         41
```

•   Enter the following command from the dBASE dot prompt:

```
APPEND FROM dw-db.asc SDF
```

When the sets of the ASCII file are copied, the following message appears:

```
10 records added
```

•   Modify the structure of the database so that it has the following structure:

```
Structure for database: DW4-DB.DBF
Number of data records:       10
Date of last update: 01/31/90
Field    Field Name  Type        Width   Dec.   Index
    1      NAME       Character     10            N
    2      STREET     Character     12            N
    3      CTY        Character      4            N
    4      SALES      Numeric        6     2      N
    5      CREDIT     Numeric        6     2      N
** TOTAL **                         39
```

The data can then be edited from within dBASE.

4.6.2 DisplayWrite 4—Microsoft Multiplan

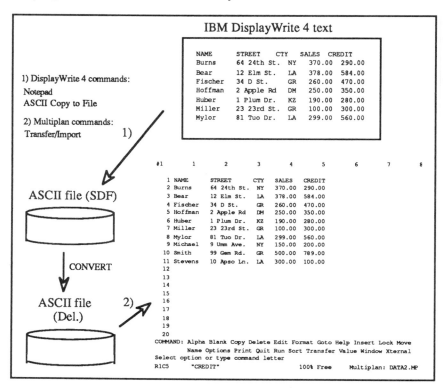

Figure 4.6.2: Importing DisplayWrite 4 data to Multiplan

The following file named DATA.DOC will be used for this example:

```
Burns    64 24th St. NY 370.00 01/01/88
Bear     12 Elm St.  LA 378.00 02/01/88
Fischer  34 D St.    GR 260.00 12/31/87
Hoffman  2 Apple Rd. DM 250.00 03/01/88
Huber    1 Plum Dr.  KZ 190.00 04/01/88
Miller   23 23rd St. GR 100.00 05/01/88
Mylor    81 Tuo Dr.  LA 299.00 07/01/88
Michael  9 Umm Ave.  NY 150.00 08/01/88
Smith    99 Gem Rd.  GR 500.00 07/20/88
Stevens  10 Apso Ln. LA 300.00 07/30/88
```

- Start DisplayWrite 4 and press the <R> key (Revise Document). When the Revise Document window appears, enter the DATA.DOC filename (including path and drive specifier if needed) and press the <Enter> key.

- Move the cursor to the beginning of the second line of text and press <Ctrl><F4> to invoke the Notepad function.

- Press the <A> key (ASCII Copy to File). DisplayWrite 4 prompts you to move the cursor to the end of the block you want transferred (select all the text from line 2 down). Press the <Enter> key once you have selected the text.

- Enter the name ASCII.ASC in the File Name field and press the <Enter> key.

The ASCII.ASC file created above must be converted to a format readable by Multiplan.

This is done using the CONVERT program, found on the companion disk for this book, and printed in the Appendix as a Turbo Pascal source code.

- Quit DisplayWrite 4 and start the CONVERT utility from the DOS prompt. The program prompts the user for the name of the source file. Enter the source filename ASCII.ASC and press the <Enter> key.

- The CONVERT utility then prompts the user for the ASCII format of the source file: Press the <S> key (SDF).

- Next the program prompts the user for the number of fields in each record (press the <5> key, then the <Enter> key).

- The program then prompts the user for the length of each field. Enter the following for each field:

  Field 1: 10
  Field 2: 12
  Field 3: 4
  Field 4: 6
  Field 5: 11

- CONVERT displays a test record. Press the <Y> key to accept this record layout or the <N> key to try again.

- The program prompts the user for the name of the target file. Enter the target filename (in this case, DW4-MP.DEL) and press the <Enter> key. If CONVERT finds an existing file of the same name, it will ask if you want to overwrite the existing file with the new data. Press the <Y> key to overwrite the existing file, or the <N> key to end the program.

- The CONVERT utility then determines that the target file is in DELIMITED format. The program prompts the user for the field separator character (press the <,> key) and the text delimiter (press the <"> key).

- CONVERT prompts the user for each field type: press <T> for the first three fields, <N> for the fourth field and <D> for the remaining field.

CONVERT then converts the file to the proper format.

The target file DW4-MP.DEL has the following contents:

```
"Burns","64 24th St.","NY",370.00,01/01/88
"Bear","12 Elm St.","LA",378.00,02/01/88
"Fischer","34 D St.","GR",260.00,12/31/87
"Hoffman","2 Apple Rd.","DM",250.00,03/01/88
"Huber","1 Plum Dr.","KZ",190.00,04/01/88
"Miller","23 23rd St.","GR",100.00,05/01/88
"Mylor","81 Tuo Dr.","LA",299.00,07/01/88
"Michael","9 Umm Ave.","NY",150.00,08/01/88
"Smith","99 Gem Rd.","GR",500.00,07/20/88
"Stevens","10 Apso Ln.","LA",300.00,07/30/88
```

- Run Multiplan and select the Transfer/Options command. Select the Other option and press the <Enter> key.

- Select the Transfer/Import command.

- Enter the filename DW4-MP.DEL in the file name: command field. Press the <Tab> key.

- The at: command field should contain the starting point of the range into which the ASCII file should be transferred. Enter the upper left corner of the range (R1C1). Press the <Tab> key.

- The cursor should be in the numbers: command field. Press the <Y> key (Yes) to accept numeric and alphanumeric data and press the <Tab> key.

- The query: command field controls whether Multiplan should prompt the user for overwriting data. Press the <N> key, then press the <Tab> key.

- The delimiters: command field determines which ASCII character should be considered as the field separator. The defaults are the space and the Tab character (^s,^t). Press the <,> key, then press the <Enter> key.

The data transfers into Multiplan. The worksheet looks like this:

```
#1        1          2          3      4        5        6        7
   1  Burns     64 24th StNY         370.00    1/1/88
   2  Bear      12 Elm St.LA         378.00    2/1/88
   3  Fischer   34 D St.  GR         260.00  12/31/87
   4  Hoffman    2 Apple RdDM        250.00    3/1/88
   5  Huber      1 Plum Dr.KZ        190.00    4/1/88
   6  Miller    23 23rd StGR         100.00    5/1/88
   7  Mylor     81 Tuo Dr.LA         299.00    7/1/88
   8  Michael    9 Umm Ave.NY        150.00    8/1/88
   9  Smith     99 Gem Rd.GR         500.00   7/20/88
  10  Stevens   10 Apso LnLA         300.00   7/30/88
  11
  12
  13
  14
  15
  16
  17
  18
  19
  20
COMMAND: Alpha Blank Copy Delete Edit Format Goto Help Insert Lock Move
         Name Options Print Quit Run Sort Transfer Value Window Xternal
Select option or type command letter
R1C1      "Burns"                  100% Free     Multiplan: TEMP
```

The data can now be edited from within Multiplan.

4.6.3 DisplayWrite 4—Microsoft Excel

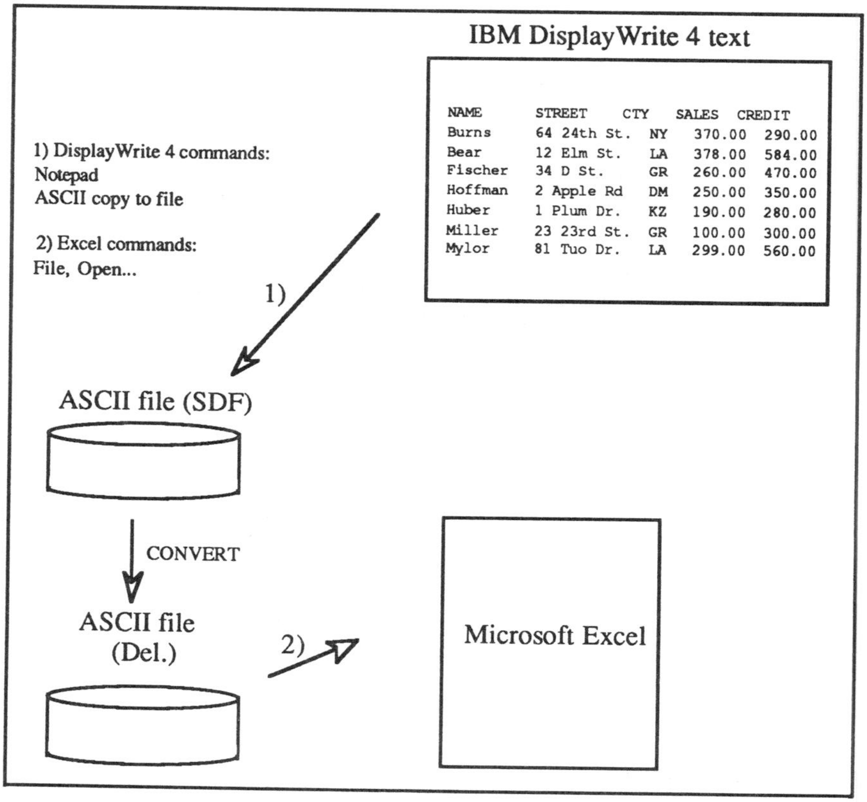

Figure 4.6.3: Importing DisplayWrite 4 data to Excel

Use the ASCII.ASC file from Section 4.6.2. This file must be converted to a format readable by Excel.

This is done using the CONVERT program, found on the companion disk for this book, and printed in the Appendix as a Turbo Pascal source code.

- Quit DisplayWrite 4 and start the CONVERT utility from the DOS prompt. The program prompts the user for the name of the source file. Enter the source filename ASCII.ASC and press the <Enter> key.

- The CONVERT utility then prompts the user for the ASCII format of the source file: Press the <S> key (SDF).

- Next the program prompts the user for the number of fields in each record (press the <5> key, then the <Enter> key).

- The program then prompts the user for the length of each field. Enter the following for each field:

  Field 1: 10
  Field 2: 12
  Field 3: 4
  Field 4: 6
  Field 5: 11

- CONVERT displays a test record. Press the <Y> key to accept this record layout or the <N> key to try again.

- The program prompts the user for the name of the target file. Enter the target filename (in this case, DW4-EXC.CSV) and press the <Enter> key. If CONVERT finds an existing file of the same name, it will ask if you want to overwrite the existing file with the new data. Press the <Y> key to overwrite the existing file, or the <N> key to end the program.

- The CONVERT utility then determines that the target file is in DELIMITED format. The program prompts the user for the field separator character (press the <,> key) and the text delimiter (press the <Space> key).

- CONVERT prompts the user for each field type: press <T> for the first three fields, <N> for the fourth field and <D> for the remaining field.

CONVERT then converts the file to the proper format.

The target file DW4-EXC.CSV has the following contents:

```
Burns , 64 24th St. , NY ,370.00,01/01/88
Bear , 12 Elm St. , LA ,378.00,02/01/88
Fischer , 34 D St. , GR ,260.00,12/31/87
Hoffman , 2 Apple Rd. , DM ,250.00,03/01/88
Huber , 1 Plum Dr. , KZ ,190.00,04/01/88
Miller , 23 23rd St. , GR ,100.00,05/01/88
Mylor , 81 Tuo Dr. , LA ,299.00,07/01/88
Michael , 9 Umm Ave. , NY ,150.00,08/01/88
Smith , 99 Gem Rd. , GR ,500.00,07/20/88
Stevens , 10 Apso Ln. , LA ,300.00,07/30/88
```

- Run Excel. Select the File/Open... command.

- Change the file extension from *.XL* to *.*.

- Click on the DW4-EXC.CSV filename and click OK.

- Insert a row at the top of the worksheet and insert the labels NAME, STREET, CITY, SALES and DATE.

You can now edit the file from within Excel.

4.6.4 DisplayWrite 4—Microsoft Chart

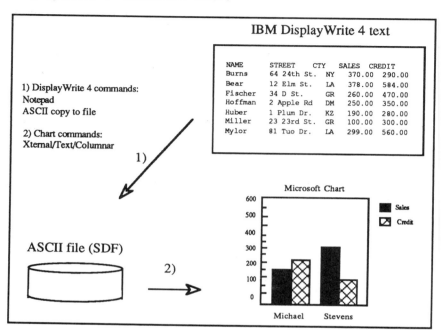

Figure 4.6.4: Importing DisplayWrite 4 data to Chart

DisplayWrite 4 data must be converted to ASCII format before it can be loaded into Microsoft Chart.

- Run DisplayWrite 4. Press the <R> key and enter the filename DATA2.DOC.

- Once the file loads, press <Ctrl><F4> to invoke the Notepad. Press the <A> key (ASCII Copy to File). Select the entire file and press the <Enter> key. When DisplayWrite prompts for a filename, enter DW4-CH.ASC and press the <Enter> key.

- Exit DisplayWrite 4.

- Run Chart. Select the Xternal/Text/Columnar command.

- Enter the name DW4-CH.ASC in the filename: command field. Press the <Tab> key to move to the linked: command field. Press the <Y> key, then press the <Tab> key to move to the selected rows: command field.

- Enter 3,6 in the selected rows: command field and press the <Tab> key to move to the selected columns: command field.

- Enter 4,5 in the selected columns: command field and press the <Tab> key to move to the orient series by: command field.

The orient series by: command field allows chart orientation by rows or columns. We'll now take you through each configuration.

If you prefer to orient the chart by rows, do the following:

- Press the <R> key (Rows), then press the <Tab> key to move to the column width: command field. Enter 10,12,4,7,6 and press the <Tab> key.

- Enter 1 in the series name(s) from: command field. Press the <Tab> key to move to the categories from: command field. Enter 1 and press the <Tab> key.

- Press <T> to select Text in the category type: command field and press the <Enter> key.

The list screen displays the following:

```
Incl.(*) Name    Source of data              Type   # pts.
1    *   Bear    Linked: a:\dw4-ch.asc:R3C4:5 Text   2
2    *   Huber   Linked: a:\dw4-ch.asc:R6C4:5 Text   2
```

- Press the <C> key to invoke the Chart command. The graphic created by Chart has the following structure:

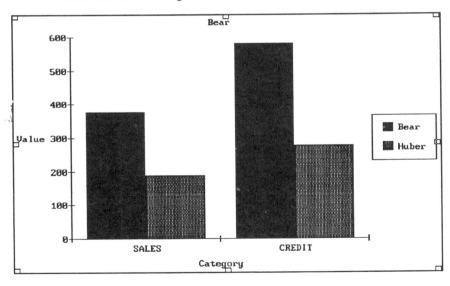

Figure 4.6.4a: Chart graphic from DisplayWrite 4 ASCII data (row orientation)

You can now edit the headings within Chart.

- Save this data under the title DW-CH-RO.CHA using the Transfer/Save command.

If you prefer to orient the chart by columns, do the following:

- Press the <C> key (Columns), then press the <Tab> key to move to the column width: command field. Enter 10,12,4,7,6 and press the <Tab> key.

- Enter 1 in the series name(s) from: command field. Press the <Tab> key to move to the categories from: command field. Enter 1 and press the <Tab> key.

- Press <T> to select Text in the category type: command field and press the <Enter> key.

The list screen displays the following:

```
Incl.(*) Name      Source of data             Type   # pts.
1    *   SALES     Linked: a:\dw4-ch.asc:R3,6C Text   2
2    *   CREDIT    Linked: a:\dw4-ch.asc R3,6C Text   2
```

- The graphic created by Chart has the following structure:

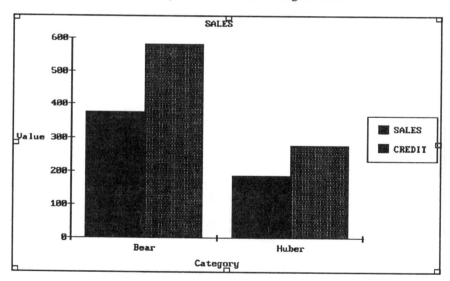

Figure 4.6.4b: Chart graphic from DisplayWrite 4 ASCII data
(column orientation)

- Save this data under the title DW-CH-CO.CHA using the Transfer/Save command.

You can now edit the headings within Chart.

4.6.5 DisplayWrite 4—Lotus Freelance Text Charts

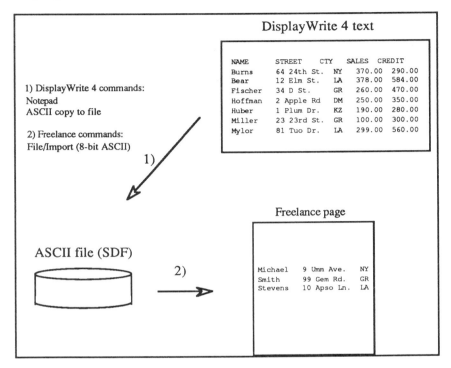

Figure 4.6.5: Importing DisplayWrite 4 data to a Freelance text chart

Use the ASCII2.ASC file created at the beginning of this section.

•   Run Freelance and select the Charts and Drawings command.

•   Select the File Import command.

•   Select the 8-bit ASCII option in the File type item and press the <Tab> key.

•   Enter the name ASCII2.ASC in the Name item and the proper path in the Path item.

•   Press the <F10> key to load the file.

You can now edit the data as a Freelance text chart.

4.6.6 DisplayWrite 4—Lotus 1-2-3

```
                          DisplayWrite 4 text

                        NAME      STREET     CTY   SALES  CREDIT
                        Burns     64 24th St. NY   370.00 290.00
  1) DisplayWrite 4 commands:     Bear      12 Elm St.  LA   378.00 584.00
  Notepad               Fischer   34 D St.   GR   260.00 470.00
  ASCII copy to file    Hoffman   2 Apple Rd  DM   250.00 350.00
                        Huber     1 Plum Dr.  KZ   190.00 280.00
  2) Lotus commands:    Miller    23 23rd St. GR   100.00 300.00
  /, File, Import, Numbers        Mylor     81 Tuo Dr.  LA   299.00 560.00

        1)

                        E1: (F2) U [W7] 'CREDIT
                        READY

  ASCII file (SDF)            A        B        C    D      E      F    G    H
                        1   NAME      STREET     CTY  SALES  CREDIT
                        2   Burns     64 24th St. NY   370.00 290.00
                        3   Bear      12 Elm St.  LA   378.00 584.00
                        4   Fischer   34 D St.    GR   260.00 470.00
                        5   Hoffman   2 Apple Rd. DM   250.00 350.00
                        6   Huber     1 Plum Dr.  KZ   190.00 280.00
       CONVERT          7   Miller    23 23rd St. GR   100.00 300.00
                        8   Mylor     81 Tuo Dr.  LA   299.00 560.00
                        9   Michael   9 Umm Ave.  NY   150.00 200.00
  ASCII file           10   Smith     99 Gem Rd.  GR   500.00 789.00
   (Del.)     2)       11   Stevens   10 Apso Ln. LA   300.00 100.00
                       12
                       13
                       14
                       15
                       16
                       17
                       18
                       19
                       20

                        30-Jan-90  02:21 PM        UNDO
```

Figure 4.6.6: Importing DisplayWrite 4 data to Lotus 1-2-3

Use the ASCII.ASC file created in Section 4.6.2 for this example. This file must be converted to a file format readable by Lotus 1-2-3 before it can be loaded into Lotus 1-2-3.

- Start the CONVERT utility from the DOS prompt. The program prompts the user for the name of the source file. Enter the source filename ASCII.ASC and press the <Enter> key.

- The CONVERT utility then prompts the user for the ASCII format of the source file: Press the <S> key (SDF).

- Next the program prompts the user for the number of fields in each record (press the <5> key, then the <Enter> key).

- The program then prompts the user for the length of each field. Enter the following for each field:

  Field 1: 10
  Field 2: 12
  Field 3: 4
  Field 4: 6
  Field 5: 11

- CONVERT displays a test record. Press the <Y> key to accept this record layout or the <N> key to try again.

- The program prompts the user for the name of the target file. Enter the target filename (in this case, DW4-LOT.DEL) and press the <Enter> key. If CONVERT finds an existing file of the same name, it will ask if you want to overwrite the existing file with the new data. Press the <Y> key to overwrite the existing file, or the <N> key to end the program.

- The CONVERT utility then determines that the target file is in DELIMITED format. The program prompts the user for the field separator character (press the <,> key) and the text delimiter (press the <"> key).

- CONVERT prompts the user for each field type: press <T> for the first three fields, <N> for the fourth field and <T> for the last field.

CONVERT then converts the file to the proper format.

The target file DW4-LOT.DEL has the following contents:

```
"Burns","64 24th St.","NY",370.00,"01/01/88"
"Bear","12 Elm St.","LA",378.00,"02/01/88"
"Fischer","34 D St.","GR",260.00,"12/31/87"
"Hoffman","2 Apple Rd.","DM",250.00,"03/01/88"
"Huber","1 Plum Dr.","KZ",190.00,"04/01/88"
"Miller","23 23rd St.","GR",100.00,"05/01/88"
"Mylor","81 Tuo Dr.","LA",299.00,"07/01/88"
"Michael","9 Umm Ave.","NY",150.00,"08/01/88"
"Smith","99 Gem Rd.","GR",500.00,"07/20/88"
"Stevens","10 Apso Ln.","LA",300.00,"07/30/88"
```

- Run Lotus 1-2-3 and select the / File Import Numbers command. Press the <Esc> key until the Enter name of file to import: file is empty.

- Enter the filename DW4-LOT.DEL and press the <Enter> key.

Lotus 1-2-3 loads the file, but some formats need specification.

- Make sure that the cell pointer is in cell A1, then select the / Worksheet Insert Row command. Press the <Enter> key to insert a row at the top of the worksheet.

- Enter NAME in cell A1, STREET in cell B1, CITY in cell C1, SALES in cell D1 and DATE in cell E1.

- Move the cell pointer to cell C1 and select the / Worksheet Column Set-Width command. Enter the number 4 and press the <Enter> key.

- Keeping the cell pointer at cell C1, select the / Range Label Center command. Select the entire range of values in column C and press the <Enter> key.

- Move the cell pointer to cell D1 and select the / Range Label Center command. Select the entire range of values in column D and press the <Enter> key.

- Keeping the cell pointer in cell D1, select the / Range Format Fixed command. Press the <2> key, then the <Enter> key.

- Move the cell pointer to cell E1.

- Select the / Worksheet Column Set-Width command. Enter the number 11 and press the <Enter> key.

- Select the / File Save command and save the file under the name DW4-LOT.WK1.

The file and date formats can now be edited from within Lotus 1-2-3.

Note: The DATE column was interpreted by 1-2-3 as labels. You must edit these fields to convert them to true 1-2-3 dates.

```
┌────────────────────────────────────────────────────────────────────────┐
│A1:  'NAME                                                          READY │
│                                                                          │
│        A         B        C       D      E        F      G       H       │
│ 1   NAME      STREET    CITY    SALES  DATE                               │
│ 2   Burns     64 24th S  NY     370.00 01/01/1988                         │
│ 3   Bear      12 Elm St  LA     378.00 02/01/1988                         │
│ 4   Fischer   34 D St.   GR     260.00 12/31/1987                         │
│ 5   Hoffman   2 Apple R  DM     250.00 03/01/1988                         │
│ 6   Huber     1 Plum Dr  KZ     190.00 04/01/1988                         │
│ 7   Miller    23 23rd S  GR     100.00 05/01/1988                         │
│ 8   Mylor     81 Tuo Dr  LA     299.00 07/01/1988                         │
│ 9   Michael   9 Umm Ave  NY     150.00 08/01/1988                         │
│10   Smith     99 Gem Rd  GR     500.00 07/20/1988                         │
│11   Stevens   10 Apso L  LA     300.00 07/30/1988                         │
│12                                                                        │
│13                                                                        │
│14                                                                        │
│15                                                                        │
│16                                                                        │
│17                                                                        │
│18                                                                        │
│19                                                                        │
│20                                                                        │
│30-Jan-90   03:43 PM          UNDO                                        │
└────────────────────────────────────────────────────────────────────────┘
```

4.6.7 DisplayWrite 4—Microsoft Word

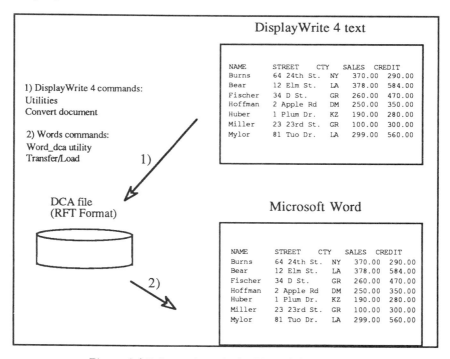

Figure 4.6.7: Importing DisplayWrite 4 data to Word

The DATA2.DOC document created in Section 4.6.2 will be used for this example.

There are some things to consider when converting a text from DisplayWrite 4 format to Word format:

- After the conversion the Word document should be repaginated.

- Comment text is converted to normal text.

- Spacing, font and characters per inch commands are not supported.

- Columnar text is converted to single, left justified columns.

- Page numbering not included in headers or footers is ignored.

- Form letter text is not supported.

- Any control characters are converted to normal text.

The text in DisplayWrite 4 must be converted to DCA/RFT format. Then the text must be converted to Word format and then processed in Word.

- Run DisplayWrite 4. The following menu appears.

```
┌─────────────────────────────────────┐
│       DisplayWrite 4 Version 2       │
├─────────────────────────────────────┤
│   1.  Create Document                │
│   2.  Revise Document                │
│   3.  View Document                  │
│                                      │
│   4.  Print                          │
│   5.  Spell                          │
│   6.  Utilities (Copy, Erase, ...)   │
│                                      │
│   7.  Merge                          │
│                                      │
│   8.  DOS Commands                   │
│   9.  Profiles                       │
├─────────────────────────────────────┤
│  Enter   Esc=Quit   F1=Help          │
└─────────────────────────────────────┘
```

- Select option 6 (Utilities):

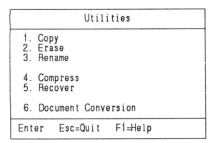

```
                    Utilities
┌─────────────────────────────────────────┐
│ 1. Copy                                   │
│ 2. Erase                                  │
│ 3. Rename                                 │
│                                           │
│ 4. Compress                               │
│ 5. Recover                                │
│                                           │
│ 6. Document Conversion                    │
├─────────────────────────────────────────┤
│ Enter   Esc=Quit   F1=Help                │
└─────────────────────────────────────────┘
```

- From Utilities select option 6 (Document Conversion). The following menu appears:

```
┌──────────────────────────────────────────────────────────┐
│                  Document Conversion                       │
├──────────────────────────────────────────────────────────┤
│ Document Name...........[                              ]   │
│ Converted Document Name..[                             ]   │
│                                                            │
│ Type of Conversion.......[1]  1 = Document to Revisable-Form Text │
│                               2 = Revisable-Form Text to Document │
│                               3 = Document to Final-Form Text     │
│                               4 = Final-Form Text to Document     │
├──────────────────────────────────────────────────────────┤
│ Enter   Esc=Quit   F1=Help   F3=List                       │
└──────────────────────────────────────────────────────────┘
```

- Enter the name DATA2.DOC in the Document Name command field. Press the <Cursor down> key to move to the Converted Document Name command field and enter the name WO-RFT.RFT, including the drive specifier and path if necessary.

- Press the <Cursor down> key to move to the next command field and press the <1> key. Press the <Enter> key to complete the task.

- Quit DisplayWrite 4 and run the WORD_DCA utility from the DOS prompt.

The WORD_DCA utility displays the following menu:

```
WORD_DCA 5.0 - DCA RFT File Conversion Utility for Microsoft (R) Word 5.0
Copyright (C) Systems Compatibility Corp., 1988-1989. All rights reserved.



                            - INTERACTIVE MODE -
Select Conversion Type:
A = Microsoft Word to DCA/RFT
B = DCA/RFT to Microsoft Word
Enter A or B ==>
```

- Press the <B> key. The program displays the following:

```
Enter the Input File List
==>
```

- Enter the name of the source file (WO-RFT.RFT) and press the <Enter> key. The program displays the following:

```
Enter the Output File List (or Output Directory)
==>
```

- Enter the name of the target file (DW-WO.DOC) and press the <Enter> key. WORD_DCA converts the file and the utility ends.

- Run Word and select the Transfer/Load command. Enter the filename DW-WO.DOC and press the <Enter> key. Word will display a message stating that a style sheet is unavailable, but will load the file anyway.

The file can now be edited from within Word.

4.6.8 DisplayWrite 4—Aldus PageMaker

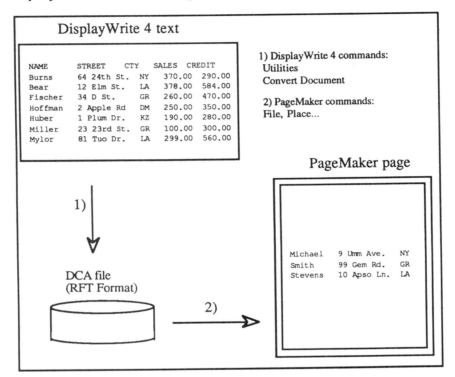

Figure 4.6.8: Importing DisplayWrite 4 data to PageMaker

The DATA2.DOC file from the beginning of this section will be used for this example.

The text in DisplayWrite 4 must be converted to DCA/RFT format. Once this conversion is done, PageMaker will load the file without problems.

• Run DisplayWrite 4. The following menu appears.

```
┌─────────────────────────────────────────────┐
│          DisplayWrite 4 Version 2            │
├─────────────────────────────────────────────┤
│   1.  Create Document                        │
│   2.  Revise Document                        │
│   3.  View Document                          │
│                                              │
│   4.  Print                                  │
│   5.  Spell                                  │
│   6.  Utilities (Copy, Erase, ...)           │
│                                              │
│   7.  Merge                                  │
│                                              │
│   8.  DOS Commands                           │
│   9.  Profiles                               │
├─────────────────────────────────────────────┤
│   Enter   Esc=Quit   F1=Help                 │
└─────────────────────────────────────────────┘
```

• Select option 6 (Utilities):

```
┌──────────────────────────────────────┐
│               Utilities              │
├──────────────────────────────────────┤
│   1.  Copy                           │
│   2.  Erase                          │
│   3.  Rename                         │
│                                      │
│   4.  Compress                       │
│   5.  Recover                        │
│                                      │
│   6.  Document Conversion            │
├──────────────────────────────────────┤
│   Enter   Esc=Quit   F1=Help         │
└──────────────────────────────────────┘
```

• From Utilities select option 6 (Document Conversion). The following menu appears:

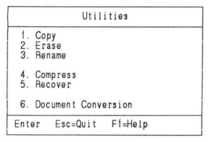

```
┌──────────────────────────────────────────────────────────────┐
│                    Document Conversion                        │
├──────────────────────────────────────────────────────────────┤
│   Document Name...........[                                 ] │
│   Converted Document Name..[                                ] │
│                                                              │
│   Type of Conversion.......[1]  1 = Document to Revisable-Form Text │
│                                 2 = Revisable-Form Text to Document │
│                                 3 = Document to Final-Form Text     │
│                                 4 = Final-Form Text to Document     │
├──────────────────────────────────────────────────────────────┤
│   Enter   Esc=Quit   F1=Help   F3=List                       │
└──────────────────────────────────────────────────────────────┘
```

• Enter the name DATA2.DOC in the Document Name command field. Press the <Cursor down> key to move to the Converted Document Name command field and enter the name PM-RFT.RFT, including the drive specifier and path if necessary.

• Press the <Cursor down> key to move to the next command field and press the <1> key. Press the <Enter> key to complete the task.

• Quit DisplayWrite 4 and run PageMaker.

• Lay out a new publication or load an existing publication.

- Select the File menu and the Place... option. Click on the PM-RFT.RFT filename and click OK.

Once the file is loaded, the mouse pointer changes to a manual flow text icon.

- Move this pointer to the location at which you want the file to begin. Press and hold the left mouse button and move the pointer down and to the right of the starting point of the pointer. Release the left mouse button. An alternate method is to click once at the desired starting point of the file.

If the file is larger than the amount of space you have created, a plus sign within a semicircle appears at the bottom of the page. This is the bottom windowshade handle. By dragging this handle down, dragging the handles at the edge of each text block, or clicking on the bottom windowshade handle and creating another block for the remaining text, you can insert the remaining text.

You can now edit your data from within PageMaker.

4.6.9 DisplayWrite 4—Ventura Publisher

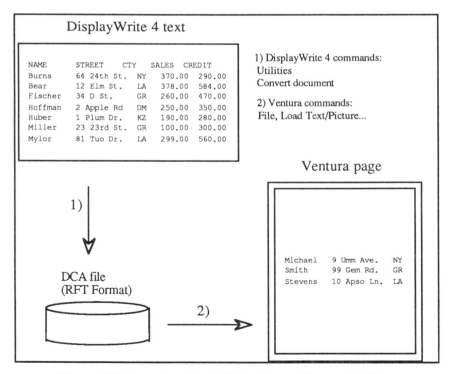

Figure 4.6.9: Importing DisplayWrite 4 data to Ventura Publisher

DisplayWrite 4 data must be converted to DCA/RFT format. Once this conversion is done, Ventura Publisher will load the file without problems. The DATA2.DOC file from the beginning of this section will be used for this example.

- Run DisplayWrite 4. The following menu appears:

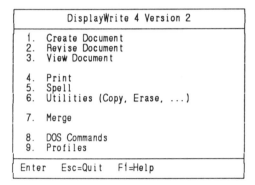

```
                DisplayWrite 4 Version 2

       1.  Create Document
       2.  Revise Document
       3.  View Document

       4.  Print
       5.  Spell
       6.  Utilities (Copy, Erase, ...)

       7.  Merge

       8.  DOS Commands
       9.  Profiles

    Enter   Esc=Quit   F1=Help
```

- Select option 6 (Utilities):

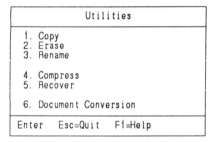

```
                    Utilities

       1.  Copy
       2.  Erase
       3.  Rename

       4.  Compress
       5.  Recover

       6.  Document Conversion

    Enter   Esc=Quit   F1=Help
```

- From Utilities select option 6 (Document Conversion). The following menu appears:

```
                    Document Conversion

    Document Name...........[                              ]
    Converted Document Name..[                             ]

    Type of Conversion.......[1]  1 = Document to Revisable-Form Text
                                  2 = Revisable-Form Text to Document
                                  3 = Document to Final-Form Text
                                  4 = Final-Form Text to Document

    Enter   Esc=Quit   F1=Help   F3=List
```

- Enter the name DATA2.DOC in the Document Name command field. Press the <Cursor down> key to move to the Converted Document Name command field and enter the name VP-RFT.RFT, including the drive specifier and path if necessary.

- Press the <Cursor down> key to move to the next command field and press the <1> key. Press the <Enter> key to complete the task.

- Quit DisplayWrite 4 and run Ventura Publisher.

- Select the File menu and the Load Text/Picture... option. Click on the Text button and the DCA button, then click on the OK button.

- When the ITEM SELECTOR box appears, click on the VP-RFT.RFT filename and click on the OK button.

The file can now be edited from within Ventura Publisher.

4.7 Freelance Graphics—Aldus PageMaker

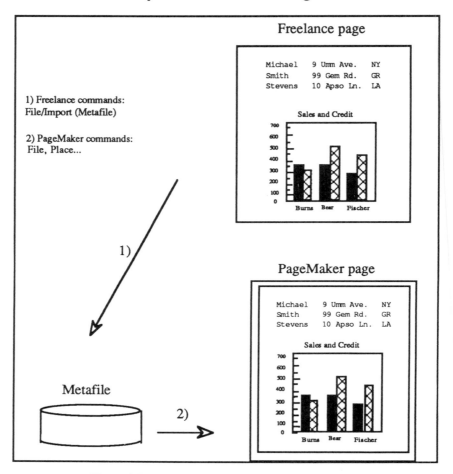

Figure 4.7: Importing Freelance charts to PageMaker

PageMaker accepts Freelance charts in metafile form, provided that the CGM metafile filter was added during installation (see your PageMaker manuals for information about filters and installation).

- Run Freelance and select the Charts and Graphics command. Select the File/Retrieve command and load the LOT-FL-GR files created in Section 4.4.5.1.

- Select the File/Export command. The File type: item should read Metafile. Move the cursor to the Path: item and enter the correct path. Press the <Enter> key.

- Move the cursor to the Name: item. Enter the name FL-DTP.CGM. Move the cursor to the DONE bar and press the <Enter> key.

- Quit Freelance and run PageMaker.

- Lay out a new publication or load an existing publication.

- Select the File menu and the Place... option. Click on the FL-DTP.CGM filename and click OK.

- Once the file is loaded, PageMaker prompts you to enter the range you want placed. Click OK to place all the worksheet data.

The mouse pointer changes to a manual flow text icon.

- Move this pointer to the location at which you want the file to begin. Press and hold the left mouse button and move the pointer down and to the right of the starting point of the pointer. Release the left mouse button. An alternate method is to click once at the desired starting point of the file.

If the file is larger than the amount of space you have created, a plus sign within a semicircle appears at the bottom of the page. This is the bottom windowshade handle. By dragging this handle down, dragging the handles at the edge of each text block, or clicking on the bottom windowshade handle and creating another block for the remaining text, you can insert the remaining text.

You can now edit your data from within PageMaker.

4.8 Chart Graphics—Aldus PageMaker

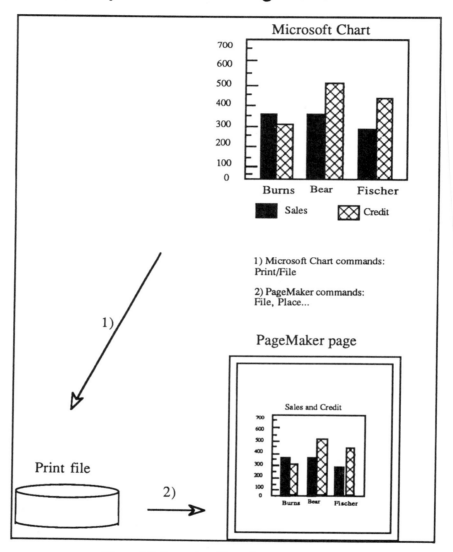

Figure 4.8: Importing Chart data to PageMaker

PageMaker accepts charts from Microsoft Chart in HPGL form, provided that the HPGL filter was added during installation (see your PageMaker manuals for information about filters and installation).

- Select the Xternal Lotus command in Chart. Enter the name DATA2.WK1 in the filename: command field (including drive specifier and path if needed).

- Press the <Tab> key to move to the linked: command field. Press the <N> key (No) and press the <Tab> key to move to the type: field. The Worksheet option should be selected; if not, press the <W> key.

- Press the <Tab> key to move to the named area or reference: command field. Enter the following:

```
R4C4:5,R7C4:5,R10C4:5
```

- Press the <Tab> key to move to the orient series by: command field.

- Press the <R> key (Rows) for row orientation.

- Press the <Tab> key until the cursor reaches the series name(s) from: command field. Press the <1> key.

- Press the <Tab> key to move to the categories from: command field. Press the <1> key. The category type: command field should be set at Text.

- Press the <Enter> key to load.

- The List screen contains the following entries:

```
Incl.(*) Name        Source of data         Type        # pts.
1        Fischer     Linked: a:\data2.wk1:R4C4:5 Text    2
2        Miller      Linked: a:\data2.wk1 R7C4:5 Text    2
3        Smith       Linked: a:\data2.wk1 R10C4: Text    2
```

- Press the <C> key. The graphic created by Chart has the following structure:

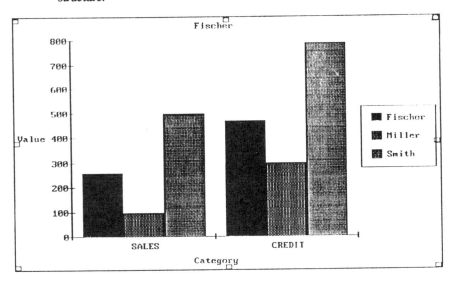

Figure 4.8: Chart graphic with data from Lotus 1-2-3 (row orientation)

The chart must be printed to disk.

- Select the Print/Setup command. Make sure that the cursor is in the device: command field and press one of the cursor keys to see a list of printers.

- Use the cursor keys to move the cursor to the HP7475A option and press the <Enter> key.

- Select the Print/File command. Enter the filename CH-DTP.PLT and press the <Enter> key. A filename with this extension is interpreted as a file in HPGL format by PageMaker.

- Quit Chart.

- Run PageMaker.

- Lay out a new publication or load an existing publication.

- Select the File menu and the Place... option. Click on the CH-DTP.PLT filename and click OK.

- Once the file is loaded, PageMaker prompts you to enter the range you want placed. Click OK to place all the worksheet data.

The mouse pointer changes to a manual flow text icon.

- Move this pointer to the location at which you want the file to begin. Press and hold the left mouse button and move the pointer down and to the right of the starting point of the pointer. Release the left mouse button. An alternate method is to click once at the desired starting point of the file.

If the file is larger than the amount of space you have created, a plus sign within a semicircle appears at the bottom of the page. This is the bottom windowshade handle. By dragging this handle down, dragging the handles at the edge of each text block, or clicking on the bottom windowshade handle and creating another block for the remaining text, you can insert the remaining text.

You can now edit your data from within PageMaker.

4.9 Freelance Graphics—Ventura Publisher

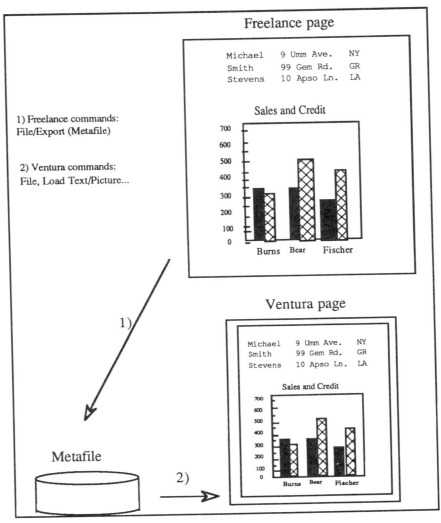

Figure 4.9: Importing Freelance graphic data to Ventura Publisher

Ventura Publisher accepts Freelance charts in metafile form. The file FL-DTP.CGM created in Section 4.7 will be used for this example.

- Create a new frame in Ventura Publisher.

- Select the File/Load Text/Picture... command. Click on the Line-Art button and the CGM button. Click on the FL-DTP.CGM filename within the ITEM SELECTOR box and click on OK.

275

4.10 Chart Graphics—Ventura Publisher

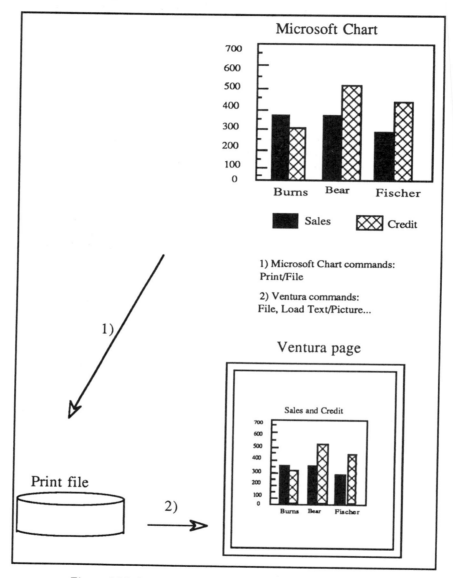

Figure 4.10: Importing Chart graphics to Ventura Publisher

Ventura Publisher accepts chart data from Microsoft Chart, provided that the chart data is saved in HPGL format. The CH-DTP.PLT example created in Section 4.8 will be used for this example.

•   Enter the following from the DOS prompt:

```
copy ch-dtp.plt ch-dtp.hpg
```

•   Run Ventura Publisher.

•   Create a new frame using the Add New Frame addition button in Ventura Publisher. Select the File menu and the Load Text/Picture... option. Click on the Line-Art button and the HPGL button. Click on the filename CH-DTP.HPG in the ITEM SELECTOR box and click on OK.

The file can then be processed by Ventura Publisher.

Note: Ventura Publisher defaults to certain file extensions (e.g., .HPG for HPGL files). By changing the Directory: line of the ITEM SELECTOR box to read *.*, Ventura will directly accept the original name of the above file (i.e., CH-DTP.PLT).

4.11 Aldus PageMaker—Ventura Publisher

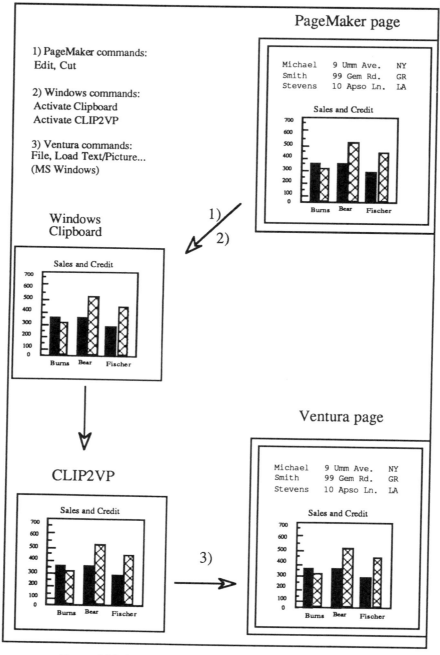

Figure 4.11: Importing PageMaker data to Ventura Publisher

Metafile data included in a PageMaker publication can be transferred to Ventura Publisher using the Windows clipboard and the CLIP2VP.EXE utility included on your Ventura Publisher Utilities disk. CLIP2VP.EXE must be accessible from Microsoft Windows.

- Run PageMaker and the Clipboard from Windows (you can toggle between them by pressing the <Alt><Esc> keys).

- Create a new file and place the FL-DTP.CGM file cited in Section 4.7.

- Select the Edit menu and the Copy or Cut option to place the data in the Clipboard. Exit PageMaker. Run the CLIP2VP utility from Windows.

- Select the Command menu and the Save As... option. Enter the filename CH-DTP.WMF (including the drive specifier and path as needed) and press the <Enter> key.

- Close any open applications in Windows and run Ventura Publisher. Memory constraints may force you to run Ventura Publisher from the DOS prompt instead of from Windows.

- Create a new frame using the Add New Frame addition button in Ventura Publisher.

- Select the File menu and the Load Text/Picture... option. Click on the Line-Art button and the MS Windows button. Click on the filename CH-DTP.WMF in the ITEM SELECTOR box and click on OK.

The file can then be processed from within Ventura Publisher.

Appendix

The CONVERT utility program listed below was written in Turbo Pascal Version 5.5. This utility is included here only as a general example of file conversion using a programming language. The program can be tailored to your own needs.

```pascal
program convert; { SDF->DELIMITED/DELIMITED->SDF file converter }

{$V-}

Uses Crt;

Type LText = String[30];

Var Source, Target : LText;                          { Filenames }
    SrcFle,
    TargetFle      : Text;                           { Text files }
    SrcFormat,
    TargetFormat   : Char;
    Character,
    Key            : Char;
    Field,
    FRecord,
    FieldAmt       : Integer;
    FieldContents,
    NullString     : String[255];
    SrcSep,
    TargetSep,
    SrcDlimiter,
    TargetDlimiter: Char;
    SrcFieldType,
    TargetFieldType : Array[1..128]of Char; { Text/Number/Date field types }
    FieldLngth    : Array[1..128]of Integer;          { Field lengths }
    Place,
    n, x, z        : Integer;                         { Counters }

Function Available(Fle : LText): Boolean;
Var Fil : File;
Begin
    Assign(Fil,Fle);                                 { Assign filename }
    {$I-}
    Reset(Fil);                                       { Reset file }
    {$I+}
    Available := IOResult = 0        { If IOResult=0, file is available }
End;

Procedure SDF_Read;
Begin
    FieldContents    := NullString;          { Clear field contents }
    FieldContents[0] := #0;                    { Set length to 0 }
    for z := 1 to FieldLngth[Field] Do Begin   { Read field contents }
        Read(SrcFle,Character);
        FieldContents := FieldContents + Character
    End;
```

```
Procedure SDF_Write;
Begin
    Case TargetFieldType[Field] of    { Insert spaces dependent on field type }
        'T' : While (Length(FieldContents)<FieldLngth[Field])
                Do FieldContents := FieldContents + ' ';
        'N' : While (Length(FieldContents)<FieldLngth[Field])
                Do FieldContents := ' ' + FieldContents;
        'D' : While (Length(FieldContents)<FieldLngth[Field])
                Do FieldContents := FieldContents + ' '
    End;
    for z := 1 to FieldLngth[Field]
                Do Write(TargetFle,FieldContents[z]);          { Write field }
    if Field = FieldAmt then Writeln(TargetFle)
                                      { Write following last field's CR/LF }
End;


Procedure Delim_Read;
Begin
    FieldContents      := NullString;              { Clear field contents }
    FieldContents[0] := #0;                        { Set field lengths to 0 }
    Repeat
        Read(SrcFle,Character);
        if not (Character in [SrcSep,#10,#13]) then
        FieldContents := FieldContents + Character{ Printable characters only }
    until Character in [SrcSep,#10,#13];
                                    { Arrange by end of field or end of record }
    for z := 1 to Length(FieldContents) Do            { Remove delimiters }
        if FieldContents[z] = SrcDlimiter then Begin
        FieldContents[z] := ' ';
        Delete(FieldContents,z,1)                  { Correct field lengths }
        End;   { if }
    if Field = FieldAmt then Read(SrcFle,Character)
                              { Start CR/LF at end of record }
End;


Procedure Delim_Write;
Begin
    if TargetFieldType[Field] = 'T' then
    Write(TargetFle,TargetDlimiter);
    if Length(FieldContents) > 0 then Begin
        Case TargetFieldType[Field] of              { Remove excess spaces }
            'T'  : While (FieldContents[Length(FieldContents)] = ' ')
                    and (Length(FieldContents)>0)
                        Do Delete(FieldContents,Length(FieldContents),1);
            'N'  : While (FieldContents[1] = ' ') and (Length(FieldContents)>0)
                        Do Delete(FieldContents,1,1);
            'D'  : While (FieldContents[1] = ' ') and (Length(FieldContents)>0)
                        Do Delete(FieldContents,1,1)
        End;   { case }
        For z := 1 to Length(FieldContents)
                    Do Write(TargetFle,FieldContents[z]) { Write fld contnts }
    End;
    if TargetFieldType[Field] = 'T' then Write(TargetFle,TargetDlimiter);      { Write text
delimiter }
    if Field <> FieldAmt then Write(TargetFle,TargetSep)   { Write separators }
    else Writeln(TargetFle)                                { Write CR/LF }
End;

Procedure SourceDefinition;
Begin
    ClrScr;
    Writeln('Please enter the name of the source file');
    Writeln;
    Writeln('(e.g., C:\DBASE\MYDATA.DBF)');
    Writeln;
    Write('Source: '); Readln(Source);
    if not Available(Source) then Begin
        ClrScr;
        Writeln('ERROR: File not found.');
```

```
      Writeln;
      Writeln('Ending program.');
      Halt
   End;
   Writeln;
   Write('Please enter source file format (<S>DF or <D>elimited): ');
   Repeat
      SrcFormat := ReadKey;
      SrcFormat := UpCase(SrcFormat)
   until SrcFormat in ['S','D'];
   Writeln(SrcFormat);
   Writeln;
   Write('How many fields does each record have? '); Readln(FieldAmt);
   if (FieldAmt > 128) or (FieldAmt < 1) then Begin
      Writeln('ERROR: You can only enter a number between 1 and 128.');
      Writeln;
      Writeln('Ending program.');
      Halt
   End
End;

Procedure TargetDefinition;
Begin
   ClrScr;
   Writeln('Please enter the name of the target file');
   Writeln;
   Writeln('(e.g., C:\DBASE\CONVDATA.DBF)');
   Writeln;
   Write('Target: '); Readln(Target);
   if Available(Target) then Begin
      Writeln;
      Writeln('WARNING: File already exists.');
      Writeln;
      Write('Do you want to overwrite it (y/n)? ');
      Repeat
         Key :=ReadKey;
         Key := UpCase(Key)
      until Key in ['Y','N'];
      Write(Key);
      if Key = 'N' then Begin
         Writeln;
         Writeln('End program.');
         Halt
      End;
   End;
   if SrcFormat = 'D' then Eegin
      Writeln;
      Write('Please enter the target file format (<S>DF or <D>elimited): ');
      Repeat
         TargetFormat := ReadKey;
         TargetFormat := UpCase(TargetFormat)
      until TargetFormat in ['S','D'];
      Writeln(TargetFormat);
      Writeln;
   End
   else TargetFormat := 'D'
End;

Procedure SDF_Definition;
Begin
   Writeln('File defined as SDF:');
   Writeln;
   For N := 1 to FieldAmt Do Begin
      Write('Field ',N:3,' length? '); Readln(FieldLngth[n]);
      if (FieldLngth[n] < 1) or (FieldLngth[n] > 255) then Begin
         Writeln;
         Writeln('ERROR: Field length can only be a number from 1 to 255.');
         Writeln;
         Writeln('End program.');
         Halt
```

283

```
         End
      End
End;

Procedure Src_Delim_Definition;
Begin
   Writeln('Source file defined as DELIMITED:');
   Writeln;
   Write('Enter the field separator character (usually ,)');
   SrcSep := ReadKey;
   WriteLn(SrcSep);
   Writeln;
   Write('Enter the text delimiter character (usually ") ');
   SrcDlimiter := ReadKey;
   WriteLn(SrcDlimiter);
   Writeln;
   Writeln('Please enter the field type: <T>ext, <N>umber or <D>ate:');
   Writeln;
   For N := 1 to FieldAmt Do Begin
      Write('Field ',N:3,' type? ');
      Repeat
         SrcFieldType[n] := ReadKey;
         SrcFieldType[n] := UpCase(SrcFieldType[n])
      until SrcFieldType[n] in ['T','N','D'];
      Writeln(SrcFieldType[n])
   End
End;

Procedure Target_Delim_Definition;
Begin
   Writeln('Target file defined as DELIMITED:');
   Writeln;
   Write('Enter the field separator character (usually ,)');
   TargetSep := ReadKey;
   WriteLn(TargetSep);
   Writeln;
   Write('Enter the text delimiter character (usually ") ');
   TargetDlimiter := ReadKey;
   WriteLn(TargetDlimiter);
   Writeln;
   Writeln('Please enter the field type: <T>ext, <N>umber or <D>ate:');
   Writeln;
   For N := 1 to FieldAmt Do Begin
      Write('Field ',N:3,' type? ');
      Repeat
         TargetFieldType[n] := ReadKey;
         TargetFieldType[n] := UpCase(TargetFieldType[n])
      until TargetFieldType[n] in ['T','N','D'];
      Writeln(TargetFieldType[n])
   End
End;

Function TestReadOK: Boolean;
Begin
   ClrScr;
   Assign(SrcFle,Source);
   Reset(SrcFle);
   Writeln('Test read:');
   Writeln;
   for Field := 1 to FieldAmt Do Begin            { Read & display 1st record }
      Write('Field ',Field:3,' :');
      Case SrcFormat of
         'S' : SDF_Read;
         'D' : Delim_Read
      End;    { case }
      Writeln(FieldContents,':');
   End;
   Close(SrcFle);
   Writeln;
   Write('Definition correct (y/n)? ');
```

```
   Repeat
      Key := ReadKey;
      Key := UpCase(Key)
   until Key in ['Y','N'];
   Writeln(Key);
   TestReadOK := Key = 'Y'
End;

Begin                    {******* Main program ********}
   ClrScr;
   for z := 1 to 255 Do NullString[z] := ' ';              { Print blank spaces }
   NullString[0] := #255;                                  { Set length }
   SourceDefinition;
   Repeat
      ClrScr;
      Writeln('Define source file format:');
      Writeln;
      if SrcFormat = 'S' then SDF_Definition else Src_Delim_Definition
   until TestReadOK;
   TargetDefinition;
   ClrScr;
   Writeln('Define target file format:');
   Writeln;
   if TargetFormat = 'S' then SDF_Definition else Target_Delim_Definition;
   ClrScr;
   Assign(SrcFle,Source);                                  { Assign source file }
   Reset(SrcFle);
   Assign(TargetFle,Target);                               { Assign target file }
   Rewrite(TargetFle);
   FRecord := 1;
   GotoXy(1,1); Write('Record #:');
   While not EOF(SrcFle) Do Begin                   { Continue until end of file }
      for Field := 1 to FieldAmt Do Begin
         GotoXy(8,1); Write(FRecord:0);                    { Display record number }
                                                           { Read source field }
         Case SrcFormat of
            'S' : SDF_Read;
            'D' : Delim_Read
         End;    { case }
         Case TargetFormat of                       { Increment target field }
            'S' : SDF_Write;
            'D' : Delim_Write
         End    { case }
      End;    { for }
      FRecord := Succ(FRecord)                       { Increment to next record }
   End;
   Close(SrcFle);                                          { Close source file }
   Close(TargetFle);                                       { Close target file }
   ClrScr;
   WriteLn('File converted.');
   Writeln;
   Writeln('Press any key to continue.');
   Repeat until KeyPressed
End.
```

Index

Companion Disk

For your convenience, the source codes and data files described in this book are available on a 5-1/4" IBM format floppy disk. You should order the companion disk if you want the programs, but don't want to type them in from the listings in the book.

All programs on the disk has been fully tested. You can change the programs to suit your particular needs. The companion disk is available for $14.95 + $2.00 for postage and handling within the U.S.A. ($5.00 for foreign orders).

When ordering, please give your name and shipping address. Enclose a check, money order or credit card information. Mail your order to:

5370 52nd Street S.E.,
Grand Rapids, MI 49512

Or for fast service, call **616/698-0330**

For orders only call **1-800-451-4319**

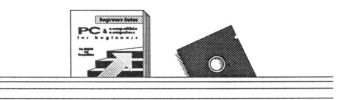

Abacus pc catalog

Order Toll Free 1-800-451-4319

5370 52nd Street SE • Grand Rapids, MI 49512
Phone: (616) 698-0330 • Fax: (616) 698-0325

Beginners Series books remove the confusing jargon and get you up and running quickly with your PC.

PC and Compatible Computers for Beginners - For the absolute newcomer to personal computers. Describes the PC and all of its components in an non-technical way. Introduces DOS commands.
ISBN 1-55755-060-3 $18.95
Canada: 52072 $22.95

MS-DOS for Beginners - Describes the most important DOS commands clearly and understandably. Teaches skills required to more effectively use your PC.
ISBN 1-55755-061-1 $18.95
Canada: 52071 $22.95

Excel for Beginners - Newcomers to this powerful spreadsheet and graphics software will learn to master Excel's many features in a short while. Dec. '90
ISBN 1-55755-067-0 $18.95
Canada: 52067 $22.95

Microsoft Works for Beginners - A thorough introduction to this "all-in-one" software package. Loaded with simple, practical examples.
ISBN 1-55755-063-8 $18.95
Canada: 52070 $22.95

Ventura Publisher for Beginners* - Presents the basics of the premier desktop publishing package. Many examples and illustrations.
ISBN 1-55755-064-6 $18.95
Canada: 52074 $22.95

To order direct call Toll Free 1-800-451-4319

In US and Canada add $4.00 shipping and handling. Foreign orders add $12.00 per item. Michigan residents add 4% sales tax

Productivity Series books are for the user who wants to become more productive sooner with their PC.

Printer Tips & Tricks describes how printers work, basic printer configurations using DIP switches, using MS-DOS commands for simple printer control and includes utilities on a 5 1/4" companion diskette to demonstrate the most popular software commands. Useful printer accessories, font editor, and printing tricks and tips. Dec. '89.
Includes companion diskette.
ISBN 1-55755-075-1 $34.95
Canada: 53903 $45.95

MS-DOS Tips & Tricks contains dozens of tips from the pros on using MS-DOS. Describes tricks and tips on finding any file on hard disk, copying data from a backup without the RESTORE commands, protecting your data, cold-starting your PC from a batch file and more. Feb. '90.
ISBN 1-55755-078-6 $17.95
Canada: 53907 $23.95

PC Tools Complete is a complete reference to the PC Tools software, the best-selling softare utility for years. It thoroughly covers all of the many features of each of the utilities that make up this all-encompassing software package. Jan. '90
ISBN 1-55755-076-X $22.95
Canada: 53905 $29.95

Complete Guide to the Atari Portfolio contains valuable information about the Atari Portfolio, the smallest PC available on the market. Designed for both the beginner and experienced PC user it covers hardware, software, built-in applications, printing and transferring data to other computers and much more.
ISBN 1-55755-058-1 $17.95
Canada: 53900 $23.95

More Titles Coming Soon!

In US and Canada add $4.00 shipping and handling. Foreign orders add $12.00 per item. Michigan residents add 4% sales tax

Quick Reference Series books are convenient, durable books made to last. You'll find clear, concise information quickly at your fingertips.

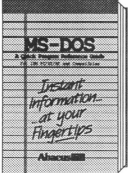

MS-DOS Versions **3.3 & 4.0**
ISBN 1-55755-000-X $9.95
Canada: 52079 $12.95

Lotus 1-2-3 Versions **2.2 & 3.0**
ISBN 1-55755-014-X $9.95
Canada: 52076 $12.95
Available Dec. '89

WordPerfect
Covers Versions **5.0 & 5.1**
ISBN 1-55755-015-8 $9.95
Canada: 52085 $12.95
Available Jan. '90

Multiplan
ISBN 1-55755-002-6 $9.95
Canada: 52080 $12.95

GW-BASIC
ISBN 1-55755-001-8 $9.95
Canada: 52078 $12.95

dBASE III Plus & IV
ISBN 1-55755-013-1 $9.95
Canada: 52077 $12.95
Available Dec. '89

PC Tools Companion
All the information you require for working with best-selling PC tools software. Features a durable hardback cover that makes the book perfect for laptop users.
ISBN 1-55755-012-3 $12.95
Canada: 53908 $16.95
Available Jan. '90

UNIX/ XENIX Reference Guide - Gain quick access to vital information on UNIX and XENIX. Commands listed with syntax, options, examples of use and reference to other commands.
Soft cover.
ISBN 1-55755-031-X $12.95
Canada: 52083 $16.95

In US and Canada add $4.00 shipping and handling. Foreign orders add $12.00 per item. Michigan residents add 4% sales tax

Program Diskette Enclosed

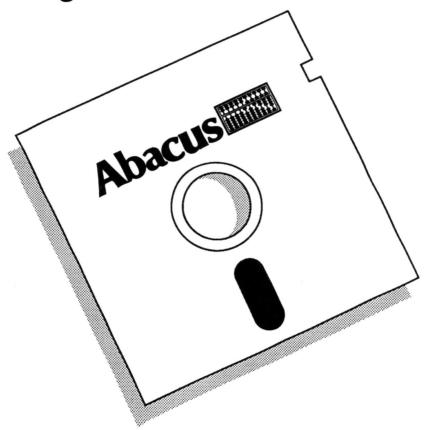